ILLINOIS CENTRAL COLLEGE
PN4121.C35
STACKS
A manner of speak
A12900 282197

W9-BXE-539

A MANNER OF SPEAKING

A Manner of Speaking

FOR EFFECTIVE COMMUNICATION

by

CARL B. CASS, Ph.D.

Professor of Drama, University of Oklahoma

G. P. PUTNAM'S SONS
New York

Library of Congress Catalog Card Number 61-6402
Manufactured in the United States of America

To

DOROTHY AND AGNES

Contents

Preface 11

Part 1 Voice and Articulation

1: INTRODUCTION 15

The Basic Function of Speech 16
How Communication Is Learned 21
Development of Speech Skills in School 26
Factors Limiting the Normal Development of Speech Skills 27
Objectives in Training Voice and Articulation 36
Summary 39
Questions 41
Exercises 42

2: PHYSICS OF SOUND 47

Air as a Medium Through Which Sound Travels 47
Sound Waves 49
The Variable Attributes of Sound Waves and Sounds 52
Intensity, Amplitude, and Loudness 52
Sound-Wave Frequency and the Pitch of Sound 54
The Quality of Sound 56
Resonance and Quality 58
Sound Duration 61
Summary 62
Questions 64
Exercises 64

3: THE PRODUCTION OF VOICE AND SPEECH 66

The Breathing Mechanism 66

The Eating and Drinking Mechanism 73
The Speech Mechanism 74
Vocal Variations While Speaking 81
Summary 82
Questions 85
Exercises 86

4: The Strength and Basic Quality of the Voice 88

A Speaker's Natural Voice 88
The Means of Changing One's Natural Voice 90
Hearing and Evaluating Voice 90
Criteria of a Good Voice 93
The Essentials of Voice Improvement 94
Elimination of Common Vocal Faults 96
Summary 103
Questions 105
Exercises 106

5: The Representation of Speech Sounds 115

Phonetic Alphabet and Webster's Collegiate Dictionary Equivalents 119
Classification of Phonetic Units 122
Supplementary Marks Used in Transcription 126
Phonetic Writing or Transcription 128
Detailed Consideration of New Symbols 130
The Use of the Phonetic Alphabet 144
Summary 145
Questions 145
Exercises 146

6: Ear Training 152

Variations in Hearing Efficiency 152
Speech and the Listeners' Hearing 154
Interdependence of Speech and Hearing 155
Improvement of Auditory Observation and Judgment 156
Auditory Memory and Guidance 158
Impersonation and Mimicry 159
The Value of Mimicry and Demonstration 161
Summary 163

Questions 165
Exercises 166

7: ENUNCIATION AND PROJECTION 171

Pronunciation and Enunciation Defined 172
Quality and Modes of Enunciation 174
Poor Enunciation 177
The Projection of Speech 179
Improvement of Enunciation and Projection 181
Summary 182
Use of Enunciation Exercises 183
Questions 183
Exercises 184

8: AMERICAN STANDARDS OF PRONUNCIATION 215

Standards of Pronunciation 215
Pronunciation Standards in the United States 219
Speech Standards and Their Relative Beauty 222
Improvement of Pronunciation 225
Summary 227
Questions 228
Exercises 229

Part II Tonal Communication

9: THE SPEECH INTONATION PATTERN AND MEANING 245

The Nature of Speech Intonation Patterns 246
Factors Determining Speech Variety 247
Vocal Variations and Meaning 248
Variations in Speech Content 251
The Inevitability of Intonation Patterns 254
Summary 256
Questions 257
Exercises 258

10: THE SPEECH PERSONALITY 266

The Speech Situation 268
An Effective Speech Personality 268

Speech Personality Not Based on Pretense 275
An Ineffective Speech Personality 276
Acting and Speech Personality 277
Summary 278
Questions 279
Exercises 280

11: DEVELOPING VOCAL FLEXIBILITIES 284

Force Variations and Control 285
Motivation and Types of Force Emphasis 286
Pitch Variety in Speech 288
Pitch Range, Key, and Optimum Pitch 290
Development of Pitch Variety and Control 291
The Variety and Control of Voice Qualities 293
The Emotional Accompaniment of Speech 295
Quality Emphasis 296
Training for Quality Variations 297
Summary 298
Questions 299
Exercises 300

12: TIME VARIETY, TEMPO, AND RHYTHM 321

Time Emphasis 323
Speech Tempo 324
Speech Rhythm 325
Improvement of Timing, Tempo, and Rhythm 327
Summary 330
Questions 331
Exercises 332

13: ON FOLLOWING THROUGH 338

Course Objective 338
Facilities for Continued Progress 339
Individual Objectives 340
Summary 341
Questions 342
Exercises 342

Selections by Authors 351
Topic Index 355

Preface

THE improvement of one's manner of speaking for effective oral communication presents a unique and very difficult problem. It is a difficult problem because, after many years of talking experience, each person has developed a "natural voice" and a "characteristic manner of speaking" that are based upon long-established muscular habits that operate well below the level of his consciousness and hence will be very hard to change. It is a unique problem because each individual (although he may admit quite readily, as an academic principle, that he should improve his speech habits) actually tends to resist any specific change in his voice or his manner of speaking because such changes seem (to his ears at least) to tend towards strained, artificial, and unnatural voice or speech. Such normal resistance to any change of one's deep-seated speech habits results from the fact that a person's critical judgment of "good voice" and "good speech" is conditioned by years of experience in listening to his own voice and speech and to similar voice and speech models that he imitated when his speech habits were initially being formed. Consequently, when a person attempts to improve his voice and oral diction he must acquire simultaneously new and improved muscular habits of speaking and a new auditory appreciation of his improved manner of speaking.

Any effective course of study and training that is aimed at the improvement of voice, articulation, and tonal expression must be specifically adapted to this unique and difficult problem. In the following pages an attempt is made to present such a course of study and training. Study of the text material (in preparation of which an attempt was made to avoid unnecessary scientific detail and any specialized vocabulary) should lead to a basic understanding of how one should go about improving his oral techniques in speaking. And a systematic use of the drill materials in daily practice sessions should result both in the formation of new and improved muscular habits of speech and in an auditory appreciation of the improved speech sounds.

The amount of practice or drill needed by different students in the various phases of the speech process will vary a great deal. Some students may need many weeks or months of vocal drills in order to develop greater strength of voice and to improve vocal qualities, while others may need only to develop greater vocal flexibility or perhaps greater precision and accuracy of articulation. Emphasis on specific drill materials must usually be adjusted to the individual needs of various students. But in all cases some sort of systematic practice or drill will be necessary if any real progress in the improvement of vocal and articulatory habits is to be accomplished. It is not enough that one should know how his speech mechanism should operate in the process of communicating effectively; he must establish by much practice effective habits of speech that will operate automatically without conscious control.

CARL B. CASS

PART I

Voice and Articulation

1.

Introduction

THE act of speaking words is accompanied inevitably by physical and tonal expression. Speech is, therefore, a blend of three types of communication which are used simultaneously to supplement and reinforce each other. An infant acquires the initial ability to communicate first by means of physical expression, then by tonal expression, and finally by verbal expression. In terms of communicative force or dominance, the three types of communication should be ranked in the same order. If, for example, a person should speak in a very friendly tone such a line as, "Please come here," but at the same time should assume a threatening or angry posture with a scowl on his face and doubled fists, the person spoken to would probably respond to the threat communicated by the physical posture rather than to the request indicated by the tone and the spoken words. Similarly, if the word "yes" were uttered with a tone and inflection that meant "no," a listener would almost always accept the negative message communicated by the tone and inflection rather than the literal meaning of the spoken word.

In spite of the dominance of the physical and tonal types of communication, however, the verbal language is by far man's most important means of communication because of its great versatility and exactness of expression. And it is the possession of capacity for verbal thought and expression that elevates man above the lower animals and makes his civilization possible.

The skills or techniques of physical, tonal, and verbal expression help to determine the effectiveness of speech; yet the initial development of such skills or techniques is started at a very early age, before the individual is aware of the importance of speech and before he is able to distinguish an effective means of communication from one that is ineffective. By the time the average person might be expected to possess a reasonably good critical judgment of effective speech, his own physical, tonal, and verbal techniques have become long-established and deep-seated habits of speech that seem to be inseparable attributes of his own personality. As a result, the average adult is not likely to regard the training of the speaking voice as an exciting opportunity. Self-complacency or a natural reluctance to change anything so much a part of oneself as the voice and manner of speaking accounts for the fact that few adults ever make a serious effort to improve their skills of vocalizing and articulating their speech.

The Basic Function of Speech

Not so many years ago, people who were interested in improving their speech studied the "art of expression"; today they study "effective communication." The difference between expression and communication may seem insignificant; but it is a difference that is of fundamental importance to anyone interested in improving his speech habits because it concerns the real function of speech.

According to Webster's Collegiate Dictionary, the word expression means "Act or process of representing, esp. by language," while the word communication means "intercourse by words, . . . interchange of thoughts or opinions." It is obvious that a person might express his thoughts and feelings when no one is within hearing distance, and, in such a case, no communication could be accomplished. It is also obvious that a person might skillfully express his thoughts and feelings aloud in the presence of others who are so preoccupied with their own thoughts and feelings that they become only vaguely conscious that someone is talking and hence they fail to respond to the thoughts and feelings expressed. Again no communication would be accomplished.

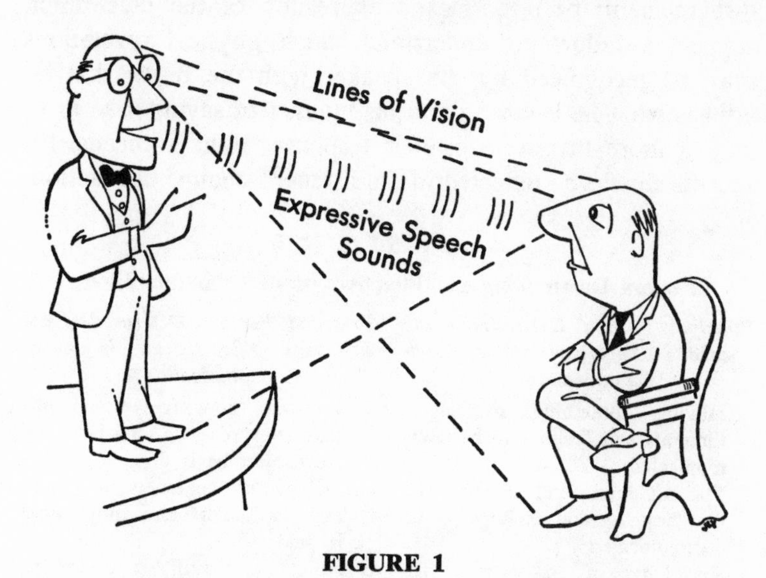

FIGURE 1

Circular Relationship of Speaker and Listener

The significance of communication as distinct from expression is indicated by Figure 1 and Table 1. Only the speaker has any part in the physical, tonal, and verbal expression of speech, but both speaker and listener are necessarily involved in the cooperative process of communication.

In Figure 1 the circular relationship that exists between any speaker and listener is represented graphically. The speaker talks and the sounds of both his words and the intonation pattern of his speech carry through the air to the ears of the listener. Simultaneously the physical expression of the speaker is perceived through the eyes of the listener. The three types of expression arouse within the listener certain thoughts and feelings that he expresses more or less unconsciously by posture and movement. Uneasy movements, for example, might indicate a faltering of attention or boredom; a slight shaking of the head and a scowl might show disagreement; or a perplexed expression of the face might suggest a failure to understand. Such physical revelations may be recognized by the speaker with the result that he adjusts what he is saying and his manner of saying it so as to gain a more favorable listener response. If he succeeds, his success should be reflected in the listener's change of reaction.

TABLE 1

Factors Determining the Effectiveness of Communication

Principal Factors Determining the Speaker's Effectiveness in Communication	*Principal Factors Determining the Listener's Effectiveness in Communication*
1. Having something to say—thoughts and feelings to be communicated	1. Previous knowledge of and attitude towards the speaker and the subject he is discussing
2. The vividness and intensity of the thoughts and feelings to be communicated	2. Degree of eagerness to listen and to understand fully what is said
3. Knowledge of and attitude towards the listener or listeners	3. Ability and skill of perceiving and interpreting the physical, tonal, and verbal expression of the speaker
4. Degree of eagerness to communicate fully	4. A readiness to react in such a manner as to reveal state of mind to the speaker
5. Perception of and adaptation to the listeners' reactions	
6. Skill of physical, tonal, and verbal expression	

Each of the factors listed in the two columns of Table 1 is variable and each represents a possible point of weakness in the whole process of communication. Thoughts and feelings are the materials to be communicated by speech.

Thoughts and feelings are really different aspects of a single state of consciousness of one individual; and it is obviously impossible for anyone to transfer his individualized state of consciousness to someone else. A speaker has thoughts and feelings that are dependent upon his own past experience. He can only hope to stimulate in other people, by means of speech, thoughts and feelings that are similar to his own. The thoughts and feelings thus stimulated by the speaker are always dependent upon the past experience of the individual listener. The effectiveness of a speaker's communication always depends upon how similar, in nature and degree of completeness, the thoughts and feelings stimulated within another person's consciousness are to those that he has conceived and attempted to communicate. Both speaker and listener take part in any process of communication and the knowledge, attitudes, and skills of both are involved.

The task of communicating may vary from the extremely difficult to the extremely easy, depending upon the degree of difference or similarity that initially exists in the backgrounds of experience and in the viewpoints or attitudes of the speaker and his listener or listeners. An easy task of communication might be illustrated by a speech given by Mr. Barnes before a meeting of a Parent-Teachers Association at a local elementary school. Although Mr. Barnes is known as a poor speaker, his announced subject is traffic control, which attracts an audience of young parents who are vitally interested. In spite of the fact that Mr. Barnes delivers only trite generalities in a dull, uninspired manner, his audience is already so close to a spontaneous reaction against the lack of traffic control in their district that, at Mr. Barnes' request, they readily sign a petition asking for a campaign against violators, and several volunteers agree to present that petition to the city manager. Thus Mr. Barnes accomplishes his purpose and his potentially dull speech is 100 per cent effective when judged in terms of gaining the desired audience response.

By way of contrast, a very difficult task of communication is illustrated by the case of Mr. Doaks and his neighbor's son. Mr. Doaks, a kindly, middle-aged man, has recently been involved in a tragic automobile accident that caused the death of a very close personal friend. Because of Mr. Doaks' part in this accident, a neighbor asks him to speak to his (the neighbor's) son, a boy of eighteen who is notoriously a reckless driver. The neighbor hopes that Mr. Doaks, because of his terrible experience and because he has the reputation of being a very persuasive speaker, can convey to the boy some idea of the tragedy that might easily result from his thoughtless and careless habits while driving. Mr. Doaks' thoughts and feelings concerning careless driving are particularly vivid and intense, and he is strongly motivated to communicate these thoughts and feelings to the boy. Moreover, he is skillful in expressing by physical, tonal, and verbal means his own acute anxiety associated with driving an automobile and his firm conviction that safe driving demands low speeds and extreme vigilance. But, unfortunately, the only thoughts and feelings that he can arouse within the boy are founded upon the boy's personality and background, and hence they bear the stamp of the boy's own reckless individuality. Although this boy may listen attentively and to a degree sympathetically to Mr. Doaks' impassioned plea, the thoughts and feelings aroused within him are still those of an immature youth who has great faith in his own skill and his seeming infallibility as an automobile driver. The thoughts and feelings that Mr. Doaks seeks to communicate and those that he does arouse in the boy are very different, and hence the effectiveness of his communication is very limited.

The function of speech is to communicate, and the efficiency of speech can be judged only in terms of successful communication. Although Mr. Doaks' speech was far more skillful than Mr. Barnes' speech in terms of expression, it was not nearly so effective in terms of communication because of the great difference in the difficulty of the tasks of communicating in the two cases.

How Communication Is Learned

As previously indicated, an infant acquires the initial ability to communicate first by means of physical expression, then by tonal expression, and finally by verbal expression. He acquires the ability to communicate physically by moving first and then learning afterwards what meanings may be conveyed by his movements. For example, a baby may struggle to avoid some unpleasant object. The baby's mother or nurse, seeing the struggling movements, promptly removes the offending object. A few repetitions of this routine is all that is needed to establish an association between the act of struggling and the removal of the object. Thus struggling movements acquire a purpose. Their repetition becomes a demand for the removal of an unpleasant object. Then as this physical reaction is repeated for the purpose of communication, it tends to become more and more refined at each repetition by becoming more and more restricted in scope. For example, the first struggling reactions of an infant are probably violent, involving all muscles from head to toe; but, as this reaction is repeated, the muscular activity tends to become more and more restricted until a mere turning of the head or a pushing movement of one hand may be all that is used to communicate the same idea.

Tonal communication lags only slightly behind physical communication in time of initial development. A cry, for example, is a natural protest or expression of distress that, at first, has no conscious purpose or communicative intent. Nevertheless, the sound of the cry conveys to the mother or nurse the idea that the baby is uncomfortable so she hastens to find and eliminate the cause of discomfort. The gentle ministrations resulting from the cry are pleasant to the baby, and it isn't long before a link is forged in the baby's mind between the act of crying and the comforting care that seems always to follow. Then the crying becomes a demand for service, and soon variations in the act of crying are used as demands for the specific kinds of service wanted. The baby's cry is not the only nonverbal sound that acquires a communicative function. Grunts, screams, gurgles, and squeals of a great variety, plus many other sounds that are natural expressions of moods and feelings, acquire a communicative function because the mother or nurse is extremely sensitive to every suggestion of the baby's slightest wish as it is normally expressed by vocal tone.

The next step in learning to communicate vocally is that of acquiring an articulate language. This is a very complicated process extending over several years and divided into three distinct but overlapping stages of development.

The first is the babbling stage, experienced by every normal child and consisting of a period of spontaneous cooing, gurgling, and playful experimentation with the muscles that will someday produce articulate speech sounds. During this period associative links are formed between the muscular means of producing different vocal sounds and the auditory impressions of the sounds produced. By way of random articulation the baby tends to vocalize through the open mouth, thus uttering something that at least resembles a vowel sound. He then interrupts the flow of sound by closing or partially closing the mouth passage in various ways, thus tending at least to approximate different consonant sounds and to form a series of syllables which, of course, he also hears. Since babbling is a kind of play, it is continued through most of the waking hours for many months. As time passes, various syllables tend to become favorites. The baby utters them often enough to recognize them and to get the knack of uttering them so that he can repeat them quite accurately at will, and he does repeat them over and over as though he were gaining a kind of satisfaction in the very monotony of the repetitions. During the babbling period the child builds up a repertory of sounds that he can both recognize and reproduce. These are the raw materials used in making an articulate language.

The second stage in the development of verbal communication consists of a sort of automatic imitation of sounds uttered by others. This is a parrotlike process since it is not accompanied by the slightest sense of the meanings of words imitated. During the babbling period the baby responds to sounds that he himself utters by repeating them; now he starts to respond to actual words that other people utter by attempting to duplicate them. His attempts may be very crude, according to an adult standard, partly because his sense of hearing is not sufficiently developed to make possible an accurate perception of the speech sounds that he hears, and partly because the repertory of speech sounds that he has learned to make does not include sounds that are exactly like those that he attempts to imitate. Consequently, he can only substitute from his limited repertory those sounds that seem to his unpracticed ear most similar to the sounds he hears. For example, a baby who is just beginning to imitate sounds might respond with a simple "da" to a variety of words such as doll, dog, darling, doctor, and dollar. However, such inaccuracies are soon eliminated quite naturally because the random practice of babbling continues many months after attempts at imitation are first started. Such random articulation not only builds a larger repertory of sounds the baby can make, but it also improves his auditory discernment of vocal sounds and his muscular dexterity in articulating them.

The final stage in the development of verbal communication is that of acquiring a vocabulary of meaningful word symbols. This is a process that usually begins early in the second year (just past the first birthday) and continues throughout one's lifetime or at least possibly until it is halted by senility.

A word is a symbol; and, according to Webster's Collegiate Dictionary, a symbol is "That which suggests something else by reason of relationship, association, convention, etc." A word is invested with meaning by an arbitrary association that must be learned. The initial utterance of a word is in no way a natural response, nor does its sound arouse any natural or unlearned reaction in the listener. It can be used as a vehicle of communication only after the speaker and the listener have learned to associate it with similar meanings.

As soon as a baby can imitate sounds uttered in his presence, he is ready to start acquiring a vocabulary of meaningful words. This process is usually started by somebody teaching the baby to name persons or objects already familiar to him. This is done simply by presenting the person or object to the baby's senses as the name of the person or object is uttered. The baby imitates the name as he observes, in one way or another, the person or object. After a few repetitions of this routine the baby can respond to the person or object by uttering the name without prompting.

If, for example, a mother presents the baby with a doll as she utters the word "doll" and the baby responds with a "da" as an imitation, only a few repetitions will be necessary before the act of presenting the doll will elicite the "da" response without prompting. At this stage the association has been established between the word "da" and the actual perception of the doll itself. But one more step has to be taken before "da" becomes a full-fledged word symbol. The baby must learn to use the word "da" or its improved version "doll" for the purpose of conveying some idea concerning the doll when the doll is not in sight. This may be accomplished either by direct teaching or by additional experience with the doll and its new name. The mother or nurse may teach the baby to associate the word with a recalled image of the doll by holding the doll out of sight as she speaks the word "doll"; then as the baby responds by imitating the word, she promptly produces the doll as a reward for speaking the word. Or, without any directed learning, the baby, by playing with the doll, soon comes to associate it with other objects in his environment; then when the doll is gone, other objects, by association, suggest a remembered image of the doll. This remembered image, by association, calls up the response of uttering the word. Then the mother or nurse, thinking that the baby has asked for the doll, hastens to fetch it for him. In either case the baby learns to utter the word in response to an idea or mental image of the actual object, and soon he learns to use the word as a means of communicating a desire for the object to a listener whose behavior is influenced in such a way that the baby obtains the desired object. In other words, the baby has successfully used a verbal symbol as a means of completing the full process of communication.

Further development of articulate language, as a means of communication, progresses along the same lines. Words must acquire conventional meanings by repeated association with objects or ideas; then these words must be uttered for the purpose of stimulating in others specific images or ideas that will cause them to react in a desired manner before communication can be said to have been accomplished.

Once started, any baby having better than subnormal intelligence learns new words very rapidly. The average child builds a vocabulary of about three thousand words by the time he reaches school age. As a person grows up, a larger and larger vocabulary is acquired through imitation of word sounds that are associated with meanings that his experience permits him to comprehend. The initial meaning that one first learns to associate with a word may be vague or inaccurate; but clearer and more accurate meaning is developed as the word is used and its associations are multiplied in the give and take of daily conversations.

Development of Speech Skills in School

When a child enters kindergarten or elementary school for the first time, the rate of his speech development is greatly accelerated. He is thrown suddenly into a social group of strangers that is much larger than any he has ever known. His need for communication is increased because of a larger number of social contacts; and the process of communicating effectively is more difficult because he is among listeners who, for the most part, are less skilled in understanding his speech and also are less amenable to his influence than members of his own family have been previously. Also the child in school soon acquires experiences both in and out of the classroom that give him new ideas to be communicated. As he begins to read and write, he makes great strides in expanding his vocabulary of word symbols and in developing a sense of language usage, as well as in broadening his intellectual horizons. Each of his school subjects provides some practice in using language as a means of communication. From books as well as from teachers he obtains verbalized information; in classroom recitations and discussions he communicates vocally some of the same information to his teachers and his classmates; and in written reports and examinations he gains practice in verbal communication in writing.

All of this indicates the kind of progress in verbal communication that inevitably accompanies mental development and practice in the interchange of ideas by conversation. But does the average school child receive any specialized training or direction that is aimed directly at improvement in the effectiveness of tonal or physical communication?

Many school systems today employ speech therapists who are concerned with diagnosis and treatment in cases of children whose speech is distinctly subnormal. But otherwise, kindergarten and elementary school teachers rarely have received, or are capable of directing, any specialized training in effective vocal communication. Of course, many teachers usually attempt to correct whatever they recognize as speech errors made by their pupils. For example, they correct what they believe (sometimes mistakenly) to be mispronunciations; they also call attention to obviously slurred articulations, to mistakes in grammar, and to awkward sentence constructions; and they sometimes help pupils to improve their stumbling attempts to communicate ideas by helping to clarify those ideas—usually by supplying words to express them more effectively. In short, nonspecialized teachers are as efficient as they can be in helping pupils to choose and utter words properly, but they usually do not attempt to help their pupils to correct or improve weak or thin voices, harsh or unpleasant voice qualities, stumbling or jarring rhythms of speech, monotonous and colorless manners of talking, or even mild cases of mumbling indistinctness of articulation.

In many high schools specialized courses in speech are available, but such courses are seldom required of all students, and they naturally appeal to students who already speak relatively well. Most colleges and universities offer a number of speech courses; and quite often at least one course in speech is required of students majoring in other fields. In such cases the required course is likely to be a general course in fundamentals of speech or public speaking rather than one aimed primarily at the development of vocal and articulatory skills. It is entirely possible, therefore, that a child might acquire ineffective and unpleasant habits of vocalizing and articulating his speech through the imitation of family models and then go through school and college without improving his manner of speaking or even becoming aware of the undesirable nature of his speech habits.

Factors Limiting the Normal Development of Speech Skills

One might ask why an adult who has practiced speaking since before he can remember should need any training and practice in vocalizing and articulating speech. One might just as well ask why a young man who has been throwing objects like a baseball all his life should need any training and practice in order that he might become a skilled baseball pitcher. The answer in both cases is the same. He needs a kind of strength, flexibility, and control that his previous practice and experience have not given him. But why, one might ask, has one's previous experience in oral communication failed to require sufficient strength, flexibility, and control to make one a skillful speaker? There are many reasons, but four are of basic importance. These are:

1. *Expert listeners.* Much of one's communicative experience has been in intimate conversations with members of his own family and with those associates who know a good deal about him—his interests, his basic attitudes, and his habits of speech. Therefore, they have become experts in understanding whatever he attempts to communicate to them.

2. *Personality.* One's personality always limits the scope of his expression and hence the variety of his speech experience.

3. *Social inhibitions.* Social conversations are conventionally inhibited or mild and reserved—most natural feelings being hidden or moderated.

4. *Social anxieties.* Social anxieties such as stage fright, self-consciousness, and embarrassment interfere with freedom of response and expression.

Expert Listeners: A child's mother is an expert listener so far as his speech is concerned. She understands what he tries to communicate long before he can say it with sufficient clarity for anyone else to understand. As long as the child needs only his mother's services and cooperation, he can depend upon her special ability to understand him and, therefore, he will feel no need to improve his communicative skills.

To some extent the special ability of mother, family, and intimate associates has the same effect upon everyone. A person develops enough communicative skill to secure understanding when and where understanding is important to him. It is relatively easy to secure understanding from intimate associates. Those with whom one has daily contacts know not only his characteristic manners of talking but also his individual attitudes and manners of thinking. It is not necessary for them to hear clearly every word he speaks in order for them to comprehend that which he wishes to communicate. Consequently, anyone's manner of communicating can be very unrevealing and still appear to be adequate in his own intimate circle. A person can use trite, generalized, and inexact verbal expression without being misunderstood; he can mumble or speak so softly that many of his words are too indistinct to be distinguished by his listeners, yet they hear enough to comprehend his meaning; he can speak in a dull, indifferent manner while hiding his feelings behind an air of casual unconcern and still his listeners will know how he feels. Most of any person's speaking experience may be in the nature of relatively trite, inanimate, and indistinct speech that is nevertheless quite adequate to communicate his routine and somewhat stereotyped thoughts and feelings to those who know him well enough to anticipate most of his thoughts and feelings anyway. Only upon relatively rare occasions when one wishes to influence or control the behavior of strangers —as, for example, when he applies for a job through a personal interview—does he feel that his communicative skills are inadequate. But such occasions are too infrequent in the life of the average person to motivate a serious and tenacious effort to improve his speech effectiveness.

Personality: Personality may be defined as individuality or as the total of all attitudes that the individual habitually assumes towards himself, towards those with whom he comes in contact, towards mankind in general, and towards the conventional opinions and ideals of his social world. Important here is the fact that as a child develops a personality, he develops tendencies towards certain attitudes and the behavior motivated by those attitudes, and at the same time he avoids other inconsistent attitudes and behavior. A surly or churlish person, for example, has as a personality trait the tendency towards sullen and ill-natured attitudes and rude behavior while at the same time he avoids happy, gracious, and carefree attitudes and polite or considerate behavior. Every developed tendency to assume certain attitudes is also a tendency to avoid others; so one might say that the development of personality inevitably decreases variation in a person's attitudes and behavior. It also decreases the variety of attitudes communicated by speech and consequently the amount of vocal practice that might be gained by expressing a great variety of attitudes in greatly varied manners of speaking.

No one ever expresses with equal frequency all kinds of attitudes in a great many different manners. A pessimistic worrier seldom if ever expresses delight in an effervescent or boisterous manner of speech; a kindly and gracious person rarely speaks sarcastically; and an arrogant and superficial dandy rarely expresses cordiality or sympathy by his manner of speaking. So it is that one's personality limits his practice in varying his manner of speaking.

Perhaps the most serious effects of personality upon speech development result from personality traits that are assumed, usually during the adolescent years, as a kind of social pose. A young girl, for example, may assume a soft, submissive pose of feminine sweetness and cultivate a thin, breathy voice quality which seems to her to be gentle and velvety but which would not be heard past the second row in any classroom and might not even reach the first row of a large auditorium. The result might be a weak and ineffective voice throughout a lifetime. Many boys assume a kind of sophistication shown by an attitude of elaborate casualness and unconcern that motivates a shuffling kind of walk as well as a mumbling indistinct-

modes of expression, and eagerness to communicate are all conditions essential to the acquiring of skill in effective communication; and social inhibitions tend to reduce the effective quality of every one of these conditions.

Social Anxieties: A social anxiety grows out of social training and is rooted in a feeling of submissiveness to, fear of, or respect for the social group and a desire for social admiration or approval. The particular social anxieties that interfere most with the development of speech skills are stage fright, embarrassment, and self-consciousness.

Although there are great individual differences in the extent to which various people are affected by the social anxieties, every normal person is affected to some extent, and most people tend to think that they are affected more than anyone else. Some of the factors that determine the extent to which any individual is affected are the following:

1. The degree of the person's sensitivity and his readiness to respond.
2. The degree of his personal aggressiveness or submissiveness.
3. The number and prestige of other people present.
4. The novelty of the social situation.

The social anxieties usually limit the development of effective speech habits indirectly by multiplying and reinforcing social inhibitions. As a result of stage fright, embarrassment, or self-consciousness, a person tends to become more reserved or retiring, and more colorless, trite, and submissive in both what he says and his manner of saying it.

Stage fright is the most intense of the social anxieties, although it is seldom very damaging to good speech. It sometimes mounts to panic stages, and it often results in obvious indications of fear such as shaking knees, lapses in memory, and a quavering voice, which usually prove very embarrassing. However, stage fright, being motivated by the novelty of facing an assembled audience, is entirely normal; and its damaging effects usually wear off as the novelty of making public appearances wears off. There is no recognized method of avoiding stage fright except by complete avoidance of any appearance before an assembled group of any kind. A person may reduce the initial shock of stage fright, however, by first making many public appearances before relatively small audiences of people who are not above his own level in age and public prestige, and who are assembled upon a relatively informal or routine occasion. A speech class is ideal for easing the early shock of panic before an audience. Members of such a class are almost always afflicted with stage fright at first, but their fright is not so intense as it would be if they were forced to make a first public appearance before a huge audience of older and relatively prominent people assembled upon a solemn or formal occasion. Of course, a person who has completed a course in speech and has eliminated the damaging effects of stage fright in the classroom may still suffer some degree of stage fright before a large audience upon an important occasion. But the damaging effects of stage fright would be greatly reduced as a result of the classroom experience, and the fright itself would be less intense.

When a person has the opportunity to make his first public appearance as a speaker, actor, or interpreter, he should accept stage fright as a thoroughly normal reaction, and he should not give way to the tendency to believe himself more frightened than others under similar circumstances. In order that he should minimize the damaging effects of stage fright, he should be governed by the following advice:

1. *Be well prepared.* Good preparation for a public appearance serves to bolster self-confidence, which is a powerful antidote to stage fright.

2. *Relax* and do not try to hide your nervousness. Fright is always accompanied by extreme muscular tensions that often cause trembling of knees and hands. The natural

tendency is to be ashamed of such evidences of fear and to try desperately to hide them. The usual method of trying to stop trembling is that of tensing muscles even more than they are, and thus the trembling is increased. The most effective way to control a tendency to tremble is to relax and stop trying to hide the trembling. Some public speakers successfully relieve their physical tensions by calling attention to their shaking knees or hands in a joking manner. After both they and their audiences have laughed at such evidences of nervousness, they no longer try to hide their trembling and their tensions seem to disappear.

3. *Become active* by responding freely to your material. Nothing relieves physical tensions quite so effectively as physical activity. Freedom of physical movement and expression, therefore, has the double function of reinforcing verbal communication and of draining off excess nervous energy and thus relieving physical tensions.

4. *Never give up to stage fright.* A lapse of memory or a panicky confusion of thoughts resulting from stage fright may cause a person to want to admit defeat and to escape from the audience without finishing what he has set out to present. But if he yields to such a temptation, his shame and embarrassment will serve to multiply his fears in any future public appearance. In fact, one or more of such failures might cause stage fright to become a fixed phobia of abnormal intensity.

Although a person may never learn to rid himself entirely of stage fright, the novelty of appearing in public wears off, and the intensity of stage fright usually falls far below the level at which it can be embarrassing to the speaker or damaging to his development of effective speech habits. In fact, heightened feelings of controlled stage fright may be very stimulating to a speaker, actor, or interpreter, increasing both his alertness and his animation, thus tending to improve rather than damage the effectiveness of his speech.

Embarrassment and self-consciousness, on the other hand, are never stimulating. They are both entirely restrictive in their effect upon a speaker or interpreter. By multiplying and reinforcing social inhibitions they cause a person to become more reserved and more timid or negative in attitude towards any audience. A high degree of self-consciousness makes the learning of effective communicative skills extremely difficult.

Embarrassment is usually more temporary than self-consciousness. It means a loss of self-possession or a sudden sense of inferiority or shame, whereas self-consciousness means an assumption of one's own social awkwardness or an expectancy, in the presence of others, of one's own failure to accomplish anything smoothly and in a manner deserving public admiration. The two terms, however, are very closely related. In fact, self-consciousness may be defined as a predisposition to be embarrassed at the least provocation.

Fortunately self-consciousness and embarrassment are troublesome to an average person only in novel social situations before large or important groups of people. Consequently, the restrictive effect of self-consciousness and embarrassment gradually fades away as novelty gives way to familiarity. But in some cases, where self-consciousness is reinforced by a so-called inferiority complex or a habitual submissiveness of attitude, the restrictive effect of this social attitude becomes a primary problem in any training program for the improvement of communicative skill.

Objectives in Training Voice and Articulation

The general objective of training the voice and articulation is the improvement of one's communicative skill as a speaker. But communication by means of speech has a very wide range of difficulty. There is, for example, a tremendous difference in difficulty between the communication of one's own casual, everyday thoughts and feelings, upon close face-to-face contact, to a member of one's own family or an intimate associate and the communication of the thoughts and feelings of one of Shakespeare's great dramatic characters to a large audience of strangers. Probably very few people have any intention of preparing themselves to become Shakespearean actors, but anyone interested in effective speech will presumably try to develop a much greater skill than that needed to reveal the daily experiences of his routine life in a conventional manner to his family and intimate friends.

As a person sets out to improve his communicative skill, one of his first and most fundamental objectives should be to develop a voice that is strong and of pleasing basic quality. It should be strong enough so that he may project it easily across any distance that may frequently separate him from any listener, and it should be pleasant enough in effect upon any new listener to inspire sympathy, confidence, and respect.

Another of the most fundamental objectives is to improve the conventional accuracy and precision of articulating words so that speech flows with a maximum of distinctness and yet with an ease and normality of sound that makes the manner of speaking unobtrusive. This involves the careful analysis of differences in the usage of speech sounds by people of different cultural levels and of different geographic regions, and a development of good taste in selecting and using the speech sounds that will give an impression that the speaker is unpretentious and well-bred.

Other objectives may be classified under the one general objective of gaining sufficient flexibility and control of speech vocalization to make a high degree of skill in vocal expression possible. This general objective is then subdivided according to the different attributes of voice and speech for which flexibility and control are essential to skillful expression. These attributes are force, pitch, quality of voice, and timing of articulate speech.

Skillful expression involves both a vivid and complete conception of the thoughts and feelings to be communicated and the spontaneous composition or recall of effective speech, consisting of both words and an expressive intonation pattern. The person who is interested in improving his voice and articulation must be concerned primarily, not with the selection of words and the construction of sentences (however important these may be), but with the enunciation of connected words and the spontaneous composition of expressive intonation patterns. It is obvious that he must develop a flexible speech mechanism that he can use with dexterity and a high degree of muscular precision, coordination, and synchronization. Although skill in the enunciation of connected words may be developed at least in part by a calisthenic type of drill that does not necessarily involve the communication of vividly perceived thoughts and feelings, an effective intonation pattern must be motivated by the impulse to communicate. It seems, therefore, that the flexibility of the vocal instrument must be developed principally by practice in communication.

It is understood, of course, that different people who undertake the improvement of their voices and manners of speaking may have vastly different goals in mind. One may wish to develop a vocal instrument that can express effectively and pleasantly nothing more unusual than his own thoughts and feelings in social conversations with friends and acquaintances; another may wish to become an effective public speaker with a vocal instrument that is capable of communicating his own most significant thoughts and feelings to an audience of any size and under any circumstances; and another may wish to become an actor or interpreter with a highly trained speech mechanism that will be capable of vocalizing and articulating in an expert fashion the power, intensity, and beauty of the world's greatest literature. However, the variation in goals will make less difference in the manner and scope of training or practice than one might suppose. Any difference should be one of degree of development in specific skills and perhaps in the variety of materials used for practice rather than in the nature of training or practice to be undertaken.

Summary

The act of speaking is supplemented and reinforced by both physical and tonal expression which have greater credibility than the articulated words. However, a verbal language is by far the most versatile medium for communicating precise or complex thoughts and feelings. A person's individual techniques of physical, tonal, and verbal expressions are acquired at an early and uncritical age so that, by the time anyone is old enough to be concerned about the effectiveness of his speech, he has already formed deep-seated habits in his manner of speaking which seem so characteristic of himself that he is usually reluctant to attempt any change which he is unable to recognize as an improvement.

The function of speech is not merely to express one's thoughts and feelings but to communicate them to others. This involves not only the speaker's perception, attitudes, and skills of speaking which are determined by his past experience but also the listener's previous knowledge, attitudes, and skills of listening that are determined by his past experience. Whether communication be very easy or very difficult, the effectiveness of speech will always depend not upon skill of expression but upon the degree of successful communication.

A baby acquires the ability to communicate first by physical expression and then by tonal expression. This is accomplished by merely associating his own natural physical and vocal reactions with the resulting behavior of his mother or mother-substitute; and then, after the associations are formed, he uses the same physical and vocal reactions as a means of demanding the same behavior.

Vocal communication develops much more slowly through several stages. First comes the babbling stage, which is a period of playful experimentation with the vocal mechanism.

This serves to establish associations between the ways of producing different sounds and the auditory impressions of the sounds produced. Next comes the stage of imitating speech sounds uttered by others. Then follows the slow process, of symbolization, or the association of the speech sounds imitated first with objects and then with remembered images or ideas. By the time the average child reaches school age he will have acquired a vocabulary of approximately three thousand words and will be composing simple sentences without difficulty.

In school the speed at which the child acquires ability in verbal communication will be greatly accelerated. However, the average child will receive little or no specialized training that would help him to improve the quality of his voice, the precision of his articulation, or the skill of his vocal and physical expression. It is entirely possible, therefore, that a person may acquire by means of imitation in infancy many bad habits of articulating and vocalizing his speech and a dull, monotonous manner of speaking, and that these faults may not be corrected as a result of his school training.

One might naturally suppose that a lifetime of practice in conversational communication would develop skill in effective speech. But the communicative problem is so simple in the average conversation that a very low grade of speech efficiency is usually quite adequate for social communication. There are four basic reasons for the usual low standard of communicative efficiency in social speech. First, one speaks most commonly to listeners who are so expert in anticipating most of what he is likely to say that they can usually understand what he attempts to say without his having to bother to express it clearly or articulate it distinctly. Second, a speaker's personality greatly decreases the variety of attitudes that he ordinarily expresses, and, consequently, it reduces his scope of practice in expressing a variety of moods and attitudes. Third, social training restricts the variety and intensity of emotions and feelings that may be expressed in social conversation so that a well-adjusted or sophisticated person is very reserved and mild in his manner of speaking. Fourth, stage fright, embarrassment, and self-consciousness tend to reinforce social inhibitions rendering a speaker extremely reserved in all novel social situations.

Any program of voice training is aimed at the development of effective communication no matter how the ability to communicate may be used. Any program of training should include strengthening the voice and improving its basic quality. It should also involve work for a maximum distinctness of articulation without loss of a smooth and unobtrusive flow of speech. It should aim to develop flexibility and control of the force, pitch, and quality of voice and the timing of articulated speech for effective communication. And, finally, it should aim to develop a positive speaking personality and a freedom of response.

QUESTIONS

1. What three kinds of expression are used simultaneously by a speaker?
2. Which type of expression is the most dominant?
3. Which type of expression is the least dominant?
4. Which type of expression is the most versatile?
5. Why is the average person very uncritical of his own speech?
6. Distinguish between communication and expression and explain why this distinction is important.
7. Name some of the factors that determine a speaker's effectiveness in communication.
8. Name some of the factors that determine a listener's effectiveness in the process of communication.
9. Cite an example of easy communication and of difficult communication.
10. In what order does an infant acquire the various types of expression?
11. Describe the various steps by which a baby learns to talk.
12. Why is babbling essential to the process of learning to talk?

13. What is meant by a symbol? Give an example of a symbol other than a word.

14. About how many words should you expect a six-year-old child to have in his vocabulary?

15. What kinds of aid in speech development does a pupil normally receive in school?

16. Why does practice in social conversations fail to develop a high degree of communicative skill?

17. Define personality and explain how personality might limit one's development of speech skills.

18. How do social inhibitions limit the development of speech skills?

19. What are the best ways of combating stage fright?

20. Would you like to be the type of person who is utterly unaffected by stage fright? Explain.

21. What are the chief objectives in training voice and articulation?

Exercises

General Method of Preparation: The preparation of exercise materials should not necessarily involve memorization of words. However, the fact that a selection may be interpreted while reading the words should never be accepted as a reason for curtailment of study.

In the process of preparing any material for oral presentation, the aim should be to develop an easy and spontaneous manner of delivery. This will necessitate a thorough assimilation of the ideas expressed, and a sensing of all imagery, all the motivations, and all the attitudes suggested, as well as a complete familiarity with all the words, in order to insure acceptable pronunciation, accurate articulation, and a rapid and unstumbling delivery. The general effect should be similar to that of conversational speech—the ideas and feelings being communicated impulsively, as though they were originated at the moment of utterance. Such a smooth and spontaneous style of delivery is not easy to develop, and it can never be developed by merely repeating the words without concentrating upon their significance during each repetition, and without consciously attempting to communicate their full significance.

Oral interpretation for platform, stage, or studio is an intensive form of study; therefore, study methods are especially important. In fact, poor methods of study may be worse than no study at all because poor study methods might result in the formation of artificial habits of vocal expression.

The following principles should serve as a guide to effective study:

1. First, read silently the material to be interpreted; then attempt to summarize the thought content in your own words. If necessary, repeat the reading and summarizing process several times until the thought content seems clear.

2. Always refer to a dictionary for the meaning or the preferred pronunciation of any word about which you have the slightest doubt. Any vagueness of speech pattern showing lack of a clear perception of meaning, as well as any error of pronunciation or stumbling indefiniteness of utterance, should be regarded as serious faults if committed by any learner who has carefully prepared the material he is reading.

3. Begin to read aloud, striving upon each repetition to increase the vividness of your own perception of the meanings, the imagery, the feelings or attitudes suggested, and the overall mood of the selection. Never repeat the material unless you are fully alert and responsive to it. In other words, each repetition must be as complete an interpretative process as the reader is capable of accomplishing at that time. Careless or mechanical repetitions of the material when the learner is not alert or is thinking of something else will only result in the memorization of dull and uninteresting patterns of speech which will be very difficult to eliminate.

Selections: Purpose—To serve as a vocal introduction demonstrating the existence or absence of basic voice problems.

Method—Prepare one or more of the following selections for your best oral delivery.

1. * The first rule shall be—OBSERVE! A simple matter—one, I dare say, which it will seem to you difficult not to follow. You have a pair of eyes; how can you fail to observe? Ah, but eyes can only look; that is not observing. You want to observe, not to look only. You want to penetrate into things, to find out what is there. There is nothing on earth which, when observed, is not of enormous interest. You cannot find anything so destitute of the principles of

* "The Glory of the Imperfect—The First Rule of Practice" from THE IDEAL TEACHER by George Herbert Palmer, Copyright 1915: Used by permission of Houghton Mifflin Company.

life that, when you come to study it, it will not disclose those principles to you. But it makes all the difference whether you do thus observe, whether you are willing to hold your attention to the thing in hand and see what it contains. After puzzling long about the charm of Homer, I once applied to a learned friend and said to him, "Can you tell me why Homer is so interesting? Why can't you and I write as he wrote? Why is it that his art was lost with him, and that today it is impossible for us to quicken such interest as he?" "Well," said my friend, "I have meditated on that a great deal, but it seems to me it comes to about this: Homer looked long at a thing. Why," said he, "do you know that if you should hold up your thumb and look at it long enough, you would find it immensely interesting?" Homer looked a great while at his thumb; he sees precisely the thing he is dealing with. He does not confuse it with anything else. It is sharp to him; and because it is sharp to him it stands out sharply for us over all these thousands of years.

from *The Ideal Teacher*
by George Herbert Palmer

2. * One of the oldest jokes in the world, which recurs in almost every number of every humorous periodical, in comic strips and stage farces, is a variant, without much variety, of the idea that woman talks too much, that she talks more and says less than her superior brother, who, of course, invented the joke.

There is underneath this joke an important fact entirely creditable to the fairer half of the human race and necessary to the intellectual development of the entire race, male and female alike, as God created us.

This is the momentous truth: Women ought to talk as much as they do, or, if possible, more. If women were not natural, instinctive, unconscious chatterers, civilization would perish, and we should all grow up more stupid, ignorant, and uneducated than we are. Women are the source and fountain of language, pouring it forth at the time we most need language, in the earliest years of childhood. We owe all that is most vital in our education to the provision of Nature that mother, grandmother, aunt, sister, nurse were garrulous women and kept the very air we breathed swarming with words from morning till night. From the moment when we wake up in the cradle and begin to cry for food until the hour when we are sung to sleep, it is women who flood our ears and brains with language.

from *About Women*
by John Macy

3. Speak the speech, I pray you, as I pronounced it to you, trippingly on the tongue: but if you mouth it, as many of your players do, I had as lief the town-crier spoke my lines. Nor do not saw the air too much with your hand, thus; but use all gently: for in the very torrent, tempest, and as I may say, the whirlwind of your passion, you must acquire and beget a temperance that may give it smoothness. O, it offends me to the soul to hear a robustious periwig-pated fellow tear a passion to tatters, to very rags, to split the ears of the groundlings; who, for the most part, are capable of nothing but inexplicable dumb shows and noise; I would have such a fellow whipp'd for o'erdoing Termagant; it out-herods Herod: pray you, avoid it. . . . Be not too tame neither, but let your own discretion be your tutor: suit the action to the word, the word to the action; with this special observance, that you o'erstep not the modesty of nature: for anything so overdone is from the purpose of playing, whose end, both at the first and now, was and is, to hold as 'twere, the mirror up to nature; to show virtue her own feature, scorn her own image, and the very age and body of the time his form and pressure. Now this overdone, or come tardy off, though it make the unskillful laugh, cannot but make the judicious grieve; the censure of the which one must, in your allowance, o'erweigh a whole theatre of others. O, there be players that I have seen play, and heard others praise, and that highly, not to speak it profanely, that, neither having the accent of Christians nor the gait of Christian, pagan, nor man, have so strutted and bellowed, that I have thought some of nature's journeymen had made men and not made them well, they imitated humanity so abominably.

from *Hamlet*
by William Shakespeare

4. True ease in writing comes from Art, not Chance,
As those move easiest who have learned to dance.
'Tis not enough no harshness gives offence,
The sound must seem an echo to the sense;
Soft is the strain when zephyr gently blows,

And the smooth stream in smoother numbers flows;
But when loud surges lash the sounding shore,
The hoarse rough verse should like the torrent roar.
When Ajax strives some rock's vast weight to throw,
The line, too, labours, and the words move slow:
Not so when swift Camilla scours the plain
Flies o'er the unbending corn, and skims along the main.

from *Essay on Criticism*
by Alexander Pope

5. Whence then cometh wisdom? and where is the place of understanding?

Seeing it is hid from the eyes of all living, and kept close from the fowls of the air.

Destruction and death say, We have heard the fame thereof with our ears.

God understandest the way thereof, and He knoweth the place thereof.

For He looketh to the ends of the earth, and seeth under the whole heaven;

To make the weight of the winds; and He weigheth the waters by measure.

When He made a decree for the rain, and a way for the lightning of the thunder:

Then did He see it, and declare it; He prepared it, yea, and searched it out

And unto men He said, Behold, the fear of the Lord, that is wisdom; and to depart from evil is understanding.

Job, XXVIII

2.

Physics of Sound

IT IS obvious that voice is a kind of sound produced by a human being and that it may be heard at some distance by other human beings; but exactly what a sound is and how it travels through space is not so obvious. Everyone knows that voice is a distinctive kind of sound that may be recognized as belonging to a particular person; but what makes it distinctive and recognizable? Anyone knows that sounds can be varied. The voice, for example, may be changed by articulation into different speech sounds, and it may also be changed to make up the intonation pattern that a speaker uses to reinforce and modify the literal meanings of his spoken words; but, in terms of sound, can everyone explain the nature of these variations? Does everyone know exactly what is meant by such words as loudness, intensity, amplitude, pitch, frequency, tone, noise, resonance, timbre, quality, and overtones? If not, he is not ready to discuss the development of voice and articulation with complete understanding. It will be well, therefore, to pause briefly and learn some of the basic fundamentals of the physics of sound.

Air as a Medium Through Which Sound Travels

The vast ocean of air that completely surrounds the earth is the most important medium through which sounds can travel. Sounds can travel also through any resilient solid substance such as steel and through a liquid such as water, but nearly all the sounds we hear come to us through the air.

Air consists of minute particles of matter (much too small to be visible) that we call air molecules. These air molecules repel one another, thus tending to remain as far apart as possible. However, air molecules have weight, and the weight of the vast ocean of air surrounding the earth and pressing down toward its surface with a force known as atmospheric pressure keeps the air molecules compressed relatively close together. Each molecule tends to fall to the earth because of its own weight and the weight of other molecules repelling it from above; but, at the same time, each molecule is repelled by others below it and on all sides of it. As a result, each molecule is suspended in space at a point where all forces acting upon it are in exact equilibrium; and all air molecules at any particular atmospheric pressure will tend to remain the same distance apart.

When any air molecules are displaced, they quickly spring back into their original places or rearrange themselves into new positions of equilibrium where all forces pushing them from different directions are exactly equal. When air is compressed—the molecules being abnormally close together, as in a toy balloon or an automobile tire— it tends to expand in all directions because of the repelling force of the molecules themselves, thus exerting an outward pressure. When, on the other hand, air is rarefied—the molecules being abnormally far apart, as in any partial vacuum—the surrounding air exerts a strong inward force because of atmospheric pressure. So we see that air resists distortion of any kind.

When any solid object is forced to move through the air, it will condense the air in front of itself and rarefy the air behind. In the condensed area in front, which may also be called a high-pressure area, the air molecules are forced relatively close together; and in the rarefied or low-pressure area behind, the air molecules are forced relatively far apart.

Normally, the excess air molecules from the high-pressure area in front will merely swirl around the sides of the moving object and quickly fill in the low-pressure area behind. When a person uses a palm-leaf fan, for example, he can easily feel the puffs of rushing air molecules as they move from the high-pressure area to the low-pressure area, first in one direction and then in the other, as the fan moves back and forth.

So we see that air is an elastic medium. At any particular atmospheric pressure it will tend to remain at a consistent density—the molecules being the same distance apart. If anything forces air molecules into condensed areas or out of rarefied areas, these molecules will always tend to rearrange themselves as soon as possible into new positions of equilibrium and at a consistent density.

Sound Waves

A sound wave may be defined as a series of condensations and rarefactions of air molecules that is projected outward from its source in all directions at a speed of approximately 1,100 feet per second. Now the question arises—is a sound wave the same as a sound?

Almost everyone has heard the riddle about the tree falling in the forest when no one is near enough to hear it fall. This riddle ends with the question as to whether or not there is any sound of the tree's falling. This question may be correctly answered with either a "yes" or a "no," depending upon which of two possible definitions of sound we are willing to accept. If we define sound as a disturbance of air molecules that is transmitted through the air in the form of a wave, then the correct answer is "yes," because the falling tree would undoubtedly create such a sound wave; but, if we define sound as the auditory sensation which is the effect of a sound wave upon the ear, then the answer should be "no," because there is no ear close enough to be affected by the sound wave created by the tree's falling. In order to avoid confusion, we shall accept the latter definition, and shall refer hereafter to the air disturbance as a sound wave and to the resulting auditory sensation as a sound.

There are an infinite variety of sounds, most of which may be classified either as tones or noises. A tone may be defined as a sound having sufficient regularity of vibration to give it a distinctive pitch and quality for an appreciable length of time. A sound wave that is perceived by the ear as a tone consists of a series of condensations and rarefactions of air molecules that is of consistent pattern. A noise, on the other hand, never has a distinctive pitch and quality for an appreciable length of time; and the sound wave that is perceived as a noise will not have a patterned regularity of condensations and rarefactions. The sound of a human voice is a tone, while the sound of articulating consonants with lips or tongue is a noise. The sound of a person speaking is made up largely of vowel tones, but a confused babble of many voices speaking at the same time may be perceived only as noise. The whistle of a steam locomotive is a tone, but the whishing sound of escaping steam is a noise.

In the following discussion of sound waves and sound, we shall consider only regular or patterned waves that are perceived as tones.

Most patterned sound waves are initiated by vibrating objects. A vibrating object oscillates, or moves to and fro, very rapidly. Most vibratory movements are too rapid to be observed accurately. If we look carefully at a vibrating violin string, for example, we may see that it looks thicker than it does normally and it appears slightly blurred, and it would give a tickling sensation to the touch; but the to-and-fro movements of the string are too rapid to be perceived as distinct movements. These movements are also too rapid to allow time for the air molecules to swirl around the string on each separate vibration and thus regain their equilibrium. A forward movement of the string quickly condenses air molecules, then a backward movement rarefies the molecules, another forward movement condenses the molecules, and so forth—never allowing sufficient time for the molecules to regain their equilibrium and come to rest. Actually the air molecules themselves are forced to oscillate in a to-and-fro movement similar to that of the vibrating string. Because of the elastic nature of the air, the movement of the molecules close to the string will force other adjacent molecules into similar motion and these transfer the movement to others father and farther away. So it is that a sound wave consisting of a series of condensations and rarefactions of oscillating air molecules is created. This sound wave moves out from its source in all directions and at a consistent speed.

FIGURE 2
A Sound Wave

The vibrating tuning fork sets the air molecules into similar oscillating movements, and a sound wave consisting of a series of condensations and rarefactions of air molecules (which are represented in Figure 2 by alternate dark and light circles) move out from the tuning fork in all directions. When a sound wave enters a person's outer ear, it represents a series of rapidly changing pressures. A condensed area, having a high pressure, would push the eardrum inward; then a rarefied area, having a low pressure, would (like a suction) pull the eardrum outward. The high and low pressures, alternating very rapidly as the sound wave moves into the ear, cause the eardrum to vibrate. The mechanism of the inner ear converts this vibration into nerve impulses which are translated by the brain as the sensation of sound.

Sound waves always travel through the air at approximately 1,100 feet per second. This means that all kinds of sound waves will travel about one mile in five seconds or approximately 720 miles per hour. It should be understood, however, that the sound wave and not the air molecules move at such a speed. The air molecules that transmit a sound wave merely oscillate back and forth while remaining approximately in their original locations.

The Variable Attributes of Sound Waves and Sounds

Sounds are of many kinds. We hear loud sounds and weak sounds; shrill sounds and low or rumbling sounds; harsh sounds and sweet sounds; sharp, staccato sounds and long-drawn-out sounds; as well as an infinite variety of sounds that we can readily distinguish from one another by ear even though it might be very difficult to describe the variations. All these differences may be classified under four variable attributes of sound which are known as (1) loudness, (2) pitch, (3) quality, and (4) duration. Any two contrasting sounds will differ in one or more of these variable attributes. And the fact that we can distinguish differences by ear indicates that the sound waves themselves must differ.

Intensity, Amplitude, and Loudness

The terms intensity and amplitude are applied to sound waves, while loudness is applied only to sound. When we speak of the intensity of a sound wave, we are referring to the amount of energy used in initiating the sound wave, or, we might say, the amount of energy that is consumed in the process of forcing the sound wave to move through the air. The amplitude of a sound wave, on the other hand, is a measure of distance of vibration. It is equal to half the total distance through which an air molecule moves in its to-and-fro motion. Intensity and amplitude may be illustrated by the movement of a pendulum. If a pendulum were hanging motionless, any push, however weak, would start it swinging to and fro. The amount of energy exerted in this initial push (and slowly consumed while the pendulum continues to swing) is analogous to the energy used in causing an object to vibrate. A measure of this energy would be the same as the measure of the intensity of the sound wave initiated by the vibrating object. The distance that the pendulum moves in the direction that it is pushed before it stops and starts to fall back is the amplitude of its movement because that distance equals half of the total distance through which the pendulum will swing. This is analogous to the amplitude of the movement of a vibrating object or the resulting vibration of air molecules.

If anyone should strike a tuning fork, each prong of the fork would move to and fro exactly as a pendulum moves, except, of course, that the movement of the tuning fork would be much more rapid and of much smaller amplitude. If one should strike a tuning fork very lightly (thus exerting very little energy upon the blow) the resulting vibration and the sound wave initiated by it would be of very weak intensity and the amplitude of the movement would be very small. The ear would perceive this sound wave of weak intensity and small amplitude as a faint tone having a very low degree of loudness. If one should then strike the same tuning fork much harder, both the intensity and the amplitude of the resulting sound wave would be much greater, and the effect upon the ear would be that of a louder tone.

The intensity of a sound wave will determine the distance the wave will carry through the air before it dies out. A sound wave of strong intensity will carry farther (although not faster) than a sound wave of weak intensity. The sound wave of strong intensity will have a relatively large amplitude close to its source, but this amplitude will get smaller and smaller as the wave travels farther and farther from its source. A sound wave having a strong intensity and large amplitude close to its source will be sensed by anyone's ear as a loud sound; but the same sound wave at a greater distance from its source will have a much smaller amplitude and will be sensed by an ear as a weak sound.

In general, we may say that a sound wave of strong intensity is that of a loud sound in the sense that it will travel relatively far through the air; but a sound wave of strong intensity may be sensed as a weak or faint sound by anyone who is far from its source. The loudness of a sound will depend upon the amplitude of the sound wave at the point where it is sensed by the ear.

Sound-Wave Frequency and the Pitch of Sound

The frequency of a sound wave is the speed at which the to-and-fro movements of the vibrating air molecules are repeated. This frequency is measured in terms of the number of cycles per second, or, one might say, the number of complete vibrations per second. When anything is repeated over and over again, each complete occurrence is called a cycle. While a swinging clock pendulum, for example, moves from any position to one extreme of its arc then back to the other extreme and back again to its initial position, it is completing one cycle. All other cycles will be exact repetitions of the first. It happens that a clock pendulum completes a cycle in two seconds; therefore, its frequency is one-half cycle per second.

The vibrating movement of air molecules involved in sound-wave transmission is a to-and-fro movement like that of a clock pendulum, but the frequencies of various sound waves are very much higher or faster. Sound waves that can be perceived as tones by the human ear will have frequencies ranging from about 20 cycles per second to perhaps 12,000 cycles per second. The upper limit of audible frequencies is rather indefinite because the ears of different individuals vary in the ability to hear high-frequency sounds. Although many people can hear frequencies that are considerably higher than 12,000 cycles per second, the auditory sensation of such high frequencies will probably not seem like a tone but rather like a slight hissing sound that will lack definiteness of impression.

Sound waves having different frequencies are sensed by the ear as sounds having different pitches. The pitch of a sound may be described as its degree of highness or lowness on the musical scale. A sound wave that we sense as a tone of high pitch has a relatively high frequency, while the sound we sense as a tone of low pitch has a relatively low frequency. If, for example, you should strike the piano key known as "middle C," you would hear a musical tone resulting from your ear's perception of a sound wave having a frequency of 256 cycles per second—assuming that the piano has been tuned at the usually accepted level. If you should strike the key just one octave (or eight steps on the musical scale) higher, you would hear the higher pitch of a sound wave having a frequency just twice as fast, or 512 cycles per second.

When any solid object can be made to vibrate so as to create a sound wave, its rate of vibration will determine the frequency of the wave and hence the pitch of the sound that is sensed by the ear. Any means of controlling the rate of vibration, therefore, is also a means of controlling the pitch. As an example of the control of pitch, let us consider a violin because a musician, in tuning or playing a violin, controls pitch by visible means. A violin has four strings of about equal lengths but of different thicknesses. Other things being equal, the thicker strings vibrate at slower frequencies and hence produce lower pitches. The musician tunes the four strings to different pitches by adjusting the tension of each string by means of pivots to which the strings are attached. If the pitch produced by a string is too low the string will be tightened by twisting the pivot to which it is attached, thus speeding up the frequency of its vibration and raising the pitch; if, on the other hand, the pitch produced by a string is too high, the frequency of vibration must be lowered by loosening the string. When playing the violin, the musician controls pitch by adjusting the length of the part of each string that is made to vibrate. He can adjust the length of a vibrating segment of string by pressing a finger down upon the string at different points, thus leaving only that part of the string between his finger and the bridge of the violin free to vibrate.

So we see that pitch may be determined to some extent by the thickness of a vibrating string or it may be controlled by adjustment of the tension or the length of that part of the string that is made to vibrate. We may expect high pitches to be produced by a vibrating string that is thin, tight, or short, while a relatively low pitch may be produced by a thicker, looser, or longer vibrating string.

The Quality of Sound

Variations in the loudness or the pitch of a sound are relatively simple changes in degree or level. The loudness of a sound can be changed only in degree to a less loud or a louder sound, and the pitch of a sound can be changed only in level to a higher or a lower pitch. But the variations in quality of sound cannot be measured according to any single scale of level or degree; and some changes may be very subtle and complicated and hence hard to describe. We may classify sound qualities according to varying degrees of pleasantness or unpleasantness, deepness or shallowness, fullness or thinness, softness or hardness, mellowness or harshness, and so on indefinitely until we run out of words that may be used to describe such changes.

Almost all substances that can be made to vibrate so as to create a sound wave, vibrate in a complex manner. For example, a violin string, when forced to vibrate, will vibrate as a whole and, at the same time, it will vibrate in several segments or subdivisions of the whole. Such a complex mode of vibration will create a complex sound wave. The whole string, vibrating at its natural frequency which (as explained previously) is determined by its thickness, length, and tension, will establish the dominant or fundamental frequency of the sound wave, and this fundamental frequency will be perceived by the ear as the pitch of the sound. The vibrating segments of the violin string will create at the same time certain harmonic vibrations or overtones which, when blended with the fundamental frequency, will be sensed by one's ear as the quality of the sound. One may say, therefore, that the quality of a sound is determined by the frequencies and relative amplitudes of its audible overtones.

Perhaps quality of sound may be easier to understand if we think of it in terms of a blend of several sounds. A violin string, because of its complex manner of vibration, produces simultaneously a number of sounds that are loud enough to be heard. The one sound produced by the vibration of the string as a whole is relatively loud, while the other sounds produced by vibrating segments of the string are relatively weak. The loud sound has a relatively low pitch, which we call the fundamental pitch. The weak sounds, which we call overtones, all have different pitches which are all higher than the fundamental pitch. All of these sounds—the loud and low-pitched and the weak and high-pitched—are blended together so that they are sensed by the ear as one sound which has a characteristic quality.

The relatively loud sound of the fundamental pitch will be predominant over the weaker overtones, thus determining usually the over-all effects of pitch and loudness; but the blended combination of all the sounds will determine that characteristic that we call the quality or sometimes the timbre of sound.

Since the quality or timbre of a sound is determined by the frequencies and relative amplitudes of the audible overtones, the quality of any sound may be changed by changing these frequencies, and relative amplitudes, and the number of audible overtones. Such changes may be made by means of a resonator.

Resonance and Quality

A resonator is a part of a sound-producing instrument that intensifies or reinforces sound waves. A resonator may operate on either or both of two general principles, which may be called the cavity principle and the sounding-board principle.

A cavity resonator consists, as the name implies, of a cavity having one or more openings. There are a great variety of cavity resonators which depend for their effects upon the size and shape of the cavities themselves, the firmness and resiliency of their walls, and the number, size, and shape of their openings. However, it is hardly necessary to consider here all the variations in operation of all different kinds of cavity resonators. In general, a resonator has the effect of reinforcing or giving greater amplitude to sound waves. Most cavity resonators are highly selective in the sense that they reinforce certain pitches to which they are best adjusted. A single cavity resonator may give maximum reinforcement to certain pitches to which it is well adjusted, while at the same time it gives some reinforcement in varying degrees to other pitches to which it is not well adjusted, and it might even "damp out" or deaden certain other pitches to which it is poorly adjusted. In general, large cavities with small openings are best adjusted for the reinforcement of low pitches and small cavities with large openings are best adjusted for the reinforcement of high pitches. A xylophone illustrates the adjustment in size of cavity resonators to certain pitches. The xylophone is made up of wooden bars of graduated lengths that initiate the various musical tones.

Directly under the wooden bars are metal cylinders that are closed at the lower ends. These cylinders are resonating cavities which are also graduated in length for the best adjustment to the various pitches. The smallest cavity is used to reinforce the highest pitch and the largest is used to reinforce the lowest pitch.

A sounding-board resonator operates as a kind of extension of the vibrator. Any resilient mass may be forced to vibrate by contact with a vibrating object. If, for example, a person should hold a tuning fork in his hand as he strikes it, the sound initiated by its vibration would be relatively weak; but if he should then press the base of the vibrating fork firmly against a table top, the sound would instantly seem much louder. The table top acts as a sounding board because it is forced to vibrate in unison with the tuning fork. The sound wave initiated by the vibrating table top adds to and reinforces that set up by the tuning fork, thus giving the combined wave a greater amplitude. A sounding-board resonator, like a cavity resonator, is somewhat selective because most resilient materials of a particular size, shape, and texture will vibrate more easily to some frequencies than to others. However, a sounding board may be forced to reinforce all frequencies to some extent.

Almost all musical instruments make use of a cavity resonator or a sounding board or both. The xylophone uses a series of cavity resonators of varied sizes; most wind instruments use single cavity resonators of adjustable sizes; the piano uses principally a sounding-board type of resonator; and the violin uses both a cavity resonator of fixed size and a sounding board consisting of the thin and highly resilient wood that encloses the cavity.

A resonator may be used chiefly to reinforce the fundamental frequency of a complex sound wave and thus increase the loudness of the sound; but the same resonator will inevitably have its effect upon the various overtone frequencies, reinforcing some and muffling others. So it is that a resonator can determine the relative frequencies and amplitudes of the overtones and thus determine the quality of the sound. So it is also that a change in the size or shape of a resonator will inevitably change the quality of a complex sound being resonated by it.

It may seem strange that a resonator that may neither create new overtones nor change the frequencies of existing overtones can, nevertheless, determine the frequencies and amplitudes as well as the number of audible overtones of a complex sound wave. The following table provides an explanation (based entirely upon hypothetical figures) of how this may be possible.

TABLE 2

The Effect of Different Resonators Upon the Same Sound

Sound Wave Resonated by Resonator #1

Fund. Frequency	200 C.P.S.
1st Overtone Freq.....	400 C.P.S.
2nd Overtone Freq.....	600 C.P.S.
3rd Overtone Freq.....	800 C.P.S.
4th Overtone Freq.....	1,000 C.P.S.
5th Overtone Freq.....	1,200 C.P.S.
6th Overtone Freq.....	1,400 C.P.S.
7th Overtone Freq.....	1,600 C.P.S.
8th Overtone Freq.....	1,800 C.P.S.
Threshold of Audibility →	

Same Sound Wave Resonated by Resonator #2

Fund. Frequency	200 C.P.S.
1st Overtone Freq.....	400 C.P.S.
2nd Overtone Freq.....	600 C.P.S.
3rd Overtone Freq.....	800 C.P.S.
4th Overtone Freq.....	1,000 C.P.S.
5th Overtone Freq.....	1,200 C.P.S.
6th Overtone Freq.....	1,400 C.P.S.
7th Overtone Freq.....	1,600 C.P.S.
8th Overtone Freq.....	1,800 C.P.S.
Threshold of Audibility →	

The above table illustrates how a change from one resonator to another, or even a change in the size or shape of a resonator, might change the number of audible overtones as well as the relative frequencies and amplitudes of those overtones by the single means of reinforcing some frequencies and weakening others. In the table the lengths of the lines to the right of the various frequencies indicate the relative loudness of each. When a line is too short to cross the vertical line marked "threshold of audibility," that means that that particular overtone is too weak to be heard by the human ear. An examination of Table 2 will reveal that the sound affected by the first resonator has a stronger fundamental pitch and more audible overtones, and some of the audible overtones are of different frequencies than the overtones that are made audible by the second resonator.

Sound Duration

The fourth variable attribute of sound is its timing or duration. Any sound lasts for a discernible length of time. It might be very short and staccato, like a gunshot, or long and drawn out, like the tone of a siren. It might start suddenly as a sound wave reaches one's ear and stop just as suddenly as the sound wave passes away beyond the ear. For example, a person might observe a steam whistle about a mile away as it suddenly releases a jet of steam for about one second. Approximately four seconds later he hears the one-second blast of that whistle. The sound wave initiated by the whistle continues to travel out from its source in all directions until its energy is exhausted and its amplitude is reduced to a degree at which it is no longer audible to the human ear. But as long as that sound is audible, anywhere within its range of audibility it is of the same one-second duration.

Although the meaning of sound duration is simple and easy to understand in terms of any single sound, the timing of a series of sounds of varying lengths of duration that are separated by intervals of silence (or breaks in sound continuity) which are also varied in terms of time duration can be very complicated. The timing of speech, for example, can be extremely complicated.

Summary

A brief study of the basic fundamentals of the physics of sound seems essential to the complete understanding of the problems involved in the development of effective speech habits.

Air is an elastic medium through which sound waves travel at a speed of approximately 1,100 feet per second. Air waves are usually initiated by a source of vibration such as a vibrating object which causes the air molecules to oscillate in a to-and-fro movement. A sound wave, consisting of a series of condensations and rarefactions of air molecules, will upon contact cause a person's eardrums to vibrate. The ears translate these vibrations into nerve impulses which are interpreted by the brain as the conscious sensation of sound. The wave movement in the air is not a sound but a sound wave. The term sound is used to refer only to the sensation of hearing.

Sounds may be roughly classified as tones and noises. We are chiefly concerned here with tones or the sound waves that are perceived as tones. These waves have sufficient regularity to be sensed as single sounds having distinctive pitches and qualities during appeciable lengths of time. Any sound that may be described as a tone has four variable attributes that are perceived by the ear as loudness, pitch, quality, and duration.

The intensity of a sound wave determines the distance the wave can travel through the air. It is measured in terms of the amount of energy exerted in initiating the sound wave. The amplitude of a sound wave, which is the distance that each vibrating molecule is displaced from the central point of its to-and-fro movement, will steadily decrease as the sound wave moves away from its source. The degree of loudness is a recognizable characteristic of sound that is determined by the ear's reaction to the amplitude of the sound wave at the point of perception. Sound waves of large amplitudes are sensed as loud sounds whereas sound waves of small amplitudes are sensed as weak sounds.

The frequency of a sound wave determines the pitch of the sound heard by the ear. Frequency is a measure of the speed of vibration. Air molecules involved in the transmission of a sound wave will be forced to vibrate to and fro. The number of cycles or complete vibrations per second is the measure of frequency. Sounds that are audible to the human ear range in frequencies from about 20 cycles per second, which is perceived as a very low pitch, to some vague limit that may be fixed at around 12,000 cycles per second, which is perceived as an extremely high pitch.

The quality or timbre of a sound is determined by the frequencies and relative amplitudes of its audible overtones. Most sound waves are complex, being made up of one relatively low and strong frequency which is known as the fundamental frequency and several higher and usually weaker frequencies that are called overtones. These different sound frequencies blend together and are sensed as one tone having a distinctive quality. Although the fundamental and all the overtone frequencies are initiated by the source of vibration, it is usually a resonator consisting of a cavity or a sounding board or both that determine the relative frequencies and amplitudes of the overtones and the number of overtones that are loud enough to be heard. Almost all musical instruments are provided with resonators of some kind or other. By reinforcing some frequencies and weakening others, a resonator determines the quality or timbre of a complex tone; and any change in the size or shape of a resonator results inevitably in a change in the quality of the tone resonated by it.

Questions

1. Why are air molecules closer together at sea level than at high altitudes?

2. When you blow up a toy balloon and seal the opening, what force keeps the rubber stretched?

3. What forces air to flow into a vacuum cleaner?

4. Does the sound of a bass drum beat travel faster or slower than the sound of a trumpet?

5. Why is the streamlining of automobiles important? Is the design of the rear end as important as the design of the front?

6. Of the two frequencies—256 cycles per second and 512 cycles per second—which is the higher pitch? How much higher?

7. Define a sound wave. How do the molecules involved move?

8. Define tone and distinguish it from a noise.

9. Why does the change in the size of a cavity resonator change the quality of any tone resonated by it?

10. Would a violin cast out of a nonresilient material such as lead sound different from one made of wood?
    a. Would there be a difference in loudness?
    b. Would there be a difference in the pitches played identically?
    c. Would there be a difference in the qualities of tone?

11. Do you believe that a sound wave could be transmitted through a vacuum?

12. Do all the sounds from a marching band travel through the air at the same speed?

13. Would you be able to hear an airplane while it was approaching at a speed of 800 miles per hour?

14. Does the pleasantness of tone depend upon loudness, pitch, quality, or duration?

15. How are the pitches of stringed musical instruments controlled?

16. Does the manner of vibrating have anything to do with the quality of the resulting sound?

Exercises

The viewing of such motion-picture films as "Sound Waves and Their Sources," "Fundamentals of Acoustics," and "Your Voice" is highly recommended. All are produced by Encyclopaedia Britannica Films.

By using such equipment as may be available or easily borrowed, it should be rather easy to demonstrate the relationship between amplitude of vibration and loudness of sound. It should also be possible to demonstrate the variable efficiency of cavity and sounding-board resonators in reinforcing sounds, and how variation in a resonator will change the quality of sound. For example, with a single tuning fork it is possible to demonstrate the following:

1. The relationship of loudness and intensity, by tapping the fork lightly and then sharply and noting the difference in degree of loudness of its tone.
2. The to-and-fro movement of a vibrating tuning fork, by bringing it in contact with a pith ball or tiny cork suspended on a thread.
3. The variation of sounding-board resonators, by pressing the base of a vibrating tuning fork against various surfaces such as a table top, a door panel, the side of an open box, etc.
4. The variation in the reinforcement of a tone by various cavity resonators, by holding a vibrating tuning fork in or above the openings of various cavities such as glass jars, tumblers, test tubes, etc.
5. The tuning of a resonator, by holding a vibrating tuning fork over a glass tumbler and then pouring water into the tumbler and adjusting the amount of water so as to attain maximum loudness of the tone resonated by it.

3.

The Production of Voice and Speech

PEOPLE often speak of the vocal instrument or the speech mechanism as though it were a special part of the body designed by nature for the specific purpose of producing voice and speech. But this is not true. The production of speech is a synchronized activity of more than one independent body mechanism, each of which has a natural or primary function other than that of voicing and articulating words. The process of learning to talk requires the adaptation and synchronization of the movements of the breathing mechanism and of the eating and drinking mechanism, and these movements must be guided by the brain with the help of the ear.

Anyone who is interested in the production and control of voice as a coordinated function will do well to consider first the breathing and the eating and drinking mechanisms and their normal functions separately. Such a consideration would give one a proper respect for the task of initially learning to speak and of the process of relearning for the sake of improving the effectiveness of speech.

The Breathing Mechanism

Breathing is an unlearned muscular activity that started at birth. It permits the blood to absorb oxygen from, and to discharge carbon dioxide into, a continually renewed air supply in the lungs. This, of course, is a vital function necessary to the continuance of life itself. The breathing mechanism may be divided into the following parts:

1. *The lungs*. These are a pair of sponge-like clusters of tiny air sacs that have only the passive function of containing air. They occupy a major portion of the chest cavity, but they take no active part in either the inhaling or the exhaling of breath. When certain muscles expand the chest cavity, atmospheric pressure forces some air into the lungs. Then when the size of the chest cavity is reduced, either with or without muscular help, some air is squeezed out of the lungs.

2. *The diaphragm*. This is a thin, dome-shaped partition

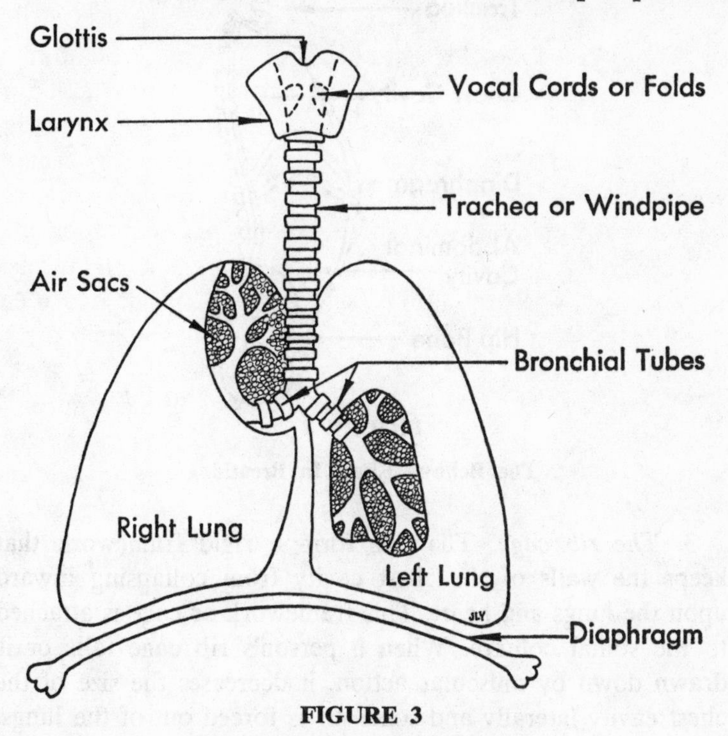

FIGURE 3

Larynx, Lungs, and Diaphragm

that separates the cavity of the chest from that of the abdomen. It is shown in Figure 3 as the curved floor upon which the lungs rest. It is composed of muscles and sinews, and during the process of breathing, it moves rhythmically downward and upward in such a way as to aid in the process of alternately enlarging and reducing the size of the chest cavity. The diaphragm itself actually contributes very little of the muscular power necessary to accomplish these downward and upward movements. Such movements are governed principally by muscles attached to the diaphragm and surrounding the abdominal walls.

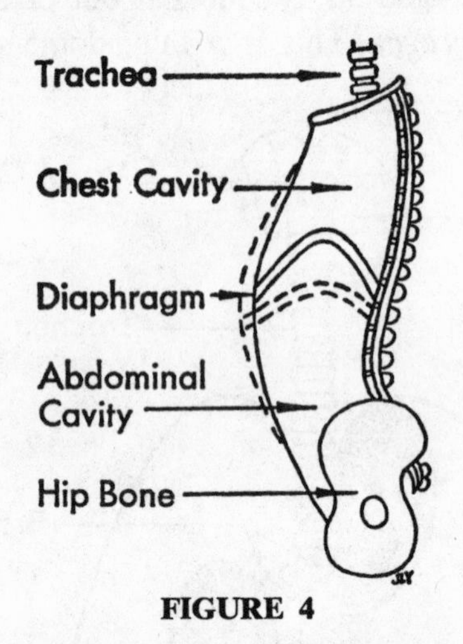

FIGURE 4

The Bellows Effect In Breathing

3. *The rib cage.* The ribs form a rigid framework that keeps the walls of the chest cavity from collapsing inward upon the lungs and heart. This framework or cage is attached to the spinal column. When a person's rib cage falls or is drawn down by muscular action, it decreases the size of the chest cavity laterally and some air is forced out of the lungs. When next the rib cage is raised, the chest cavity is enlarged

and atmospheric pressure forces some air into the lungs. The dotted lines in Figure 4 indicate the enlargement of the chest cavity by the action of both flattening the diaphragm and raising the rib cage.

4. *The muscles controlling breathing.* As indicated above, breathing is a two-way process. First some air is drawn into the lungs by enlarging the chest cavity and then some air is forced out of the lungs by reducing the size of the chest cavity. The amounts of air transferred in and out of the lungs may vary a great deal as different quantities of oxygen are needed by the body because of different degrees of physical exertion. And the muscular process of breathing may also vary as different quantities of air are required.

In the case of deep and labored breathing accompanying extremes of exertion, both phases of the breathing process require rather widespread muscular activity of two complex sets of muscles that have opposing functions. For the first phase, which is that of drawing air into the lungs, some muscles raise the rib cage slightly while other muscles lower the diaphragm and flatten it out, thus expanding the chest cavity both laterally and downward. At the same time, muscles of the abdominal wall must relax and allow the abdomen to swell outward enough to compensate for the downward push of the diaphragm upon the digestive organs. For the second phase, the exhaling of breath from the lungs, opposing muscles lower the rib cage and force the diaphragm up into its relaxed position, which is relatively high and arched. Also, the muscles of the abdominal wall contract enough to hold the digestive organs against the raised diaphragm. The whole process of deep and labored breathing is often called diaphragmatic breathing. It is an efficient type of breathing that is invariably used when maximum quantities of air are required by the body.

In the modern world, however, deep or diaphragmatic breathing is seldom necessary. Life is relatively inactive and most people rarely exert themselves enough to need maximum quantities of breath. In fact, a large proportion of the adult population spends most of its waking hours in sitting positions and seldom moves faster than a walk. This means that a relatively shallow type of breathing is quite adequate for most people most of the time.

Habitual shallow breathing movements vary with different individuals. Some people, especially those who are occasionally very active, use a modified form of diaphragmatic breathing. The first phase, or inhalation in such cases, is accomplished in the same manner as described above except that the rib cage is raised and the diaphragm is depressed only very slightly. But the second phase, or exhalation, becomes almost completely passive because it can be accomplished merely by relaxing the muscles that activated inhalation. The rib cage drops because of its own weight and the diaphragm returns to its high, relaxed position because of the natural elasticity of the muscle fibers plus the pressure of the compressed internal organs below rather than any actual muscular exertion. Consequently, only the muscles used in inhaling breath are strengthened by the exercise of this type of shallow breathing.

Other shallow breathers tend to avoid the use of muscles that are located as low as the diaphragm and use instead muscles of the upper chest and shoulders. There is no clearly defined pattern of muscular movements that is consistently used by everyone who employs this type of upper-chest breathing. There is a general tendency to raise the upper chest and shoulders when inhaling breath, and to let the chest and shoulders fall when exhaling breath, with the result that breathing is accompanied by rather obvious heaving movements of chest and shoulders while muscular activity around the diaphragm and abdominal walls seems to be minimized.

In all types of shallow breathing, muscular power is used to draw air into the lungs but little or no muscular power is used to force air out of the lungs. Consequently, the average person should expect to have only weak and under-exercised muscles supporting his exhaled breath.

5. *The air passage.* As air is pumped in and out of the lungs it passes through a fairly long air passage consisting of the nasal cavities, the throat or pharynx, the windpipe or trachea, and the bronchial tubes that are directly attached by treelike branches to the tiny air sacs of the lungs. The nasal cavities, which open to the outside air through the nostrils, serve to filter and moisten the air and to regulate to some extent its temperature before it reaches the lungs. Otherwise, the air passage has no special function except the obvious one of providing a free passageway for air. Part of the same passage, however, is shared by the eating and drinking mechanism; so, in order to keep air passages free and open, two valvelike devices are provided to protect the nasal cavities and the windpipe and lungs from food, drink, and other foreign substances. These are the soft palate and the larynx, discussed separately below.

6. *The soft palate.* The thin, soft membrane that comprises the back part of the roof of the mouth is called the soft palate. Attached to the middle of the back edge of the soft palate is the fleshy lobe called the uvula, which has no known function—although some believe that it aids in gaining a firm closure of the opening into the nasal cavity. It is readily recognized as a familiar appendage hanging above the entrance to the throat. The back of the soft palate can be raised, as indicated in Figure 5, and brought into firm contact with the back wall of the throat cavity, thus completely shutting off the nasal cavities from the mouth and throat. Such a closure is made automatically when a person swallows so that no food or drink can be forced up into the nasal cavities.

7. *The larynx.* In spite of the fact that the larynx is commonly called the voice box and, as such, contains a pair of

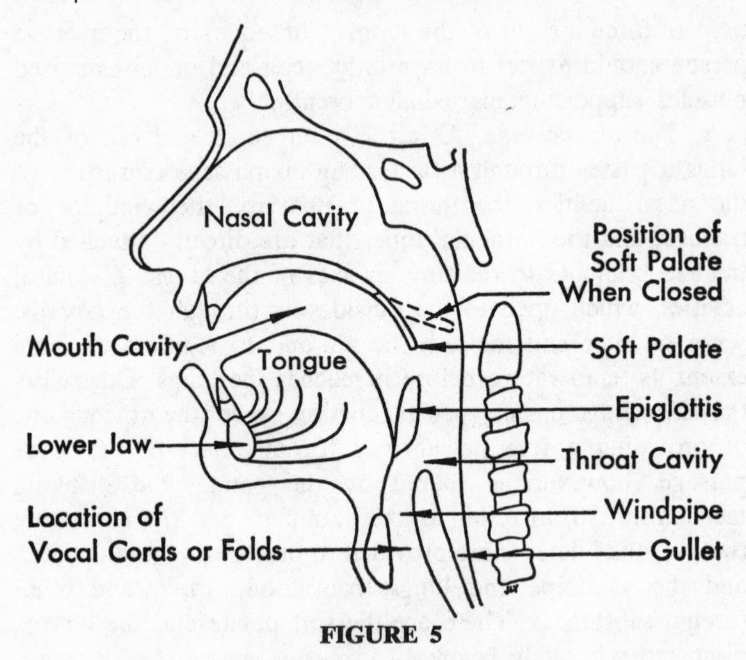

FIGURE 5

Chief Head and Throat Cavities

wedge-shaped lips or folds that are usually called the vocal cords, the primary function of the larynx is believed to be that of protection rather than the production of vocal sounds. The larynx protects the windpipe and the lungs by keeping out food and drink and other foreign substances, and it makes possible the expelling of anything from the air tract by means of coughing. A cough results from suddenly releasing air that has been compressed by the breathing muscles below the valvelike closure, accomplished by compressing the vocal cords together. (The valvelike opening between the vocal cords, called the glottis, is illustrated in Figure 3.) This same valve makes it possible to hold the breath when lifting heavy weights, thus bracing the shoulders with an air cushion which prevents the chest cavity from collapsing under the strain of the downward pull.

The Eating and Drinking Mechanism

The eating and drinking mechanism is that part of the digestive system that accepts food and drink, prepares it for the stomach, and starts it on its journey down the esophagus or gullet to the stomach. Its actions are unlearned and have operated from birth. Parts of the mechanism are:

1. *The lips.* The lips form a flexible opening that can be adjusted to help convey food or drink into the mouth. They also may help to hold solid foods in a position to be chewed.

2. *The mouth.* The mouth is the cavity in which food is prepared for the stomach. During the process of chewing, the salivary glands help the preparation of food by moistening it with saliva.

3. *The jaws and teeth.* The upper and lower teeth, mounted upon the upper and lower jaws, have the function of biting off and grinding up solid foods.

4. *The tongue.* Although the tongue is so closely associated with the act of speaking that its name is used as a word meaning a spoken language, the primary function of the tongue is that of manipulating food and pushing the unchewed portions of it between the grinding teeth. On the back of the tongue are located the taste buds which initiate the neural impulses that are translated by the brain as the conscious sensations of taste. Taste, of course, has the function of helping to determine which foods or drinks should be accepted and which should be rejected.

5. *The throat or pharynx.* The throat, which is also called the pharynx, is a cavity which provides a passageway for food or drink from the mouth to the esophagus or gullet. This cavity also serves as a part of the air passage from the lungs to the nasal cavities.

6. *The muscles used in swallowing.* Swallowing is a patterned muscular reaction involving muscles of the tongue as well as muscles surrounding the throat cavity and the muscles

that automatically close off the nasal cavities by means of the soft palate.

The Speech Mechanism

The vocal instrument or speech mechanism is made up of the same parts of the body included in the breathing and the eating and drinking mechanisms. In combination these parts have the secondary function of producing voice and speech. Except for such a natural reaction as crying, the production of voice and speech must be learned. And such secondary functions are far more complex than the primary function of breathing and eating or drinking.

The human voice, as it is used in speaking, may be thought of as a kind of wind instrument that has four mechanical elements—the *motivating power or energy,* the *vibrator,* the *resonators,* and the *articulators.* The motivating power and the vibrator can produce a sound wave. The resonators reinforce that sound wave and determine the frequencies and relative amplitudes of its audible overtones and thus cause the sound wave to give the ear an impression of human-voice quality. The articulators mold the vocal tones, and add to them certain nonvocal noises, to make up the arbitrary and audible symbols of speech. Finally, the synchronized activity of the whole speech mechanism serves to vary the force, pitch, quality, and timing of speech so as to give to it an expressive intonation pattern.

The Motivating Power: A person uses almost exclusively his exhaled breath for the production of voice or speech; so the motivating power is the muscular energy used to initiate voice by forcing it out through the closed glottis (as the opening between the vocal cords is called), thus causing the vocal cords to vibrate. This muscular pressure or motivating power is commonly called breath support. The effectiveness of breath support depends upon three factors—(1) the strength of breath pressure, (2) the ability to sustain breath pressure, and (3) the degree of precision in controlling changes of breath pressure.

1. *The strength of breath pressure* depends upon the strength of the muscles that are used to exert pressure upon the exhaled breath. As previously indicated, most modern living is too easy and inactive to have developed for the average adult person anything but relatively shallow breathing habits and relatively weak breath support. Consequently, most people who wish to develop strong breath support for singing or for any relatively strong type of public speaking will need to strengthen the muscles that exert pressure upon the exhaled breath.

2. *The ability to sustain breath pressure* for a relatively long span of rapidly flowing speech that is uninterrupted by inhalation of breath depends upon both the quantity of breath initially inhaled and the economic use of breath while speaking.

There is some controversy over the best method of developing an ability to sustain breath pressure. Some speech teachers, like nearly all teachers of vocal music, believe that the learner should be taught a deep diaphragmatic breathing method which can supply breath in maximum quantities and build up maximum breath pressures. Other teachers believe that a speaker needs only to learn to use his breath economically, and that his normal manner of breathing will supply air in sufficient quantities to sustain breath pressures long enough for any normal speech demands.

Much can be said for both contentions. If a speaker needs to develop an exceptionally strong voice capable of loud and vigorous speaking for long periods of time and with apparent ease, he probably needs to learn to inhale greater than normal quantities of breath by deep or diaphragmatic breathing so that he can sustain relatively high breath pressures for relatively long periods while speaking. If, on the other hand, a speaker needs only to develop a voice for a normal variety of speech situations including most modern styles of acting and public speaking, he can probably learn to sustain breath pressure sufficiently by merely developing greater economy in the use of breath.

Learning to conserve breath is a problem that varies with the individual. Some speakers are very wasteful of breath while others are not. One way of wasting breath is by a so-called breathy quality of voice caused by speaking with a partially open glottis and giving the effect of speaking and whispering at the same time. Other ways of wasting breath result from a lack of precision in articulation. Some consonant sounds used in speech are voiceless or whispered sounds, as for example, the sound associated with the letter "h." By prolonging such a sound slightly, great quantities of breath could be wasted. Means of conserving breath may be discovered by practice in attempting to speak increasing numbers of words on a single breath.

3. *Precision in controlling changes of breath pressures* while speaking is necessary because of great variations in breath pressure that must be carefully timed. The syllables receiving primary and secondary accents, for example, in such a word as "dictionary" are uttered with the aid of variation in breath pressure. Words uttered with different degrees of emphasis or subordination also demand many very rapid and precisely controlled changes of breath pressure. Then between syllables there are divisions that vary from almost imperceptible breaks in sound continuity to definite or prolonged pauses. A speaker makes such variations with the help of changes in breath pressure that must be carefully controlled both in degree and in exact timing by his muscles supporting breath.

The Vibrator: The vibrator consists principally of muscles and cartilages that make up the larynx or voice box. The larynx, mentioned previously as a protective valve in the breathing mechanism, accomplishes a much more intricate and delicate secondary function as a voice box. It is attached to the top of the trachea or windpipe, and its front cartilage may often protrude forward enough to be recognized as the Adam's apple.

Air that is forced from the lungs must pass through the larynx and between the vocal cords. The common name, vocal cords, is not a descriptive name. In other words, the vocal cords are not like the strings of a violin as the name seems to imply. As indicated previously, they are more like lips or folds that project from the inner walls of the larynx. These cords or lips are fairly thick, wedge-shaped muscles that are covered with a tough membrane and are rounded on the inner or free edges. The opening between them is called the glottis. The vocal cords may be flattened against the sides of the larynx, thus leaving the glottis wide open as for breathing, or the vocal cords may be brought together, thus closing the glottis (as illustrated in Figure 3). When air is forced out through the slit formed by the closed glottis, the inner edges of the vocal cords will vibrate in much the same manner as the lips of a trumpet player may be made to vibrate when he plays the trumpet. The fundamental frequency of vocal-cord vibration as well as the overtone frequencies that are initiated by the vocal cords depend upon such factors as the length, the texture, the elasticity, the mass or thickness, and the tension of the vocal cords. The length, texture, and elasticity of a person's vocal cords may change considerably over a period of months or years as a result of growth and exercise, but they can be changed only very slightly by any rapid muscular adjustment. Consequently, these factors may help to determine the pitch level at which a person habitually speaks and certain characteristics of his vocal quality, but they have little part in controlling his pitch and quality changes while speaking. The tension or tightness with which the vocal cords are stretched across the air passage, and to some extent the mass or thickness of the vocal cords, can be controlled by muscles of the larynx. As these muscles press the vocal cords together and stretch them tighter and perhaps thinner, their fundamental frequency of vibration increases and the pitch of the voice rises; and conversely, as the muscles allow the vocal cords to slacken, the pitch of the voice is lowered. At the same time that pitch changes are made by controlling the tension of the vocal cords, quality changes are inevitably brought about by overtone variations. Therefore, the muscles controlling the tension of the vocal cords control the major pitch changes of the voice and certain incidental changes in vocal quality.

Although the muscles in and around the vocal cords are very small, they do not need to be strengthened for the purpose of improving voice production. The primary function of these muscles as part of a protective valve requires them to be much stronger than they need to be in order to accomplish their secondary function in the vibrator. These muscles may be trained with the help of the ear to make extremely precise adjustments of the vocal cords for exact control of vocal pitch and some partial control of voice qualities. The particular vocal qualities that are described as tense or harsh and relaxed or easy probably result primarily from muscular adjustments of the larynx or vibrator. There are also several speech sounds that are described as voiceless because they are whispered, or frictional because they are uttered with the glottis open so that the vocal cords do not vibrate.

The Resonators: These are the resonating cavities of the throat, the mouth, the nose, and the chest, as well as any hard and resilient bony structures that are located in or near the walls of any of these cavities and may thus have the additional effect of sounding-board resonators.

How much reinforcement of voice is gained from the chest as a cavity resonator is not known. But it is quite apparent that the chest is not an adjustable resonator. At any rate, muscular action controlling the size of the chest cavity has as its purpose the control of breath support rather than adjustment for vocal reinforcement. Consequently, if the chest does affect vocal resonance to a significant degree, that effect is entirely incidental and not subject to muscular control.

The two nasal cavities also are somewhat limited in terms of muscular control. These cavities are fixed in shape and are capable of only negligible expansion or contraction of size. By means of the soft palate, however, the opening between the throat and the nasal cavities can be adjusted to any size or closed completely (see Figure 5). And even the complete closure of this opening does not eliminate the nasal cavities as resonators, because the sound-wave vibrations of the voice are easily communicated through the soft palate into the nasal cavities even when direct passage for air is completely closed. Therefore, the nasal cavities are important resonators in determining the basic qualities of a person's voice even though his control of them is virtually limited to his ability to close or open the port between them and his throat by means of the soft palate.

The most important resonating cavities are those of the mouth and throat because a speaker is capable of making a great variety of changes in the shapes and sizes of these cavities, and it is known that a change in the shape or size of a resonating cavity will change the quality of any sound that is reinforced by it. When a person speaks, the shape and size of his mouth and throat cavities are in a constant process of being changed or adjusted. These changes or adjustments are made automatically or subconsciously. Most of them are undoubtedly learned, at least in part, during the babbling period in infancy (see Chapter 1) when random muscular manipulation of the vocal instrument resulted in the production of a variety of random sounds, and associations were formed between the sounds heard by the ear and the muscular means of producing them. Because of such associations one may hear a vocal sound and be able to imitate it quite accurately but have not the slightest idea of the muscular means he uses in doing so.

As an example of an unconscious adjustment of a resonator, you have probably observed that a singer's larynx (seen as his Adam's apple) moves up and down as the pitches of his voice range upward and downward. For a high pitch the larynx always rises and for a low pitch it always moves downward. This seems to be an unconscious adjustment of the size of the throat cavity because when the larynx rises, it shortens the throat cavity above it, thus adjusting the throat resonator for better reinforcement of a high pitch; and when the larynx is lowered the throat cavity above is lengthened for better reinforcement of a lower pitch.

The Articulators: Obviously, a sustained vocal tone uttered through an open mouth passage is voice but not speech. Voice must be modified and broken up into conventional speech sounds and syllables that are combined into words, phrases, and sentences before it becomes speech. The process of modifying voice and breaking it up into a rapid series of syllables is called articulation, and it is accomplished by the articulators.

Usually the lips, tongue, teeth, lower jaw, and soft palate are listed as the articulators. However, articulation is a dynamic process; so it is really the muscles that activate or manipulate these parts of the speech mechanism that accomplish articulation. The teeth, for example, can accomplish nothing alone. Only the movements of the tongue, lips, and lower jaw can bring the teeth into the proper relationships with the other articulators and thus render them useful in the process of articulation. Although they are usually not mentioned as articulators, the muscles that open and close the glottis and the muscles that control the pressure of exhaled breath are actively involved in the process of articulating a series of speech sounds and hence they probably should be added to the list of articulators.

Any adult speaker has been articulating speech sounds as a subconscious habit for so many years that he is not aware of the intricate nature of his articulatory movements. His habits of articulation are usually as vigorous, precise, and well synchronized as his experience in social communication has demanded. Usually these demands have not been very exacting because conversational standards permit a relatively low grade of distinctness in articulation, and the slurring or omission of many speech sounds in subordinate words and phrases is accepted as normal.

Vocal Variations While Speaking

The production of voice and the articulation of words is all that is needed for the verbal expression of an idea; but, as indicated in Chapter 1, speech is a blend of three types of communication—physical, tonal, and verbal. Physical expression is not directly involved in the production and control of voice or in the articulation of speech; so there is no point in considering it here. However, the relationship between one's physical reaction to an idea or feeling and the effectiveness of his tonal communication of it is much closer than many people realize. Tonal expression, on the other hand, is a very important part of oral speech. It supplies the intonation pattern of speech which is made up of controlled variations of loudness, pitch, quality, and timing.

From a technical point of view, different variations of the voice are controlled in the following manners:

1. *Loudness or force* is controlled by an individual while speaking chiefly by the muscles that exert pressure upon his exhaled breath. Other things being equal, the greater the breath pressure the louder will be the voice. Loudness of voice is determined also by the degree of efficiency with which

the vocal cords are controlled and by the degree of vocal reinforcement given by the resonators. However, these latter factors are more likely to determine why one person's voice is louder than that of another rather than accounting for the variations in loudness used by one speaker. A person does not usually control his loudness by varying the use of his vocal cords and resonators so that they operate more or less efficiently.

2. *The pitch* of the voice is controlled chiefly by muscles of the larynx that regulate the tension and thickness (and perhaps to a very slight extent the length) of the vocal cords.

3. *The quality* of the voice is controlled by both the muscles of the larynx that regulate the operation of the vocal cords and by the muscles that adjust the size and shape of the resonating cavities. The muscles that bring the vocal cords together and regulate their tension and thickness determine the overtone frequencies initiated, and it is these muscles that determine the degree of tension or ease shown in the voice quality. However, the changes in vocal-cord adjustments are used principally to control pitch; so any changes of voice quality that result from muscular control of the vocal cords are probably purely incidental.

4. *The duration or timing* of any syllable or break between syllables in a series of speech sounds is controlled by the articulatory muscles.

The effectiveness of a speaker's intonation pattern, or his tonal communication, depends not only upon the strength of his impulses to communicate certain vividly conceived thoughts and feelings but also upon the mechanical skill and flexibility of his speech mechanism.

Summary

The speech mechanism consists of the breathing mechanism and the eating and drinking mechanism; and the production of voice and speech is a secondary function calling for the learning of adaptations and a high degree of precision and synchronization of naturally independent parts of the body. The breathing mechanism consists of:

1. *The lungs,* which are merely passive containers of air.
2. *The diaphragm* that separates the chest and abdominal cavities and is moved upward and downward to help the process of breathing.
3. *The rib cage,* which is raised and lowered in order to increase and decrease the size of the chest cavity laterally and thus help in the process of breathing.
4. *The muscles controlling breathing,* which activate the movements of the diaphragm and rib cage as well as a slight expansion and contraction of the abdominal walls during deep or labored breathing. For shallow breathing, which is very common, exhalation is accomplished almost entirely by muscular relaxation rather than by muscular force. Consequently, the muscular exercise gained through shallow breathing does not strengthen the muscles that might exert strong pressure on the exhaled breath.
5. *The air passage,* which consists of the nasal cavities, the pharynx or throat, the windpipe or trachea, and the bronchial tubes that are attached to the air sacs that make up the lungs.
6. *The soft palate,* which acts as a valve or door between the throat and nasal cavities.
7. *The larynx,* which acts as a protective valve that keeps food, drink, and other foreign substances out of the air tract leading to the lungs. The vocal cords can be brought together like lips to close the air passage through the larynx.

The eating and drinking mechanism consists of the lips, the mouth, the jaws, the teeth, the tongue, the throat, and the muscles that are used for swallowing.

The so-called speech mechanism consists of the combination of the breathing and the eating and drinking mechanisms. In its operation, it uses four mechanical elements:

1. *The motivating power,* which consists of the muscular

energy used to force air out of the lungs and through the closed glottis. The efficiency of the motivating power depends upon the strength of the muscles exerting pressure on the exhaled breath, an ability to sustain breath pressure for relatively long, uninterrupted units of speech, and the degree of precision possible in controlling breath pressures.

2. *The vibrator,* which consists of the larynx or voice box that contains the vocal cords. When the vocal cords or folds are brought together—thus closing the glottis—and air is forced through the slit between the vocal folds, they start to vibrate like the lips of a musician playing a trumpet. The vibrating vocal folds initiate a vocal tone.

3. *The resonators,* which consist of the cavities of the chest, the throat, the mouth, and the nose plus the bony structures surrounding these cavities. The sound waves initiated by the vibrator are reinforced by the resonators.

4. *The articulators* are usually listed as the lips, tongue, teeth, lower jaw, and soft palate but should include also the muscles that control breath pressure and open and close the glottis.

Tonal expression, which is an important part of the process of oral communication, supplies the intonation pattern of speech. The intonation pattern is made up of controlled changes in the loudness, pitch, and quality of the voice, and in the timing of articulated speech. Loudness is regulated principally by the muscles exerting pressure upon the exhaled breath; pitch is controlled principally by the muscles of the larynx that adjust the closure of the glottis and the tension and thickness of the vocal folds; quality is changed chiefly by altering the sizes and shapes of the resonating cavities; and the timing of speech is regulated by the articulators. All variations of the intonation pattern are dependent upon the flexibility of the speech mechanism as well as upon the speaker's vividness of conception and an active desire to communicate.

QUESTIONS

1. Describe the lungs and explain their function.
2. What is the diaphragm? Do muscles of the diaphragm itself exert much pressure upon the exhaled breath?
3. What is the primary function of the rib cage? How is it used in the process of breathing?
4. Why is breath support not usually strengthened by the exercise of quiet or shallow breathing?
5. Explain the function of the soft palate.
6. What are the primary functions of the larynx?
7. Name and explain the primary functions of the various parts of the eating and drinking mechanism.
8. Do the primary functions of the breathing and the eating and the drinking mechanisms have to be learned?
9. What are the four mechanical elements of the speech mechanism?
10. Can a person produce voice through an open glottis? Explain.
11. Explain the nature and operation of the vocal cords as they initiate vocal tones.
12. Name the cavity resonators.
13. List the various articulators.
14. Does it require more or less breath to:

    a. Whisper a line or speak the same line aloud?
    b. Speak a line normally or to shout the same line?
    c. Scream at a high pitch or shout at a low pitch?

15. Can you explain one's tendency to grunt when lifting something heavy?
16. Why does a singer's Adam's apple rise when he sings a high pitch?
17. Do you believe that speaking through a megaphone will change the quality of your voice? Explain.
18. How may the loudness of one's voice be changed? What is one's chief method of changing vocal loudness?
19. How is the pitch of the voice controlled?
20. In what ways may the quality of the voice be changed? What method of controlling voice quality is probably used most often?

Exercises

I—*Purpose:* To observe and differentiate the vocal attributes known as force, pitch, quality, and timing. Prolonged practice of this exercise is not recommended because no one needs to be able to control vocal variations consciously and independently of each other. However, a few attempts to do so should help the individual to become vividly aware of the differences and the interrelationships that exist between the variable attributes of speech sounds.

Method: Try to control independently the various vocal attributes in the following ways. Three or four attempts of each should be sufficient.

1. Count from 1 to 10, attempting to utter each number with exactly the same degree of loudness, the same pitch level, the same vocal quality, and the same time duration. Try also to avoid any inflection or change of pitch when uttering each number. The effect should be more like chanting or singing than like normal speaking.
2. Count from 1 to 10, attempting to stress every alternate number by increasing its loudness but without raising its pitch, prolonging its duration, or changing its quality.
3. Count from 1 to 10, attempting to raise the pitch of every alternate number without increasing loudness, prolonging the duration, or changing the quality.
4. Count from 1 to 10, attempting to prolong the duration of every alternate number without increasing loudness, raising pitch, or changing quality.
5. Count from 1 to 10, attempting to utter every alternate number with a different vocal quality. This process may be repeated several times—making a different change each time. For example, alternate first between a normal quality (like that used in daily conversations) and a deep, gutteral quality, then between a normal quality and a nasal quality, then between a normal quality and a tense or angry quality, etc.

II—*Purpose:* To learn by experimentation and observation how your breath support compares with that of others and to try out various methods of improvement.

Method 1: Assume an easy standing position, take a deep breath, and start counting aloud at a normal volume of voice and at a rate of about two numbers per second. See how far you can count on a single breath. Notice upon which sounds you lose the most breath. Then repeat several times, attempting each time to conserve more breath on these wasteful sounds.

Method 2: Vocalize the sound of "ah" for as long as you can on a single breath. Try to hold the voice steady at a normal volume and without fluctuation of pitch or quality. Time yourself. Try often to increase your length of vocalization. Repeat this exercise at different levels of loudness and at different pitch levels and compare the times. Then repeat while uttering different vowel sounds such as the vowel sounds in the words: beat, bit, bait, bet, bat, bought, boat, boot, but, Bert.

III—*Purpose:* To experiment with your control of breath pressure.

Method: Assume an easy standing position, take a deep breath, and then silently whistle (by blowing through rounded lips but without sound) a well-known tune. Blow hard enough to bulge out your cheeks rhythmically. See if anyone can recognize the tune from watching your cheek movements.

4.

The Strength and Basic Quality of the Voice

IN the preceding chapter the vocal instrument and its general operation are described. In the present chapter the chief concern is with one's skill of operating his vocal instrument in the production of vocal tones, so that the attention of the reader is directed to the evaluation and improvement of his own voice in terms of its strength and basic tonal quality.

A Speaker's Natural Voice

Although it is possible for anyone to change the sound of his voice in many ways, everyone has characteristic vocal tones that may be referred to collectively as his natural voice because they are tones that he uses often in his daily speech and hence his friends and acquaintances recognize these tones as belonging to him. Any person's natural voice is produced by a vocal instrument that has a complex physical structure which is muscularly controlled. His characteristic tones of voice are determined partly by the physical structure of his vocal instrument and partly by his individual habits of vocalization.

In terms of physical structure, some vocal instruments are much better than others, just as a Stradivarius violin is better than a cheaper instrument. How good a person's voice might become, if it has the best possible training and practice, depends upon the structural perfection of his vocal instrument, which may be described as a gift of nature since it is chiefly a product of heredity. In the field of vocal music, the physical structure of one's vocal instrument is of primary importance because some vocal instruments are considered to be worthy of both extensive and expensive training while others are not. In the field of speech, however, there can be no question as to whether or not a person's vocal instrument is worth training. A person who is not gifted with a good vocal instrument does not need to sing, but everybody needs to speak whether his vocal instrument is good or bad. The improvement of the speaking voice is almost always possible, and any degree of improvement in the speaking voice is always worthwhile. Consequently, everyone should be concerned with how much he can improve his natural voice by modifying his muscular habits of vocalization. Just as a skillful violinist can draw fairly pleasing music from an inferior violin, so a person with an inferior vocal instrument can develop skill of vocalization that would result in a fairly good voice or at least a voice that would not be described by the average listener as a bad voice.

The initial formation of one's muscular habits of vocalization, whether they be good, bad, or indifferent, depends upon many factors such as the following:

1. The tonal qualities of the voices heard most often and imitated during early childhood.
2. The accuracy and acuity of one's sense of hearing.
3. One's strength, vitality, and state of health, especially in the early years of childhood, when habits of vocalization were being formed.
4. One's personality, particularly such traits as poise and self-assurance.
5. One's vocal experiences, particularly experiences in singing, shouting, or loud speaking.

The Means of Changing One's Natural Voice

If a person is made to realize suddenly that he has unconsciously developed a bad voice, he will find that his long-established habit of vocalization will be hard to break. New habits may be formed, however, with relative ease. A person with a poor speaking voice may, for example, learn to sing beautifully by forming new habits of vocalization for singing. These habits will not automatically have any effect, however, upon his bad habits of vocalizing his speech. It is also possible for an actor, interpreter, or ventriloquist to develop new manners of vocalizing speech for the purpose of impersonating different characters without affecting at all his old manner of vocalizing his daily conversations.

A new manner of vocalizing speech may be developed that is far superior to one's normal manner of vocalization. This new manner may become a habit that can be substituted consciously for one's natural voice just as "company manners" may be substituted for normal behavior. If a person wishes to make such a substitution permanent, he may do so, in time, by constantly increasing the frequency of the conscious substitution until he loses the tendency to revert back subconsciously to his old habit. In this way a person may actually acquire a new and improved natural voice.

Hearing and Evaluating Voice

From the physical standpoint, making the necessary muscular adjustments for the improvement of one's voice quality should not usually be very difficult. The real difficulty lies in the search for precisely the right muscular adjustments that will bring about the greatest vocal improvement. This search must be guided by one's sense of hearing and his critical judgment of vocal tones. Therein lies the chief obstacle in the way of improving the voice, because most people can neither observe nor evaluate with any degree of accuracy the tonal qualities of the voices they hear.

The accuracy with which any listener can observe and evaluate a speaking voice is determined chiefly by the following factors:

1. *His degree of familiarity with the voice.* When a person hears a voice nearly every day, he becomes so accustomed to it that he seldom thinks of or reacts to its tonal qualities—either favorably or unfavorably. A person is most likely to observe and react to the sound of a voice that is relatively new or strange to him.

2. *His attitude towards the person whose voice it is.* Vocal qualities and personal qualities tend to become confused with each other. When one likes or dislikes a person, he tends to like or dislike everything that is characteristic of that person, including his voice.

3. *The degree to which he focuses his attention upon the voice itself.* Since everyone knows that the voice of a singer is supposed to be beautiful, the attention of even an untrained listener is focused upon the tonal qualities of a singer's voice, and such a listener will almost invariably form an opinion as to whether that voice is good or bad. On the other hand, anyone untrained in speech will usually fail to notice and evaluate the voices that he hears speaking because his attention is focused upon the ideas communicated rather than upon the sounds of the speaking voices.

4. *The degree to which the voice is unique or exceptional.* Exceptionally good or extremely bad voices and odd or unusual voices tend to attract the attention of any unfamiliar listener and as a result the listener may form critical evaluations of them. For this reason there is a tendency for untrained listeners to evaluate the great majority of speaking voices (which they do not really notice) as indifferent, average, or ordinary; whereas they describe the few exceptional

or unusual voices (that they do notice and react to) as either good or bad—pleasant or unpleasant.

The average untrained speaker is perhaps the worst possible judge of his own natural voice. He is too familiar with it to notice and evaluate its tonal qualities. If for any reason he does attempt to evaluate his own voice, his attitude towards himself prevents a detached and objective viewpoint. Also, when a person speaks, his attention is usually centered upon the ideas to be communicated rather than upon the tonal qualities of his voice. Members of one's immediate family and other intimate associates are hardly better qualified to observe and evaluate his speaking voice than he is himself. Even an exceptionally pleasing, a very irritating, or a peculiar voice is seldom consciously observed by anyone who hears it every day. A person could have the most offensive speaking voice in his community without being offended by it and without even being able to detect anything wrong with it.

Since it is obviously impossible to correct an error or fault that is not perceived or to improve the voice when neither improvement nor the need for improvement can be recognized, it is apparent that any specialized training and practice aimed at voice improvement must include ear training and the improvement of one's judgment of voices, especially of his own.

Learning to evaluate one's own voice requires experience in careful observation aided, at least initially, by a specialist in speech training who can help one to recognize the accepted criteria of good voice and the changes necessary for vocal improvement. Equipment that can be used to record and reproduce the natural qualities of one's voice is always a very valuable aid, because listening to a recording permits a detached and objective observation that cannot be attained while speaking. To some extent, experience in careful observation and evaluation of the voices of other people will help to improve one's critical judgment of vocal tones, but the best experience comes from the critical observation of one's own voice while practicing vocal exercises. Such self-criticism should be supplemented whenever possible by the criticisms of others. Vocal exercises should usually be in the nature of oral reading rather than any form of ad-libbing or extemporaneous speaking in order to permit relatively more attention to be focused upon the voice itself rather than upon the process of translating ideas and feelings into words and sentences.

Criteria of a Good Voice

A good speaking voice is both pleasant to listen to and effective as a medium of communication. A pleasant voice is one that makes a favorable impression upon anyone that notices it—as, for example, a relative stranger whose reactions are not predetermined by past acquaintance. An effective voice is one having tonal qualities that reinforce with accuracy and vividness the speaker's intended meanings.

The pleasantness of the speaking voice should not be confused with the beauty of the singing voice. In singing, beautiful and melodious sound is supposed to elicit admiration and to be an end in itself; but the sound of the speaking voice is only a means to an end. Any attempt to emphasize or sustain the most beautiful tones of the voice while speaking is certain to give an impression of affectation and artificiality. The pleasantness and effectiveness of a speaking voice should be perceived by the average listener more as a characteristic of the speaker than as an attribute of his voice. A pleasant and effective voice is a clear voice having a brilliant or unmuffled tone and a depth or fullness of quality resulting from efficient use of the resonators. Such a voice gives an impression of such personal traits of the speaker as sympathy, warmth, friendliness, and graciousness. A voice is both effective and pleasant when it results from relaxed and easy vocalization that is completely free of unnecessary muscular tensions. Such a voice gives the impression of a well-adjusted, poised, and relaxed speaker; and it is a comfortable voice to listen to because it puts the listener at his ease. An effective voice that is also pleasant is a strong voice that is easily audible but not unnecessarily loud; it gives the impression that the speaker is energetic, confident, and self-assured; and that, no matter how loudly he speaks, he could speak still more loudly without vocal strain.

The Essentials of Voice Improvement

Improving the voice through the development of greater skill of vocalization most commonly involves four essential objectives: (1) To improve breath support; (2) to improve the habitual adjustments of the vibrator muscles in and around the vocal cords; (3) to improve the habitual adjustments of the resonators; and (4) to eliminate all unnecessary muscle tensions that might affect the sound of the voice.

The Improvement of Breath Support: As indicated in the preceding chapter, good breath support demands strong muscular pressures occasionally upon the exhaled breath, an ability to sustain breath pressure without running out of breath too often, and the control of precisely timed changes in breath pressure.

Whether or not a person needs to change his whole manner of breathing by developing a so-called diaphragmatic type of breath control depends upon the degree of vocal power that he wants or needs. If he wishes to develop vocal power equivalent to that of an opera singer, he should probably undergo the same type of breathing exercises and vocal drills that the student of vocal music practices as one means of developing vocal strength. If one aspires to become an actor capable of playing some of the titanic roles of classic tragedy, or perhaps a spellbinding orator or minister, then he should probably attempt to develop a similar diaphragmatic breathing habit and maximum strength of breath support. However, in these modern times when drama is distributed electronically into nearly every living room, and electronic amplifiers are standard equipment in nearly every lecture hall, it seems entirely unnecessary that the average aspiring speaker should do any more than strengthen somewhat the muscles that he normally uses to support his exhaled breath. He may accomplish this usually by merely practicing loud speaking.

Learning to sustain breath pressure during forceful speaking, without having to damage one's speech by gasping for breath at wrong times, may involve learning to breathe a little more deeply; but it usually should not involve any more than learning to use breath more economically by practice in sustaining breath and eliminating wasteful loss of breath while speaking.

Learning to control breath pressures while speaking will involve much practice in speaking at various levels of loudness while striving for smoothness of delivery.

Improving the Adjustments of the Vocal Folds and the Resonators: These adjustments have the purpose of improving the basic quality of the voice by improving muscular manipulation of both the vocal folds and the resonators. We might describe desirable qualities of voice that a person might strive for as being clear, brilliant, deep, resonant, mellow, or rich in warmth or color. Such descriptive words may have some meaning but they give no hint as to the muscular means of producing such qualities, or how to recognize them if they are produced.

Improvement in the basic quality of one's voice may be acquired through muscular experimentation with the vocal mechanism and critical observation of the resulting sounds, thus accomplishing the training of voice and ear simultaneously in a kind of adult "babbling stage." The adult learner, however, although handicapped by long-established habits, is better qualified than the infant to profit from such vocal experimentation because he can take better advantage of expert help and criticism and he has better perception and judgment of vocal qualifications and objectives.

The Elimination of Unnecessary Tensions: Muscular tensions in the vocal mechanism may be perceived as harsh or strained qualities of voice. Such tensions almost inevitably accompany any new or consciously controlled process of vocalization. If, for example, a person attempts to speak with an unusual depth or fullness of tonal quality, he will feel muscular strain; and a listener can detect evidence of muscular strain in his vocal quality. If one should continue to practice such a manner of vocalization, one of his primary problems should be that of eliminating such evidences of strain as soon as possible. Otherwise certain unnecessary muscle tensions might become fixed by habit and result in a permanently strained quality of his voice. To the average listener, nothing is more unpleasant or quite so apparent as a vocal fault in the nature of a strained quality of voice that results from excessive tensions of the muscles involved in vocalization.

Elimination of Common Vocal Faults

To the ears of an average listener, a vocal fault is a weakness or defect that keeps one voice from comparing favorably with others. The most common vocal faults result from lack of muscular strength or bad habits of vocalization rather than from structural faults of vocal instruments; hence such faults may be eliminated by exercise and practice.

1. *A Combination of Weakness of Voice, Thin Tonal Qualities, and a High Pitch Level:* This is perhpas the most common of all vocal faults, particularly among women. The initial causes might include physical weakness particularly of breath support, a cultivated social reserve or politeness, and perhaps an early pose of feminine sweetness or submissiveness. Both the thinness of tonal quality and the highness of pitch level might result from natural vocal adjustments that are made

subconsciously for the sake of conserving the muscular energy needed for supporting breath.

Weakness, thinness, and highness are all relative terms. How weak, thin, and high-pitched a voice must be before it is considered faulty depends upon how the voice is used. A voice used in daily conversations can be quite weak, thin, and high-pitched without giving anyone an unfavorable impression; but when such a voice is magnified either by increasing its loudness, for the sake of projecting speech to most distant listeners, or by an electronic amplifier of radio, television, or public-address system, the vocal fault becomes distressingly apparent and unpleasant to most listeners. It suggests not only that the speaker lacks physical strength but also that he lacks emotional vitality and a positive personality. Such a vocal fault must be extremely marked before it is a serious drawback to the face-to-face conversationalist, but even a slight fault of this kind is greatly magnified whenever circumstances demand that the voice be enlarged or amplified. To the public speaker, actor, or public reader who faces many listeners or who transmits his voice to an audience by means of radio, movie screen, or television, even a slight weakness or thinness of voice is sure to be a critical handicap.

The means of eliminating this vocal fault is similar to the means of overcoming any kind of muscular weakness. It calls for a great amount of distributed practice in relatively loud speaking while attempting to deepen the tonal qualities and lower the pitch level of the voice. Special care should also be taken during such practice sessions to minimize tensions that give a strained quality to the voice.

Deeper tonal qualities probably result from expanding the resonance cavities during vocalization—chiefly the cavity of the throat. But the most effective means of deepening the tonal qualities of one's voice can be discovered only by vocal experimentation. While vocalizing, one may change the size and shape of his resonance cavities at random and listen to the resulting sounds. The critical guidance of a trained observer is always valuable. In the initial stages of trying to discover a means of producing deeper tonal qualities, the following suggestion often helps: Open the throat cavity as though you were yawning; then hold it open while speaking at a lower than usual pitch level. Once the muscular means of producing deeper tonal qualities has been discovered, it should be practiced frequently and systematically.

Anyone practicing a manner of producing a stronger, deeper, and lower-pitched voice than he commonly uses probably feels that this new manner of speaking is strained and unnatural. Any new and complex activity that calls for careful muscular coordination is sure to seem strained at first. As practice continues, the gradual elimination of strain becomes one of the chief objectives. One should never allow a feeling of strain to keep him from practicing any new manner of vocalization which produces a stronger, deeper, and lower-pitched voice (if he needs to make such a change) because the elimination of strain is always a necessary procedure in any process of voice improvement.

2. *Vocal Nasality:* This is almost as common as the weak, thin, and high-pitched voice. It is generally acknowledged to be a vocal fault, even though the average listener—especially in regions where nasality is most common—can seldom detect it and is seldom offended by it except in very extreme cases.

Nasality may be defined as a potentially unpleasant vocal quality that results from an imbalance of nasal resonance. There are two types of nasality—positive and negative. Positive nasality, which is most common, results in a sharp, brassy quality of voice that is commonly used, for example, by an impersonator who attempts to caricature a rural character of advanced age. Such a quality is supposed to result from the soft palate being too low, thus leaving the port between the throat and nasal cavities too far open during the vocalization of all or certain vowel sounds. The nasal resonance recognized as positive nasality results from a kind of cavity resonance with openings at both ends. Negative nasality, on the other hand, although similar in sound, may result from holding the nose completely closed by pressure of thumb and finger. Such a complete stoppage of the nasal passages, which might result normally from adenoids or a "cold in the head," gives a vocal quality produced by nasal-cavity resonance with only one opening—that made by an open soft palate.

In most cases, positive nasality is apparent only on certain vowel sounds, especially when these sounds precede or follow one of the three nasal consonant sounds, the "m," "n," and "ng" sounds. The vowel sounds most commonly nasalized are found in such words as: mean, man, mine, main, mount.

Nasality is seldom noticed by the average listener in intimate conversations, especially with close associates; but any magnification of the voice for a large audience or by means of an electronic amplifier will usually bring out the unpleasant effect and make it quite obvious even when only a few vowel sounds are nasalized. Any untrained observer may fail to identify a nasal twang consciously but he usually gets an impression of a poor voice that is decidedly uncultured; this suggests to him that the speaker himself is uncultured.

When a person attempts to eliminate nasality, he must first learn to recognize its distinctive quality in his own voice and he must become aware of the particular sounds that he usually nasalizes and which of these sounds he nasalizes to the greatest extent. The use of some device for recording and reproducing one's voice is very helpful in making a study of one's own tendency towards nasality; and usually the critical judgment of a trained listener is also needed during the initial stages of training one's ear to detect nasality.

When a person becomes completely aware of his nasality so that he can identify every speech sound that is nasalized, he is ready to start eliminating this fault. By vocal experimentation it should not be difficult to discover the means of producing pleasant tones that are free of nasality. Then practice in substituting non-nasal for nasal sounds will, in time, make possible a permanent substitution. Drills for combating nasality are given at the end of Chapter 6.

3. *Breathiness or an Aspirate Quality of Voice:* Breathiness —which is mentioned in the preceding chapter as being wasteful of breath—is a fairly frequent fault, especially among women. As a vocal quality it is not actually unpleasant, but merely inefficient for any type of forceful speaking. It suggests a soft, velvety intimacy that might be very appropriate for hushed and familiar conversations. It is only when the voice must be projected in strong, positive speech that the weakness and inadequacy of a breathy quality become obvious.

A breathy voice is a sort of vocalized whisper that results from not quite closing the glottis firmly enough during vocalization. Although the vocal cords are close enough together in order to be forced to vibrate by the exhaled breath, an excess of air escapes and dilutes the sound wave that is initiated by the vibrating cords. Failure to close the glottis tightly enough for efficient vocalization usually is only a bad habit to be corrected by guided practice; but occasionally a growth or obstruction prevents complete closure of the glottis which may require the attention and treatment of a physician before any progress may be made in eliminating breathy tones.

The glottis can always be closed consciously, as for the purpose of holding the breath; but the proper adjustment of the vocal cords for efficient vocalization can be discovered only by experimental muscular manipulation guided by the ear and aided perhaps by the criticism of a specialized observer. Practice in loud speaking, or being forced repeatedly to project speech to a distant listener, will usually result in an almost automatic elimination of breathiness because under such circumstances a breathy voice is obviously inadequate and very wasteful of the energy used to support the breath.

4. *A Harsh or Husky Voice Quality:* This is a vocal fault that is fairly common, particularly among men who have abused their vocal instruments by overly tense use in shouting or bombastic speaking. A school cheerleader or the type of political speaker or clergyman who attempts to demonstrate the strength of his convictions by the degree of his physical and vocal tensions while speaking is likely to develop some kind of unpleasant harshness or hoarseness of voice. The harsh voice and the hoarse or husky voice are not exactly alike and might be considered as different vocal faults. However, there are so many variations in degree and kinds of harshness and huskiness that it seems impossible to draw any clearly defined line of division between them in terms of either cause or the resulting sounds. Consequently, the whole range of unpleasant vocal qualities that are suggested by such descriptive terms as "gravel voice," "whiskey tone," or hoarse, strained, and rasping voice are considered together as variations of the same general fault.

These vocal variations can usually be traced back to the single initial cause of excessive muscle tension in the vocal instrument around the vocal cords. In some cases these tensions have caused irritations that have resulted in temporary or chronic damage to the vocal cords, which may be inflamed or swollen or have their edges roughened with calluslike nodules. Usually such damage can be repaired by a good rest of the voice. In other cases the harsh or husky voice is produced by nothing more serious or enduring than a bad habit that results in poor muscular adjustments of the vocal instrument and excessive muscular tensions or constrictions.

The first step in eliminating a harsh or strained quality of voice is to study the exact nature of the fault, to get a clear auditory perception of it, and to learn under what circumstances and upon which speech sounds the fault is most apparent. Voice recordings and expert criticisms of one's voice will be invaluable aids in making such a study. The second step is to discover, by means of vocal experimentation, the manner of producing more pleasant tones that are free of habitual tensions or constrictions. Then finally by means of vocal drills, one must form a habit of speaking with easy relaxed muscles of larynx and throat until he can consciously substitute that habit for his harsh or strident manner of speaking.

In some cases one may find it impossible to complete the second step because of damage already done to the vocal instrument. As indicated above, a period of rest is usually all that is needed to correct such damage. In a few cases, however, a physician's care will be needed to correct abnormalities or to repair damage.

In some cases the final step of substituting a new manner of voice production for the old one may be extremely difficult because the old and strident manner of voice production has become part of the habitual emotional response to any public-speech situation. When a bombastic approach to any audience has become a fixed habit, and a harsh and rasping voice is merely an incidental accompaniment to a general condition of emotional and physical tension, then the problem is primarily one of personality adjustment, which is discussed in Chapter 10.

5. *A Muffled Quality of Voice:* A muffled tone is sometimes called a pectoral quality. It sounds strained and unnatural and usually interferes with clarity of speech, although otherwise it is not particularly unpleasant. The use of this quality is often accompanied by a tendency to mouthe one's words in a way that is obviously affected.

The muffled or pectoral quality seems to result from a person's conscious effort to deepen his vocal tones by lowering the back of his tongue so as to produce a so-called back placement of voice. The best remedy for this fault is to discover by means of vocal experimentation the method of producing a so-called forward placement of the voice that will result in a clear and relatively brilliant quality. This might be done by raising the back of the tongue and perhaps by making a conscious effort to project the voice forward towards the front of the mouth.

Summary

For daily conversations, a person uses characteristic vocal tones that are described collectively as his natural voice. The sounds of one's characteristic tones are determined partly by the structural singularity of vocal mechanism and partly by his individual habits of vocalization. One's muscular habits of vocalization represent the chief source of vocal inadequacy for speech and the only avenue for vocal improvement.

The formation of one's muscular habits of vocalization has been determined largely by the tonal qualities of voices he imitated during childhood, the proficiency of his sense of hearing, his general strength and vitality, the degree of his self-assurance, and his vocal experiences. Although habits of vocalization are deep-seated and impossible to break immediately, other habits of vocalization may be formed with relative ease and may be substituted consciously for the old habits. In time, such a substitution can be made permanent.

Any improvement of the muscular habits of vocalization must be guided by one's sense of hearing and critical judgment. The average listener is poorly qualified to evaluate speaking voices—particularly voices with which he is very familiar—because he tends to confuse vocal qualities with the personal qualities of the speaker, and (except in cases of exceptional or unique voices) his attention is centered upon what the speaker says rather than upon his speaking voice. Ear training is, therefore, a prerequisite to voice improvement. Ear training may be aided by an initial dependence upon the critical judgment of a speech specialist and the study of recordings of one's own voice, as well as by the critical observation of the voices of others.

A good voice is a pleasant voice that is effective as a medium of communication. A pleasant voice enables a speaker to make a favorable personal impression upon the listener. It should never give the listener a conscious impression of vocal beauty. The effective and pleasant voice is clear and easy to hear and it gives an impression of ease of vocalization.

The improvement of voice usually requires the improvement of breath support, of vocal-cord adjustment, and of resonator adjustment as well as the elimination of all unnecessary muscle tensions in and around the vocal cords. The improvement of breath support usually entails some strengthening of the muscles exerting pressure upon the exhaled breath, somewhat deeper inhalation, greater economy in the use of breath, and greater skill in the control of breath pressures while speaking. The improvement of the resonator adjustment is usually aimed at the production of deeper, fuller, and richer vocal tones and greater clarity or brilliance of quality which may be accomplished by experimental vocalization and the development of better critical judgment. The elimination of unnecessary muscle tensions is aimed at the elimination of all evidence of muscular strain in the voice itself.

The most common vocal faults to be eliminated are apparent in weak, thin, and high-pitched voices, in voices of obvious nasality, in breathy voices, in harsh and husky voices, and in voices that are muffled and lacking in clarity or brilliance. Correction of these faults requires, first, the development of a consciousness of the fault; second, the discovery (usually through vocal experimentation) of a vocal adjustment that will eliminate the fault; and third, frequent and regular practice in the formation of new vocal habits that, in time, may be substituted for the old and faulty ones.

Questions

1. What two factors determine the characteristic sounds of one's natural voice?
2. Which of these two factors determines how good a person's voice might become as a result of training and practice?
3. Would the possession of a poor vocal instrument frustrate one's efforts to improve his speaking voice?
4. What factors determine how good one's vocal habits are as a result of normal development?
5. How should a person attempt to improve his habits of vocalization?
6. How may one tell what vocal adjustments will result in vocal improvement?
7. What factors determine one's skill in observing and evaluating the voice?
8. Why is a person more apt to form a definite estimate of a singing voice than of a speaking voice?
9. Why is a person usually a poorer judge of his own voice than of other voices?
10. Can a person who is completely tone-deaf improve his voice by practice?
11. What are the criteria of a good speaking voice?
12. What are the three essentials for voice improvement?
13. Should a person ever try to impress listeners with the beauty of his speaking voice? Explain.
14. When a person attempts to improve his breath support, exactly what should he attempt to accomplish?
15. Why is flexibility of breath pressure important to a speaker?
16. For what reason should a speaker try to improve the adjustment of his resonators?
17. In what way does unnecessary or excessive muscular tension affect the sound of one's voice?
18. What are the commonest vocal faults?
19. What causes positive and negative nasality? How may they be eliminated?
20. What causes a breathy quality of voice? Why should such a quality be eliminated?
21. What is the cause of harshness or huskiness of voice? How may it be eliminated?

22. How may one attempt to eliminate a muffled tonal quality?

23. Might a person develop a fine singing voice and still have a poor speaking voice? Explain.

24. Would you expect a long-distance runner to have strong breath support? When running would he use diaphragmatic breathing? Would he have good breath control for speaking as a result of his practice of running?

EXERCISES

I—*Purpose:* To strengthen the muscles supporting breath.

Method 1: Laugh heartily. An individual in a private place should have no difficulty in laughing heartily at will. At first, one should probably not try to laugh steadily for more than the length of time that he can laugh on one breath. Then after pausing long enough to breathe several times normally, he should laugh again, and repeat often enough to make up approximately five minutes of continuous laughter. This exercise should be repeated daily, gradually increasing the length of time one laughs without interruption until he can laugh steadily for perhaps ten minutes.

When several persons are working together, it is not difficult to laugh together. Most people find it seemingly impossible to laugh alone before others because of self-consciousness. A leader of a group might raise his hand as a signal for everyone to laugh together; then after a moment he might lower his hand to point out one person as a signal for all except that one person to stop laughing.

Method 2: Devise a game to be played on a small table equipped with cardboard walls at the edges that are six to eight inches high. Play the game according to hockey rules, using a ping-pong ball that is to be propelled only by breath blown through rubber tubes.

II—*Purpose:* To develop a strong voice—a deep and resonant voice that is relatively low-pitched and relaxed.

Method 1: Practice the following military commands often. Shout the commands as though they were addressed to a drill group about one city block away. Keep the pitch of the voice as near to the normal level of conversational speech as possible. Also keep the throat open and relaxed and strive for a deep quality of tone with no roughness or evidence of vocal strain.

The first part of a military command (called the preparatory command) is usually sung out with prolonged vowel sound. The last part (called the command of execution) is barked out with a sudden explosive effect. For example, the first command below might be timed as follows: "Compane-e-e-e ate-e-e-en TION!"

Commands: Company, attention—Right face—Forward march—One, two, three, four, One, two, three, four, One, two, three, four, One, two, three, four—Company, halt—Left face—Port arms—Present arms—Order arms—Right shoulder arms—Forward march—Column right march—To the rear march—Company, halt—About face—Company, dismissed.

Method 2: Vocalize sharply and vigorously the syllables listed below. Repeat in turn a single syllable repeating it in various rhythms—for example, the familiar "a shave and a haircut, bay rum" rhythm, the drum-beat rhythm of a marching band, or the rhythm of a familiar popular tune. Note variations in breath consumption by the different syllables.

1. Ha	5. Rah	9. Ah	13. Lou
2. Ho	6. Yah	10. Hay	14. Whee
3. Ma	7. Haw	11. Why	15. Thee
4. Oh	8. Who	12. Yea	16. Thaw

Selections: Practice delivering the following selections as though addressing a huge outdoor audience without the aid of a public-address system. Keep the pitch of your voice as near as possible to your normal conversational level and work for deep and sonorous quality, strong breath support, and no apparent vocal strain. Repeat often and regularly for several weeks until you are satisfied that you have actually strengthened your voice to a degree that permits you to project your voice as far as you might ever be called upon to project it.

1. Thou, too, sail on, O ship of State!
Sail on, O Union, strong and great!
Humanity, with all its fears,
With all its hope of future years,
Is hanging breathless on thy fate!
We know what Master laid thy keel,
What Workman wrought thy ribs of steel,
Who made each mast, and sail, and rope,
What anvils rang, what hammers beat,

In what a forge, and what a heat,
Were shaped the anchors of thy hope!

Fear not each sudden sound and shock;
'Tis of the wave, and not the rock;
'Tis but the flapping of the sail,
And not a rent made by the gale.
In spite of rocks and tempest's roar,
In spite of false lights on the shore,

Sail on, nor fear to breast the sea!
Our hearts, our hopes, are all with thee,
Our hearts, our hopes, our prayers, our tears,
Our faith triumphant o'er our fears
Are all with thee—are all with thee!

by Henry Wadsworth Longfellow

2. Romans, countrymen, and lovers! hear me for my cause, and be silent that you may hear: believe me for mine honour, and have respect to mine honour, that you may believe: censure me in your wisdom, and awake your senses, that you may the better judge. If there be any in this assembly, any dear friend of Caesar's, to him I say, that Brutus' love to Caesar was no less than his. If then that friend demand why Brutus rose against Caesar, this is my answer: Not that I lov'd Caesar less, but that I lov'd Rome more. Had you rather Caesar were living and die all slaves, than that Caesar were dead, to live all free men? As Caesar lov'd me, I weep for him; as he was fortunate, I rejoice at it; as he was valiant, I honour him: but, as he was ambitious, I slew him. There is tears for his love; joy for his fortune; honour for his valour; and death for his ambition. Who is here so base that would be a bondman? If any, speak; for him have I offended. Who is here so rude that would not be a Roman? If any, speak; for him have I offended. Who is here so vile that will not love his country? If any, speak; for him have I offended. I pause for a reply.

from *Julius Caesar*
by William Shakespeare

3. Friends, Romans, countrymen, lend me your ears!
I come to bury Caesar, not to praise him.
The evil that men do lives after them,
The good is oft interred with their bones;

So let it be with Caesar. The noble Brutus
Hath told you Caesar was ambitious;
If it were so, it was a grievous fault,
And grievously hath Caesar answer'd it.
Here, under leave of Brutus and the rest—
For Brutus is an honourable man;
So are they all, all honourable men—
Come I to speak in Caesar's funeral.
He was my friend, faithful and just to me;
But Brutus says he was ambitious,
And Brutus is an honourable man.
He hath brought many captives home to Rome,
Whose ransoms did the general coffers fill;
Did this in Caesar seem ambitious?
When that the poor have cried, Caesar hath wept;
Ambition should be made of sterner stuff:
Yet Brutus says he was ambitious,
And Brutus is an honourable man.
You all did see that on the Lupercal
I thrice presented him a kingly crown,
Which he did thrice refuse. Was this ambition?
Yet Brutus says he was ambitious,
And, sure, he is an honourable man.
I speak not to disprove what Brutus spoke,
But here I am to speak what I do know.
You all did love him once, not without cause;
What cause withholds you then to mourn for him?
O judgment! thou art fled to brutish beasts,
And men have lost their reason. Bear with me;
My heart is in the coffin there with Caesar,
And I must pause till it come back to me.

from *Julius Caesar*
by William Shakespeare

4. Fourscore and seven years ago our fathers brought forth upon this continent a new nation, conceived in liberty, and dedicated to the proposition that all men are created equal. Now we are engaged in a great civil war, testing whether that nation, or any nation so conceived and so dedicated, can long endure. We are met on a great battlefield of that war. We have come to dedicate a portion of that

field as a final resting place for those who here gave their lives that that nation might live. It is altogether fitting and proper that we should do this. But in a larger sense we cannot dedicate, we cannot consecrate, we cannot hallow this ground. The brave men, living and dead, who struggled here, have consecrated it far above our poor power to add or detract. The world will little note, nor long remember, what we say here; but it can never forget what they did here. It is for us, the living, rather to be dedicated here to the unfinished work which they who fought here have thus far so nobly advanced. It is rather for us to be here dedicated to the great task remaining before us, that from these honoured dead we take increased devotion to that cause for which they gave the last full measure of devotion; that we here highly resolve that these dead shall not have died in vain; that this nation, under God, shall have a new birth of freedom, and that government of the people, by the people, and for the people, shall not perish from the earth.

Gettysburg Address
by Abraham Lincoln

5. They tell us, Sir, that we are weak,—unable to cope with so formidable an adversary. But when shall we be stronger? Will it be the next week, or the next year? Will it be when we are totally disarmed, and when a British guard shall be stationed in every house? Shall we gather strength by irresolution and inaction? Shall we acquire the means of effectual resistance by lying supinely on our backs, and hugging the delusive phantom of hope, until our enemies make a proper use of those means which the God of nature hath placed in our power.

Three million of People, armed in the holy cause of liberty, and in such a country as that which we possess, are invincible by any force which our enemy can send against us. Besides, Sir, we shall not fight our battles alone. There is a just God who presides over the destinies of Nations, and who will raise up friends to fight our battle for us. The battle, Sir, is not to the strong alone; it is to the vigilant, the active, the brave. Besides, Sir, we have no election. If we were base enough to desire it, it is now too late to retire from the contest. There is no retreat but in submission and slavery! Our chains are forged! Their clanking may be heard on the plains of Boston! The wave is inevitable; and let it come! I repeat, Sir, let it come!

It is vain, Sir, to extenuate the matter. Gentlemen may cry, Peace, Peace!—but there is no peace. The war is actually begun! The next gale that sweeps from the North will bring to our ears the clash of resounding arms! Our brethren are already in the field! Why stand we here idle? What is it that the Gentlemen wish? What would they have? Is life so dear, or peace so sweet, as to be purchased at the price of chains and slavery? Forbid it, Almighty God! I know not what course others may take; but as for me, give me liberty or give me death!

The War Inevitable
by Patrick Henry

6. Though I speak with the tongue of men and of angels, and have not charity, I am become as sounding brass, or a tinkling cymbal.

And though I have the gift of prophecy, and understand all mysteries, and all knowledge; and though I have all faith, so that I could remove mountains, and have not charity, I am nothing.

And though I bestow all my goods to feed the poor, and though I give my body to be burned, and have not charity it profiteth me nothing.

Charity suffereth long, and is kind; charity envieth not; charity vaunteth not itself, is not puffed up.

Doth not behave itself unseemly, seeketh not her own, is not easily provoked, thinketh no evil;

Rejoiceth not in iniquity, but rejoiceth in the truth;

Beareth all things, believeth all things; hopeth all things, endureth all things.

Charity never faileth; but whether there be prophecies, they shall fail; whether there be tongues, they shall cease; whether there be knowledge, it shall vanish away.

When I was a child, I spake as a child, I understood as a child, I thought as a child; but when I became a man, I put away childish things.

For now we see through a glass darkly; but then face to face: now I know in part; but then shall I know even as also I am known.

And now abideth faith, hope, charity, these three; but the greatest of these is charity.

Corinthians, XIII

7. Roll on, thou deep and dark blue ocean, roll!
   Ten thousand fleets sweep over thee in vain;
Man marks the earth with ruin, his control
   Stops with the shore; upon the watery plain

The wrecks are all thy deed, nor doth remain
A shadow of man's ravage, save his own,
When for a moment, like a drop of rain,
He sinks into thy depths with bubbling groan,
Without a grave, unknelled, uncoffined, and unknown.

from *Childe Harold's Pilgrimage*
by George Gordon (Sixth Lord) Byron

III—*Purpose:* To eliminate tensions that might result in harshness or a strained quality of voice.

Method 1: Practice relaxation of the muscles of the larynx and throat. Relax the muscles of the neck and jaw, allowing the head to drop forward because of its own weight. Then rotate the head slowly, allowing the mouth to drop open when the head is rolled to the back. Then straighten the head with a minimum of effort and open and relax throat with a yawn. Then repeat each of the following syllables as often as you can comfortably on a single breath—first with a breathy tone, and then with full voice but with minimum of effort.

1. He
2. Hay
3. Ha
4. Haw
5. Hoe
6. Who

Method 2: Practice reading the following selections while striving for ease and smoothness, giving full value to the lyric qualities of the verse.

1. In May, when sea-winds pierced our solitudes,
I found the fresh Rhodora in the woods,
Spreading its leafless blooms in a damp nook,
To please the desert and the sluggish brook.
The purple petals, fallen in the pool,
Made the black with their beauty gay;
Here might the redbird come his plumes to cool,
And court the flower that cheapens his array.
Rhodora! if the sages ask thee why
This charm is wasted on the earth and sky,
Tell them dear, that if eyes were made for seeing,
Then Beauty is its own excuse for being:
Why thou wert there, O rival of the rose!
I never thought to ask, I never knew;

But, in my simple ignorance, suppose
The self-same Power that brought me there brought you.

"The Rhodora"
by Ralph Waldo Emerson

2. How sweet the moonlight sleeps upon this bank!
Here will we sit and let the sounds of music
Creep in our ears. Soft stillness and the night
Become the torches of sweet harmony.
Sit, Jessica. Look how the floor of heaven
Is thick inlaid with patines of bright gold.
There's not the smallest orb which thou behold'st
But in his motion like an angel sings,
Still quiring to the young-ey'd cherrubins;
Such harmony is in immortal souls;
But whilst this muddy vesture of decay
Doth grossly close it in, we cannot hear it.

from *The Merchant of Venice*
by William Shakespeare

3. I wandered lonely as a cloud
That floats on high o'er vales and hills,
When all at once I saw a crowd,
A host of golden daffodils,
Beside the lake, beneath the trees,
Fluttering and dancing in the breeze.

Continuous as the stars that shine
And twinkle on the Milky Way,
They stretched in never-ending line
Along the margin of a bay:
Ten thousand saw I at a glance,
Tossing their heads in sprightly dance.

The waves beside them danced, but they
Outdid the sparkling waves in glee;
A poet could not but feel gay
In such a jocund company.
I gazed, and gazed, but little thought
What wealth the show to me had brought;

For oft, when on my couch I lie
In vacant or in pensive mood,

They flash upon that inward eye
Which is the bliss of solitude;
And then my heart with pleasure fills,
And dances with the daffodils.

"The Daffodils"
by William Wordsworth

4. To be, or not to be: that is the question:
Whether 'tis nobler in the mind to suffer
The slings and arrows of outrageous fortune,
Or to take arms against a sea of troubles,
And by opposing end them? To die: to sleep;
No more; and by a sleep to say we end
The heart-ache and the thousand natural shocks
That flesh is heir to, 'tis a consummation
Devoutly to be wish'd. To die, to sleep;
To sleep: perchance to dream: ay, there's the rub;
For in that sleep of death what dreams may come
When we have shuffled off this mortal coil,
Must give us pause: there's the respect
That makes calamity of so long life;
For who would bear the whips and scorns of time,
The oppressor's wrong, the proud man's contumely,
The pangs of despised love, the law's delay,
The insolence of office and the spurns
That patient merit of the unworthy takes,
When he himself might his quietus make
With a bare bodkin? who would fardels bear
To grunt and sweat under a weary life,
But that the dread of something after death,
The undiscover'd country from whose bourn
No traveler returns, puzzles the will
And makes us rather bear those ills we have
Than fly to others that we know not of?
Thus conscience does make cowards of us all;
And thus the native hue of resolution
Is sicklied o'er with the pale cast of thought,
And enterprises of great pitch and moment
With this regard their currents turn awry,
And lose the name of action.

from *Hamlet*
by William Shakespeare

5.

The Representation of Speech Sounds

AS WE turn to the general problem of articulation, our first concern is with the means of indicating in writing the sounds used in speaking. There are three ways of representing more or less consistently the sounds of our spoken language. Each one has its use and advantages. All three depend upon an alphabet made up of letters or symbols which may be supplemented by diacritical markings. And each is intended to represent all the speech sounds of the spoken language.

The least consistent method of representing speech sounds is the written language. The letters used in writing words are intended (or at least they were originally intended) to represent not only the whole words but also the exact sounds combined in pronouncing those words. A relatively fast change of word pronunciations as compared to very slow changes of word spellings has resulted in the development of many gross inconsistencies between the spelling and the pronunciation of words. It is perhaps fortunate that the spelling of words is very rigid and slow-changing because, as it is, English literature can be read without difficulty by succeeding generations for hundreds of years and by people using widely divergent dialects of the English language. However, the fact that there are occasionally as many as a dozen different ways of representing a single speech sound by means of conventional English spelling is very exasperating to anyone learning to spell or to any foreigner attempting to master the English language.

Sometimes English scholars become quite concerned about the inconsistencies in English spelling; and occasionally they attempt to initiate a movement to simplify spelling so as to re-establish consistent phonetic relationships between spelling and pronunciation. The late George Bernard Shaw, for example, was an inveterate champion of simplified spelling. To illustrate the extreme inconsistency of some spelling, he once suggested the word "fish" might be spelled "gh-o-ti" if the "gh" were given the same sound as in "enough," if the "o" were pronounced like that in "women," and if the "ti" were given the same phonetic value as in "nation." However ridiculous such a suggestion may seem, it is no more ridiculous than the spellings of hundreds of English words, if we believe that spelling should represent accurately current English pronunciations.

A greater weakening of the phonetic tie between spelling and pronunciation is encouraged by many modern teachers of reading. They believe that children should not be taught to associate letters with speech sounds because a child can learn more rapidly and, after learning, can read more rapidly, if he learns originally to recognize the general patterns of whole words rather than learning initially the sounds of each letter and then having to go through the process of building up pronunciations by combining the sounds of the individual letters making up the word. This is undoubtedly true. Greater speed in silent reading can be attained when the reader does not have to bother with individual speech sounds associated with letters, and speed in silent reading is very important. But skills in reading aloud and in pronouncing words accurately according to conventional standards is also important; and to attain such skills, one must learn at some time the relationships that usually exist (in spite of numerous inconsistencies) between letters and speech sounds. A reader who has no sense of phonetic values of letters may be able to read silently with speed and understanding, but he is prone to ridiculous confusions in pronunciations and he may often be unable even to make a shrewd guess at the pronunciation of words that are strange to him.

Another method of representing speech sounds is commonly used by most dictionaries for the purpose of indicating conventional pronunciations. With some variations, most dictionaries use a system of simplified spelling and diacritical markings. A key to the interpretation of these markings usually appears at the bottom or top of the exposed pages of the dictionary. This system has the advantage of being consistent and accurate enough in indicating the pronunciation of individual words to individual readers; yet it is flexible enough to be interpreted differently by people using different speech standards or local conventions of English pronunciation. In Webster's Collegiate Dictionary, for example, the pronunciation of the word "further" is indicated by "fûr t̶h̶ẽr." The key includes the words "ûrn," "t̶h̶en," and "makẽr" in which the same diacritical markings occur. It happens that both the key words "urn" and "maker" are pronounced differently by people using the general American and by those using the Eastern or Southern standards of speech. In effect, therefore, the dictionary succeeds in representing different pronunciations that are properly used in different regions by means of one system of simplified spelling and diacritical markings. It should be noted also that the dictionaries are concerned only with the ideal pronunciations of single words standing alone. There is no need to indicate changes in pronunciation that might occur in rapidly flowing speech as a result of subordination, speed of utterance, and the influence of speech sounds preceding and following any particular word.

The third method of representing speech sounds is a phonetic alphabet. It is the most exact method because a different symbol is used to represent each speech sound, and each symbol is supposed to indicate the same sound to all speakers regardless of variations in their standards of speech. Phonetic writing or transcription is also commonly used to indicate the sounds of connected speech and the variations of speech sounds used in different localities, and at different speeds or degrees of care in speaking. It provides a very valuable tool to the person interested in exact pronunciation and precise enunciation.

The phonetic alphabet presented here is an adaptation of that part of the International Phonetic Alphabet (originated by the International Phonetic Association) that designates the sounds used in American standards of English speech. Each symbol in this alphabet represents a basic phonetic unit or speech sound, and it always stands for the same speech sound.

A phonetic unit or speech sound is called a phoneme. A phoneme includes all the slight variations of a sound that are perceived by a listener as the same sound. For example, the "h" phoneme includes all the sounds that are recognized as the "h" sound. An "h" sound is like a whispered vowel and it varies with each different vowel that is whispered. For example, in the words "heel," "hill," "Hal," "Hail," "hall," "hole," "hull," and "hurl" the first sound in each case is easily recognized as an "h" sound although every one is slightly different because it is like the whispered sound of the vowel following.

The same sound may seem, to different people, to belong in different phonemes especially if these people use different languages or different standards of the same language. Since a vowel sound is formed by a specific adjustment of the mouth cavity and another vowel is formed by a slightly different adjustment, then it seems apparent that a compromise sound might be formed by stopping a half-completed glide from one adjustment to the other. This compromise sound may be recognized by one person as one of the two vowel sounds while another person may recognize it as the other. In either case, it is recognized as a vowel sound to which it is similar and which is used by the listener. It is also quite possible that any person with an untrained ear might recognize the same compromise sound as belonging to first one phoneme and then to another when heard at different times.

Phonetic units or phonemes are of two general types, called consonants and vowels. Most of the consonants are articulated noises made by momentarily closing or nearly closing the vocal passage in some manner. The vowels, on the other hand, are vocal tones that are uttered through a relatively open, though precisely shaped, vocal passage. A combination of two vowel sounds in the same syllable, so that there is a continuous or unbroken glide from one vowel to the other, is called a diphthong.

Phonetic Alphabet and Webster's Collegiate Dictionary Equivalents

Consonants

PHONETIC SYMBOLS	KEY WORDS	PHONETIC TRANSCRIPTION	WEBSTER'S EQUIVALENT
p	pop	pɑp	p
b	babe	beɪb	b
t	toot	tut	t
d	deed	did	d
k	cook	kʊk	k
g	gag	gæg	g
m	mum	mʌm	m
n	noon	nun	n
ŋ	ringing	rɪŋɪŋ	ng
f	fife	faɪf	f
v	valve	vælv	v.
θ	thirteenth	θɚtinθ	th
ð	that	ðæt	t̶h̶

Phonetic Alphabet and Webster's Collegiate Dictionary Equivalents

Consonants

PHONETIC SYMBOLS	KEY WORDS	PHONETIC TRANSCRIPTION	WEBSTER'S EQUIVALENT
s	sauce	sɔs	s
z	scissors	sɪzɚz	z
ʃ	shellfish	ʃɛlfɪʃ	sh
ʒ	garage	gəraʒ	zh
h	hot	hɑt	h
l	level	lɛvl̩	l
w	wow	waʊ	w
hw	which	hwɪtʃ	wh
j	yet	jɛt	y
r	roar	ror or roə	r
tʃ	church	tʃɝtʃ	ch
dʒ	judge	dʒʌdʒ	j
ʔ	uh uh	ʔʌʔə	[none]

Vowels

PHONETIC SYMBOLS	KEY WORDS	PHONETIC TRANSCRIPTION	WEBSTER'S EQUIVALENT
i	eat	it	ē
ɪ	it	ɪt	ĭ
e(ɪ)	ate	et	ā
ɛ	pet	pɛt	ĕ
æ	pat	pæt	ă
a*	ask	ask	ȧ
ɑ	father	fɑðɚ	ä
ɒ*	wash	wɒʃ	ŏ
ɔ	law	lɔ	ô
o(ʊ)	oak	ok	ō

Vowels

PHONETIC SYMBOLS	KEY WORDS	PHONETIC TRANSCRIPTION	WEBSTER'S EQUIVALENT
ʊ	put	pʊt	o͝o
u	fool	ful	o͞o
ʌ	up	ʌp	ŭ
ə	above	əbʌv	ȧ
ɜ**	bird	bɜd	ir, er, or, ur
ɝ**	bird	bɝd	ûr
ɚ***	murder	mɝdɚ or mɜdə	ẽr

Diphthongs

PHONETIC SYMBOLS	KEY WORDS	PHONETIC TRANSCRIPTION	WEBSTER'S EQUIVALENT
eɪ	bay	beɪ	ā
aɪ	buy	baɪ	ī
ɔɪ	boy	bɔɪ	oi
aʊ	about	əbaʊt	ou
oʊ	boat	boʊt	ō
ju	music	mjuzɪk	ū
ɪu	nature	neɪtɪur	ṻ
eə or æə****	hair	heə or hæə	ar or er

* The sounds "a" and "ɒ" are not used by all American speakers, at least not consciously. By some speakers, the word "ask" is pronounced "æsk" and "wash" is pronounced "wɑʃ." Such speakers have little or no use for either the "a" and "ɒ" sounds or their symbols.

** The "ɜ" sound is used commonly by many Eastern and Southern American speakers; but those who use the General American standard of speech commonly substitute the "ɝ" sound, which is often called the syllabic "r" sound. The same speakers seldom use both sounds.

*** The Eastern and Southern speakers who use the "ɜ" sound instead of the "ɝ" sound will also commonly substitute an "ə" sound for "ɚ."

**** These are examples of a long series of diphthongs used by the Eastern and Southern speakers who substitute the "ə" for the "ɚ" sound. In the speech of such speakers the "ə" vowel combines with other vowels to form diphthong sin such words as "here," "care," "poor," "door," and "war."

Classification of Phonetic Units

In the process of articulating various consonants, the vocal passage is either partially or completely obstructed for an appreciable length of time by the articulators. Some consonants are said to be voiceless since they are whispered through an open glottis. In other words, they are uttered with a sound of breath friction but no voice. Other consonants are voiced since they are uttered with the glottis nearly enough closed for the vocal cords to be vibrating. The consonant sounds may be classified according to their manner of articulation as follows:

Stops or Plosives: Formed by complete closure of the vocal passage, which closure is then suddenly released under breath pressure:

p—voiceless b—voiced	Closure made with the lips.
t—voiceless d—voiced	Closure made with the tongue on the gum ridge.
k—voiceless g—voiced	Closure made with the back of tongue against the soft palate.
ʔ—voiced	Closure by the glottis. This sound (called a glottal click or stop) is seldom made in the nature of a speech sound in any American standard of speech. When it occurs, it is usually recognized as an unintentional sound.

Plosive consonants are articulated in three steps as follows:

1. Closing the mouth or throat passage completely in a particular way, the sound caused by such a closure being called the implosion.
2. Building up breath pressure behind the closure.
3. Suddenly releasing the pent-up breath, the sound being called the explosion. A complete plosive consonant sound

consists of both implosion and explosion, but one of the two elements is often missing. In the sentence, "Put that down," for example, there are four plosive consonant sounds, none of which would be completely enunciated in rapid speech. Only the explosion of the "p" sound would be heard because of its initial position; only the implosion of the first "t" sound would be heard because the explosion would be softened by the following fricative "ð" sound; and only the implosion of the second "t" sound would be heard because the explosion would be that of the following "d." An incomplete consonant sound resulting from the omission of either the implosion or explosion is very common and is usually in good taste.

Nasals: All voiced through the nasal passages with the mouth passage closed:

m—closure made by means of the lips.
n—closure made by the tongue on the gum ridge behind upper teeth.
ŋ—closure made by the base of the tongue against the soft palate.

Nasal consonants all pass freely through the nasal passages with continuant, humming sounds that are easily articulated and easily recognized.

Fricatives: Formed by nearly closing the vocal passage:

f—voiceless v—voiced	Lower lip near the upper teeth.
θ—voiceless ð—voiced	Tongue tip near the upper teeth.
s—voiceless z—voiced	Teeth nearly closed with tongue near the gum ridge directing a jet of air against the edge of the lower teeth.
ʃ—voiceless ʒ—voiced	Teeth nearly closed and tongue arched near the hard palate with the lips slightly rounded and extended.

h—voiceless Glottis open but narrowed enough to cause breath friction. It is really a whispered form of the vowel that follows.

Fricative consonants probably owe their name to the frictional nature of the sounds caused by near closures of the mouth or throat passage. The fricatives are not particularly difficult to articulate, but they are commonly rather unstable and they include the weakest sounds in the spoken language—the hardest sounds to project. Some of the fricatives seem to be relatively difficult to distinguish from each other since substitutions of one for another are relatively frequent. A lisp, for example, is such a substitution. The common confusions of certain fricative sounds may result partly from the fact that their distinctive sound characteristics are of very high frequencies which some ears cannot hear, and partly from the fact that some speakers, because of jaw or tooth structure, find these particular sounds relatively difficult to articulate.

The accuracy of a fricative consonant sound depends upon the precision in the adjustment of the articulators involved so as to constrict sufficiently and in an exact manner the size and shape of the mouth or throat passage. The loudness of the fricative sounds depends principally upon the degree of breath pressure behind the constricted opening.

Continuant: Like a vowel sound, in that it can be continued without change for some time:

l—voiced, the tongue against the gum ridge leaving an opening at each side. The "l" sound varies, tending to split into two distinct types of "l" sound, that are called light "l" and dark "l." Both types are used, as a rule, in the word "level." The first "l" sound is light, the back of the tongue being high; while the second "l" is dark, the back of the tongue being low. The variations in the "l" sounds are not particularly significant since both are used by all speakers, and both varieties are consistently used and easily recognized as "l" sounds.

Glides: Each sound unit is initiated in a particular manner but then the articulators move immediately to form the following sound:

w—voiced, Lips initially rounded and extended as for the vowel "u" but they move immediately to the proper position for the following sound. For example in uttering "we" and "woe" the "w" sounds in the two words are initiated in the same manner but then glide quickly to quite different vowel adjustments, which result in glides that are initiated alike but end differently.

r—voiced, Tip of the tongue initially raised and curled back towards the hard palate but moving immediately to form the following sound.

j—voiced, Initially the sides of the tongue are pressed against the inner sides of the upper teeth narrowing the opening between the tongue and the hard palate; then the articulators move to form the following vowel sound.

Vowels: The different vowel sounds are vocal tones that differ in quality because of differences in the size and shape of the mouth, which operates as a cavity resonator. The size and shape of the mouth is regulated chiefly by the tongue, the lower jaw, and the lips. The tongue comprises a very flexible floor of the mouth cavity. It may be thrust forward or drawn back, and it can be raised in the front, middle, or back. The lower jaw may be raised or lowered to open or close the mouth to any degree. And the lips may be rounded and extended forward or they may be flattened and stretched to the sides. Variations of the mouth cavity are usually represented by a kind of quadrangle like that in Figure 6. The placement of vowels on this quadrangular chart indicates roughly the location of the highest part of the tongue in forming each vowel, assuming a view of the mouth from the left side. The little drawings at each corner in Figure 6 indicate the approximate tongue and jaw positions when uttering the vowels at the respective corners of the chart.

The terms "front," "central," and "back" refer primarily to positions of the tongue or that part of the tongue that is raised the highest when the vowel sound is articulated. The terms "high," "middle," and "low" refer to the position of the lower

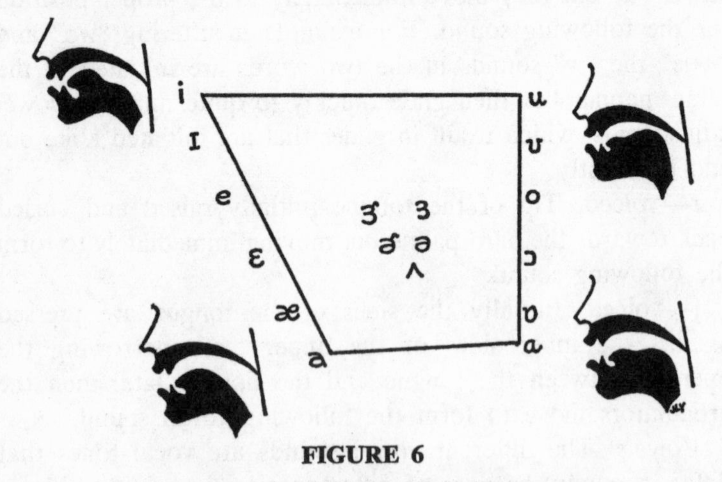

FIGURE 6

Vowel Diagram and Relative Tongue Positions

jaw and the tongue as they regulate the floor of the mouth cavity and hence the degree to which the mouth is open. According to the diagram (Figure 6) it is easy to see, for example, that the "u" sound is a high, back vowel while the "eɪ" sound is a middle, front vowel, and the "ʌ" sound is a middle, central vowel. Such indications of the modifications of the mouth cavity for the articulation of the vowel sounds may help some, but the principal guide for improvement of vowel articulation will always be the ear.

Supplementary Marks Used in Transcription

Diacritical markings are not used with the phonetic alphabet for the purpose of designating specific sound. However, a few diacritical marks are used to indicate certain modifications in articulation.

A small mark (ˌ) like an inverted accent mark, placed under a consonant symbol, indicates that the consonant sound is syllabic or that it accomplishes the function of a vowel. For example, the words "level" and "button" are transcribed "lɛvl̩" and "bʌtn̩." The little marks under the "l" and the "n" symbols indicate that each is pronounced as a separate syllable.

A colon (ː) following a symbol indicates that the sound represented by that symbol is prolonged. In Eastern or Southern speech (see Chapter 8), for example, the colon is needed to distinguish the pronunciations of words like "heart" and "hot," which are transcribed "hɑːt" and "hɑt." Sometimes a colon may be used to indicate a kind of prolonged consonant sound as in "bookcase" where the "k" sound is actually divided into two halves by a slight break in sound continuity (we hear an implosion, a slight pause, then an explosion). However, many people would prefer to use double consonants in such a case—"bukkeɪs"—on the grounds that the double consonant is not so likely to confuse a reader. Of course, double consonants should never be used except in such cases where the prolonged consonant gives the impression that the consonant sound is repeated or broken in two, so as to occur once in each of two syllables or words.

Accent marks used in phonetic transcription are different from those in most dictionaries. The accent marks used in phonetic writing are vertical and they precede rather than follow the syllables accented. A primary accent mark is placed above the word while a secondary accent mark is placed below. The primary and secondary accents of the word "dictionary," for example, are indicated conventionally thus "dik′ shun er′ i," and in phonetic transcription thus "ˈdɪk ʃən ˌɛrɪ."

Occasionally the same diacritical mark used by many dictionaries to indicate a nasalized sound is used also for phonetic transcription. This mark is a wavy line placed above the symbol representing the sound that is nasalized. Such sounds usually occur in French words adopted into English that have not been entirely anglicized as, for example, the word "lingerie" which may be pronounced "læ̃nʒə'ri"—the mark above the "æ" indicates that it is nasalized.

For phonetic transcription the conventional marks of punctuation (periods, commas, semicolons, etc.) are commonly used, but capital letters are never used either at the beginnings of sentences or proper names. Phonetic symbols that are the same as conventional letters are all small letters that are printed, never properly written in longhand script. The apostrophe denoting the possessive case or the omission of one or more letters is not considered necessary in phonetic transcription since its use would indicate no difference in sound.

Phonetic Writing or Transcription

Phonetic transcription is a means of indicating exactly what speech sounds are used in rapid sequence while speaking. Words are transcribed to indicate the way they are pronounced, whether the pronunciations be good or bad according to cultured standards. There are as many different ways of transcribing a word correctly as there are ways of pronouncing that word. For example, there are five different ways of transcribing the word "and," thus indicating five variations in pronunciation that are in common use. For relatively slow and careful speech, the word is pronounced "ænd" but as it is uttered with progressively greater subordination and speed, it may be pronounced "ənd," "ən," "nd," or merely "n." The word "the" has three common variations—"ði," "ðə," "ðɪ." The "ði" usually is used only when it is emphasized; the "ðə" is used as the most common unemphasized pronunciation; and "ðɪ" is commonly used when it is unemphasized and followed by a word beginning with a vowel—for example, "the other" is commonly pronounced "ðɪ ʌðɚ."

It should be noted that four letters in the conventional alphabet are not included in our simplified version of the phonetic alphabet. These are the letters "c," "q," "x," and "y." The letters are not needed because the sounds usually associated with the letter "c" are represented by the phonetic symbols "k" and "s"; the sound usually associated with "q" is transcribed "kw"; the sound of "x" is represented phonetically by "ɛks"; and the sound conventionally indicated by "y" is indicated by the phonetic symbol "j." Any use of "c," "q," "x," and "y" in phonetic transcription is obviously in error.

When learning to read phonetic transcription, a person should try to avoid relying upon habits formed in rapid reading of conventional printing. He should be careful, for example, to pronounce every syllable of each word exactly as it is transcribed rather than to sound out only enough sounds to be able to recognize words and then complete the pronunciation according to his habitual way of pronouncing these words. Beginners reading transcription sometimes read whole sentences by recognizing only a few key words and filling in the rest from context. Practice in reading phonetic transcription in such a manner is of no particular value, but very valuable practice may be obtained from carefully sounding out every syllable transcribed and comparing the sounds indicated with those habitually used by the reader in his daily speech.

In making a first attempt to read phonetic transcription, a person should always attempt to combine the symbols into syllabic units immediately rather than to try to sound out every symbol individually. A syllable is the smallest uninterrupted unit of utterance; so an attempt to sound out individually the symbols making up a syllable would result only in a distortion of speech sounds. Also it should be remembered that most phonetic transcription is written to represent rapid speech; hence it is likely to seem strange and distorted to a beginner who can only read very slowly a syllable at a time, because in rapid speech sounds are often omitted, shortened, or modified.

Detailed Consideration of New Symbols

Many of the phonetic symbols representing consonant sounds are identical to the letters and sounds represented in conventional writing. Any detailed consideration of these symbols and sounds, therefore, seems unnecessary. A few consonant symbols and all the vowel and diphthong symbols, however, are new in the sense that they are either unlike any symbols of the conventional alphabet or they represent sounds that are not consistently represented by the same letter symbols in conventional writing. We shall, therefore, consider these new symbols or sounds individually in some detail.

ŋ

The "ŋ" is a new symbol representing the sound commonly associated with "ng" in conventional spelling. It is a voiced nasal continuant that is formed by means of shutting off the mouth passage at the back by raising the back of the tongue against the soft palate, which is lowered enough to allow free passage for the sound through the nasal passages. This sound occurs in such words as: bank, blanket, bungalow, hunger, congress, conquer, finger, gang, language, length, pink, singing, thinking, and wrangle. In most cases any combination of "ng" or "nk" is pronounced with an "ŋ" sound which may or may not be followed by a "g" or a "k" sound. Contrast the pronunciations, for example, of the words "singer," "sinker," and "finger." There are two notable exceptions to this rule. First, an "n" preceding a "g" is pronounced with an "n" sound when the "g" is pronounced with a "dʒ" sound, as in the words "hinge" and "lunge." Second, an "n" followed by a "g" or "k" may be pronounced with an "n" sound when the "g" or "k" sound is in a different syllable that is accented —for example, in words like "congruity" and "concur."

Speakers seldom have difficulty in distinguishing the "ŋ" sound either in articulation or in auditory perception, but there is a common tendency to substitute the "n" for the "ŋ" sound in words ending in "ing." For example, the words, "ending, going, coming," and "beginning" are often pronounced "ɛndɪn, goʊɪn, kʌmɪn," and "begɪnɪn." There is also some confusion over whether or not to articulate a "g" or a "k" sound after a "ŋ" sound. Because of foreign-language influence, some speakers pronounce "singing," and "going," for example, "sɪŋgɪŋg" and "goʊɪŋk." A few speakers even tend to omit the "g" or "k" sounds when they are properly pronounced in such words as "finger" and "language," which become "fɪŋɚ" and "læŋwɪdʒ." Exercises to help clear up such confusions are found on Page 212.

θ

The sound represented by "θ" might be called the voiceless "th" sound. It is made by forcing unvoiced breath between the flattened tip of the tongue and the inner edge of the upper teeth. This sound occurs in such words as: both, booth, cloth, death, earth, froth, hearth, mouth, teeth, path, think, thirst, and wreath.

ð

The sound represented by "ð" might be called the voiced "th" sound. It is made in practically the same manner as the "θ" sound except that it is voiced instead of voiceless. However, a slight difference in the manner of articulation may be noted if one tries to make a distinctive difference in whispered speech between such word-pairs as: either and ether, thigh and thy, sooth and soothe, mouth and mouthe. The "ð" sound occurs in such words as: then, the, they, those, that, this, bathe, bother, brother, southern, rather, weather, and mother.

Some speakers tend to "thicken" their "θ" and "ð" sounds making them tend towards "ʃ" and "ʒ" sounds, probably by having the tongue tip too thick or by allowing too much of the tongue to approach too close to the area behind the upper teeth. Other speakers tend to substitute "t" and "d" sounds for those of "θ" and "ð."

ʃ

The "ʃ" sound is made by allowing a thin jet of unvoiced breath to escape between the tip of the tongue and the gum ridge behind the upper teeth. The lips are usually slightly rounded and extended forward. This sound is most commonly represented in conventional spelling by "sh" and it occurs in such words as: ash, bush, cash, dish, flash, hush, push, shade, shield, shut, sash, and wish. Represented by other spellings the "ʃ" sound occurs in such words as: ocean, sure, nation, sugar, schottische, chassis, chef, cautious, and rational.

ʒ

The "ʒ" sound is articulated in approximately the same manner as the "ʃ" sound except that the "ʒ" is voiced. Although the dictionaries commonly use "zh" as a means of representing this sound, there is no common manner of representing it in conventional spelling. The sound occurs on such words as: Asia, azure, beige, bijou, closure, garage, glazier, measure, pleasure, prestige, and rouge. The exact distinction between the manner of articulating the "z" and the "ʒ" or "ʃ" sounds can be made apparent by observing carefully one's utterance of the following pairs: glacier and glazier, beige and bays, rues and rouge, as her and azure, close her and closure.

j

The "j" sound is that usually associated in English with the letter "y." It is a voiced glide that is initiated through a narrowed opening between the tongue and the hard palate, but the tongue glides immediately to the proper position for the vowel following. The tongue position in initiating a "j" sound is very similar to the position of the tongue in uttering the high, front, tense vowel "i." This may become apparent if one observes carefully the movement of his tongue in uttering the word "ye"; then compare that movement with that made in uttering the words "you" and "yah." The "j" sound occurs in such words as: yet, yield, use, yell, university, union, onion, few, cute, William, yacht, butte, accuse, yoke, peculiar, and cue.

tʃ

The "tʃ" sound that results from exploding a "t" into an "ʃ" sound is commonly represented in conventional spelling by "ch." This blend of two voiceless consonant sounds occurs in such words as: church, choice, charge, cheap, catch, watch, which, cello, and cherish.

dʒ

The "dʒ" blend of two voiced consonant sounds which results from exploding a "d" into a "ʒ" sound, is usually represented in conventional spelling by either "j" or "g." This sound combination occurs in such words as: judge, Jim, gem, cordial, adjacent, dirigible, gadget, gauge, gesture, and jargon.

hw

The "hw" sound (which some phoneticians prefer to represent with the symbol "ʍ") is represented in conventional spelling by "wh." It is a glide initiated with the lips rounded to a small circular opening and the tongue high in back—as for the sound of "u"—then both the lips and the tongue move rapidly to the proper positions for the following vowel sound. The sound is initially voiceless. The time that vocalization starts varies with different speakers. Some speakers may complete the entire "hw" before vocalization starts (thus uttering merely a voiceless "w") while other speakers may start vocalization before the glide really starts (thus uttering a distinct "hw"). Some American and many British speakers eliminate the initial voiceless sound entirely, thus eliminating the need for the initial "h" symbol. Such speakers make no distinctive differences in their pronunciations of the following paired words: Which and witch, whale and wail, while and wile, where and wear, whither and wither. Other words in which the "hw" sound commonly occurs, according to American usage are: when, what, whim, whip, whirl, whisper, and white.

Vowels

i

The "i" sound may be described as a high, front, tense, unrounded vowel. The words high, front, and tense refer to the tongue since, during utterance of "i," the tongue is high in the front of the mouth and relatively tense. The word unrounded refers to the lips, since they are spread to the sides and thus are not rounded. The "i" sound is often referred to as a "long e" sound and it is designated in most dictionaries by "ē." It is represented by quite a number of different spellings in such words as: meat, meet, machine, people, me, Phoebe, key, quay, receive, believe, Caesar, and clique.

English speakers usually have no difficulty in distinguishing the "i" sounds from other vowel sounds in accented words or syllables either in utterance or in auditory recognition; but in unaccented words and syllables of rapid speech, most speakers tend to substitute "ɪ" sounds (which are less tense) for "i" sounds; or they use compromise sounds that are between "i" and "ɪ" sounds and might be recognized as "ɪ" sounds. For example, in rapid speech, the sentence, "she wants me to stay at home" might sound like "ʃɪ wɑnts mɪ tə steɪ æt hoʊm." Also, in rapid speech, such words as berry, pretty, merry, and tiny may be pronounced to sound like "bɛrɪ, prɪtɪ, mɛrɪ, taɪnɪ"; but the word "lingerie" is pronounced "læn͡ʒə'ri" with a distinct "i" sound at the end because the final syllable is accented.

ɪ

The sound "ɪ" may be described as a high, front, unrounded vowel. Its manner of utterance is very similar to that of the "i" sound. If a person utters alternately "i" "ɪ" "i" "ɪ" he may notice that the tongue is slightly lower and more relaxed for the "ɪ" sound and this seems to be the only apparent difference. The "ɪ" sound is represented by a variety of spellings in such words as: him, hymn, pretty, women, been, English, sieve, business, and build. Many speakers tend to confuse the "ɪ" and the "i" sounds when they are followed by "r." For example, such words as fear, weird, mere, here, beer, and pier are pronounced variously by different speakers, some using the "ɪ" sound and others using the "i" sound. Otherwise, the only common confusion between the "i" and "ɪ" sounds (mentioned previously) is brought about by the tendency to substitute "ɪ" for "i" in unaccented words and syllables. In many foreign dialects, however, the "ɪ" sound is consistently replaced by an "i" or a compromise sound that is very close to an "i."

ɛ

The "ɛ" sound may be described as a slightly lower than middle, front vowel that is relaxed and unrounded. It is commonly called a "short e" sound and is represented in most dictionaries by "ĕ." It is variously spelled in such words as:

again, aesthetic, breath, bury, friend, guest, heifer, leopard, many, says, and set.

There is a widespread tendency especially in the South and Southwest, to substitute an "ɪ" for an "ɛ" sound. This tendency is treated as a fault of "Substitution" in Chapter 7.

æ

The "æ" is a low, front vowel that is relaxed and unrounded. It is commonly called a "short a" and it is represented in most dictionaries by "ă." It is one of the most consistently spelled of all vowel sounds, being used in such words as: add, cat, hand, lamb, matter, guarantee, hair, heir, and wear. Many speakers, however, pronounce the last four of these words with an "ɛ" instead of an "æ" sound.

The "æ" sound is often uttered with tense, metallic quality or an ugly nasality or with both. For this reason it is treated as a fault of "Distortion" in Chapter 7.

In some sections of the country, particularly in the South, the "æ" sound tends to be prolonged or drawled. Any prolongation usually is accompanied by a glide or movement of the articulators resulting in a modification of the vowel sound itself. This fault is treated under the "Additions" classification in Chapter 7.

a

The "a" sound may be described as a low, front, relaxed, and unrounded vowel that is often called a "short Italian a." It is represented in most dictionaries by a single dot over the letter—"ȧ." To the majority of American speakers—the users of general American and Southern standards—the "a" sound is not clearly distinguishable as belonging to a separate and recognizable phoneme because these speakers commonly substitute the "æ" sound for it, and when they hear the "a" sound in the speech of others they recognize it as belonging to either the "æ" or the "ɑ" phoneme. Speakers who use the

Eastern standard and a few Southerners commonly use the "a" sound in such words as: after, ask, aunt, bath, chance, class, dance, fast, last, laugh, pass, path, and vast. Such speakers should have little difficulty in recognizing the "a" sound as an easily distinguished phoneme. But general American speakers and the majority of Southern speakers use the "æ" sound in all the words listed above; so they would use the "æ" symbol in transcribing them.

Some Southern speakers use a prolonged "a" as a substitute for the "ai" diphthong. This tendency is treated under the heading of "Omissions" in Chapter 7.

ɑ

The "ɑ" sound may be called a low, back, relaxed, and unrounded vowel that is often referred to as a broad Italian "a." It is represented in most dictionaries by two dots above the letter—"ä." It is conventionally indicated by various spellings in such words as: alms, arm, bazaar, father, guardian, hearth, sergeant, large, knowledge and star.

One way in which various standards of English speech deviate from each other involves the use of the "ɑ," "a," and "æ" sounds. The words in the following list, for example, are pronounced by most general American and Southern speakers with "æ" sounds, by most Eastern speakers with "a" sounds, and by some Eastern speakers and by many speakers using stage diction with "ɑ" sounds:

after	can't	fast	half	path
answer	cast	flask	lance	plant
ask	chance	France	last	raft
aunt	class	ghastly	laugh	shaft
basket	craft	glance	mask	task
bath	dance	glass	mast	trance
blast	draft	grant	master	vast
brass	example	grasp	pass	waft
calf	fancy	grass	past	wrath

ɒ

The "ɒ" sound may be described as a low, back, slightly tensed, and slightly rounded vowel that is relatively restricted in use. It is an intermediate phoneme between the "ɑ" and "ɔ" phonemes. Many speakers have great difficulty in recognizing it as a distinct and separate phoneme because they use it so seldom and when they do use it (more or less accidentally) it seems to them like only a slight modification of the "ɑ" or the "ɔ" sound. Conscious use of the "ɒ" sound may be held to represent one of the distinctive deviations in standards. This deviation may be illustrated by the following words which are pronounced by most general American and many Southern speakers with an "ɑ" sound, while they are pronounced by most Eastern and a few Southern speakers with an "ɒ" sound. The list should also contain most of the words ending in -oss, -ost, -oft, such as loss, cost, and soft.

box	drop	hot	palm	shod
clot	fop	log	pot	stop
cot	fox	lot	rod	top
clog	got	mop	rot	wash
dog	gods	nod	sod	watch
doll	hod	not	solid	watt

ɔ

The "ɔ" sound is a low-middle, back, fairly tense, and rounded vowel that is represented in most dictionaries by "ô." It is variously spelled in such words as: awe, bought, call, caught, fall, fault, flaw, abroad, George.

This sound is used quite generally and consistently with slight variations; however, when "ɔ" occurs before an "r," most speakers tend to raise the tongue enough so that the resulting sound resembles an "o" or "oʊ" sound. In words like aboard, bore, door, for, George, pore, store, and war, many speakers believe they use the "ɔ" sound while others are just as sure that they use the "oʊ" sound because the sound actually used is so near the border line between the "ɔ" and "oʊ" phonemes. Either symbol may be used in transcribing such words.

Southern speakers occasionally prolong or drawl the "ɔ" sound so that it becomes a dipthong like "ɔo" or "ɔʊ"; this tendency is referred to as a fault under the heading of "Additions" in Chapter 7.

o *or* oʊ

The "o" sound in its short and pure form seldom occurs in American speech except in very short and unaccented syllables in such words as: obey, follow, tomato, and willow. Usually the "o" sound is prolonged and combined with the "ʊ" sound to form the diphthong "oʊ." The two sounds are middle, back, tense, and rounded sounds that make up a diphthong that is usually called a "long o" sound. This sound is commonly represented in most dictionaries by "ō," and is variously spelled in such words as: ago, beau, boat, bow, brooch, dough, hoe, own, sew, so, and yeoman.

There is a tendency (mentioned above) to confuse "oʊ" with "ɔ" before "r" which is a fairly general tendency in all sections of the country. Some Eastern speakers tend to modify the "o" sound toward the "ʌ" sound. A few Southern speakers use the "oʊ" sound in place of "ɑ," "ɒ," or "ɔ." These tendencies are discussed under "Substitutions" in Chapter 7.

ʊ

The "ʊ" sound is a high, back, relaxed, and rounded vowel. It is represented in most dictionaries by "o͝o" and is variously spelled in such words as: bosom, could, pull, and wood. It is used with a fair consistency of sound in all sections of America.

u

The "u" sound is a high, back, tense, and rounded vowel that is represented in most dictionaries by "o͞o." It is variously spelled in such words as: crew, fool, fruit, group, move, rheumatic, rule, Sault Sainte Marie, shoe, Sioux, and true. In all standards of American speech, the "u" sound is used quite consistently. There is a widespread tendency to substitute "ʊ" for the "u" sound in such words as: broom, hoof, roof, room, and root. And in some foreign dialects, the "u" sound is commonly substituted for "ʊ." These tendencies are discussed in Chapter 7 as "Substitution" faults.

ʌ

The "ʌ" sound is a fairly low, central, relaxed, and unrounded vowel that is represented in most dictionaries by "ŭ." It is a sound that occurs only in accented syllables, being replaced by the "ə" sound in all unaccented syllables. It is represented by various spellings in such words as: cut, does, flood, love, and tough.

American speakers use the "ʌ" quite consistently but in some foreign dialects there is a tendency to substitute either a "u" or an "ɑ" sound so that the word "cup" would be pronounced "kɑp" or "kup."

ə

The "ə" sound is a middle, central, relaxed, and unrounded vowel that is often called the "schwa" vowel. It occurs only in unaccented syllables. As a matter of fact, many other vowel sounds tend to be shortened to the "ə" sound in unaccented syllables. It is very much like the "ʌ" sound except that it is much shorter, weaker, and usually less clear or more muffled. It occurs in the unaccented syllables of such words as: market, foreign, circus, delicious, machine, onion, surgeon, tosses, analysis, and carnival.

ɜ

The "ɜ" sound may be described as a middle, central, fairly tense, and half-rounded vowel. It is a sound used by most Eastern and Southern speakers and those trained in stage diction, but it is not normally used by general American speakers. It occurs in such words as: bird, colonel, fur, German, journey, learn, myrtle, were, and work. The letter "r" usually appears in these words as a kind of silent indicator of the "ɜ" sound. This sound always occurs in accented syllables.

ɝ

The "ɝ" sound is a middle, central, tense vowel that is uttered with the tip of the tongue curled up towards the center of the hard palate and the lips slightly rounded. It is the sound that general American speakers substitute for the "ɜ" sound; and it is called the "vowel r" sound or a "syllabic r." It occurs only in accented syllables where the "r" takes the place of a vowel. Either "ɝ" or "ɜ" sounds occur in such words as: burn, curve, dirt, earn, fern, hurt, insert, pearl, term, and word; but they do not occur in words in which the vowel appearing with the "r" is pronounced, as in: bear, care, dear, for, gore, horn, leer, poor, roar, star, steer, and wire.

It is the "ɝ" sound that some users of the Eastern standard or of a cultivated stage diction single out as being offensive in general American speech. It is a sound that can easily be made offensive even to the ears of a general American speaker if the tongue is too tense and is curled up too close to the hard palate. This fault is treated as one of "Distortion" in Chapter 7.

ɚ

The "ɚ" sound is a middle, central, relaxed, and half-rounded vowel uttered with the tip or near-tip of the tongue curled up towards the hard palate. This sound occurs only in unaccented syllables and it may be spelled by any vowel that is followed by an "r." It is found in such words as: altar, butter, circuitous, honor, and survive.

The "ɚ" sound is used by general American speakers almost exclusively. Eastern and Southern speakers usually substitute the "ə" sound so that the word murder, which is pronounced "mɝdɚ" according to general American standards, is pronounced "mɜdə" according to Eastern or Southern standards.

e *or* eɪ

The "eɪ" diphthong, being a glide from an "e" sound to and "ɪ" sound in the same syllable, is commonly called a "long a" sound. It is represented in most dictionaries by "ā." The "e" sound hardly ever occurs alone in American speech, although the single symbol may be used without danger of confusion in free or inexact transcription. The "eɪ" sound occurs, variously spelled, in such words as: bait, day, gauge, great, grey, lazy, and veil. Confusion of other vowels or diphthongs with the "eɪ" sound is quite rare.

aɪ

The "aɪ" diphthong is commonly called the "long i" sound, and it is represented in most dictionaries by "ī." It is variously spelled in such words as: aisle, buy, die, eye, flies, guide, guy, height, ice, right, and rye.

There are several slight variations of this diphthong—"aɪ," "ai," "ɑɪ" or "ɑi"—any one of which would readily be recognized as belonging to the same phoneme. To determine exactly which variation might be used by each individual each time he utters the so-called "long i" sound would be extremely difficult. Consequently, "aɪ" is recommended as an arbitrary choice for all of these variations.

ɔɪ

The "ɔɪ" diphthong is represented in most dictionaries by "oi." It is variously spelled in such words as: boy, buoy, coil, Boyd, oil, and voice.

One may hear such variations as "oɪ," "oi," "ɔɪ," "ɔi," but all would be recognized as the same diphthong; so the consistent use of "ɔɪ" to represent this diphthong is recommended.

Occasionally there is a tendency, particularly in New York City, to substitute either "ɔɪ" or "ɔi" for "ɜ" or "ɝ" in such words as: bird, first, learn, and worst. The same speakers who exhibit this confusion might also substitute an "ɜɪ" or "ɝ" for "ɔɪ" in such words as: boil, joint, oil, and point. Such faults are discussed under "Substitutions" in Chapter 7.

aʊ

The "aʊ" diphthong is represented in most dictionaries by "ou." It is variously spelled in such words as: Faust, mouse, and now. One may hear such slight variations of this diphthong as: "aʊ," "au," "ɑʊ," and "ɑu"—all of which would be recognized as the same diphthong. The "aʊ" is recommended, therefore, as an arbitrary choice of symbols to represent all such slight variations in order to avoid confusion.

There is a tendency, particularly in the South, to drawl and broaden out this diphthong to "æʊ," "æu," or even "ɪæu" or "jæu" which is discussed in Chapter 7 under "Additions."

oʊ

The "oʊ" diphthong is discussed above under the heading of "o."

ju

The "ju" combination of a consonant and a vowel is commonly called the "long u" sound and is represented in most dictionaries by "ū." There are many words in which the "ju" sound is used by speakers of all standards of American speech —for example: beauty, bugle, cues, cute, feud, few, fume, fuse, huge, humid, mew, muse, music, pewter, pure, pupil, and regulate. There are many other words in which the "ju" sound is generally used by Eastern and Southern speakers but not by general American speakers—for example: chew, dew, duke, during, duty, enthusiasm, knew, neutral, news, nude, presume, pursuit, student, stupid, suit, Tuesday, and tune.

The Use of the Phonetic Alphabet

The phonetic alphabet has many uses. It may be used as a means of showing contrasts between different standards of English speech; it may be used to indicate variations in pronunciation and to show the effects of varying degrees of care or speed upon enunciation; but its chief purpose here is that of helping the individual to correct faulty pronunciation and enunciation largely by providing practice in precise auditory observation of speech sounds.

Just as one's natural voice is largely dependent upon his habits of vocalization, so also are his normal speech sounds chiefly dependent upon his habits of articulation. And a person's critical judgment of his speech sounds is no better than his judgment of his natural voice quality. The phonetic alphabet is a very valuable analytical tool that serves to make one conscious of the exact nature of his speech sounds as they compare or contrast with the speech sounds of others.

A person can improve his pronunciation and enunciation by eliminating faults only if he is able to detect those faults, and he can learn to detect faults only if he is able to hear speech sounds with a degree of accuracy that should result from experience in using a means of representing exactly the sounds used in rapid speech. Such a means is provided by the phonetic alphabet.

Summary

Speech sounds are represented in three ways—by conventional spelling, by simplified spelling plus diacritical markings, and by phonetic transcription. Each of these ways has its advantages. Conventional spelling, although the least consistent, can be read the most rapidly. Simplified spelling plus diacritical markings is used by most dictionaries because it is subject to different interpretations by users of different pronunciation standards. The phonetic alphabet is the most accurate method of indicating speech sounds and can be used to indicate even slight modifications of sounds used by different speakers in the rapid flow of connected speech.

Each speech sound or phoneme (which may be defined as a family of similar sounds that are recognized as the same sound) is classified according to its manner of articulation. Consonants are either voiced or unvoiced and are further classified as plosives, nasals, fricatives, continuants, or glides. The vowels are classified according to tongue and jaw positions and according to the relative tension of the tongue muscles and the degree to which the lips are extended and rounded. Diphthongs are a combination of two vowel sounds in the same syllable.

The chief value of a study of the phonetic alphabet and the process of transcribing into phonetic symbols a rapid flow of connected speech sounds is the incidental ear training leading towards the accurate observation of speech which is a prerequisite to the correction of speech faults.

QUESTIONS

1. What are the three ways of representing pronunciation?
2. Why does conventional spelling often fail to indicate the pronunciation of a word?
3. Why are simplified spellings and diacritical markings preferred by most dictionary editors as a means of indicating pronunciations?

4. What are the advantages of the phonetic alphabet as a means of indicating pronunciation?

5. Define a phoneme.

6. Is the "a" sound a separate phoneme that you can easily distinguish from the "æ" and the "ɑ" phonemes?

7. Describe the articulation of "p," "b," "t," "d," "k," and "g." In what way is the articulation of all these sounds alike?

8. Describe the articulation of "f," "v," "θ," "ð," "s," "z," "ʃ," "ʒ," and "h." In what way is the articulation of all these alike?

9. What is meant by a glide, a continuant, and a nasal?

10. An "i" sound is described as a high, front, tense, and unrounded vowel. What is the significance of each descriptive adjective?

11. Can a word be correctly transcribed in phonetics in only one way?

12. Explain and illustrate the three ways of pronouncing the word "the."

13. In what way are "p," "f," "s," "t," and "ʃ" alike?

14. In what way is the articulation of the "b" and "m" sounds alike?

15. What four letters of the conventional alphabet are omitted from the phonetic alphabet? Why are these letters unnecessary?

16. How do the "h" sounds in the words "hat" and "hot" differ?

17. What is the chief value of a study of the phonetic alphabet and the process of transcribing?

18. Describe the articulation of "m," "n," and "ŋ." In what way is the articulation of all these sounds alike?

19. How may consonants be distinguished from vowels?

20. Compare and contrast phonetic transcription with conventional writing.

Exercises

I—*Purpose:* To learn to read phonetic transcription and to contrast different regional standards of pronunciation.

Method: "Sound out" carefully the following transcription. When symbols of alternative sounds are placed in a vertical column, select the one indicating the sound that you believe you would normally use when speaking rapidly. When a symbol is enclosed in parentheses, indicate whether or not you would normally use or omit the sound represented.

oə oə ə iə ə ə oə ɒ
fɔrskɔr æn(d) sɛv(ə)n jɪrz əgo(ʊ) aʊr fɑðɚz brɔt fɔrθ əpɑn ðɪs
ɒ əɪ ə i ə ə ɪ ə
kɑntɪnə(n)t ə n(j)u neɪʃən kənsivd ɪn lɪbɚtɪ æn(d) dɛdɪkeɪtəd tu ðə
ɒɪ ə ɒ ə ɪ ə ɪ ɪ əɪ
prɑpəzɪʃ(ə)n ðæt ɔl mɛn ɑ(r) krieɪtɪd ikwəl naʊ wi ɑ(r) ɛngeɪdʒd ɪn ə
(ɪ) oə ə oəɪ i
greɪt sɪv(ə)l̩ wɔr tɛstɪŋ (h)wɛðɚ ðæt neɪʃ(ə)n ɔr ɛnɪ neɪʃ(ə)n soʊ kənsivd
(ə) ə ə ə ɒɪ uə ɪ ə ɒ ɒ
(æ)nd soʊ dɛdɪkeɪtɪd kæn lɔŋ ɛnd(j)ʊr. wi ɑ(r) mɛt ɑn ə greɪt bætl̩fild əv
ə oə ɪ ə ə ə ɒ ə ə eɪ
ðæt wɔr. wi hæv kʌm tu dɛdɪkeɪt ə pɔrʃ(ə)n əv ðæt fild æz ə faɪnl̩ rɛstɪŋ
oə iə æə ə
pleɪs fɔr ðoʊz hu hɪr geɪv ðɛr laɪvz ðæt ðæt neɪʃən maɪt lɪv. ɪt ɪz
ɒ ʊ ə ə ɒ ə ə ɪ ə ɒ ə
ɔltəgɛðɚ fɪtɪŋ (æ)nd prɑpɚ ðæt wi ʃʊd du ðɪs. bʌt ɪn ə lɑ(r)dʒɚ sɛn(t)s
ɪ ə ɒ ɪə ɪ ə ɒ ɒɪ ɪ ə ɒ
wi kænɑt dɛdɪkeɪt, wi kænɑt kɑnsikreɪt, wi kænɑt hælou ðɪs graʊnd. ðə
ə iə ə ɒ ɪ ə ə
breɪv mɛn, lɪvɪŋ æn(d) dɛd, hu strʌgl̩d hɪr hæv kɑnsikreɪtɪd ɪt fɑ(r) əbʌv
ə ə ə ə oə ɪ ɜ oə ɪ ə
aʊr pʊr paʊr tu æd ɔr ditrækt. ðə wɜld wɪl lɪtl̩ no(ʊ)t nɔr lɔŋ rimɛmbɚ
ə ɪ iə ə ə ə oə ə iə oə
hwʌt wi seɪ hɪr, bʌt ɪt kæn nɛvɚ fɔrgɛt hwʌt ðeɪ dɪd hɪr, ɪt ɪz fɔr ʌs, ðə
ə ʊ ə ə iə ʊ ɜ iə
lɪvɪŋ, ræðɚ tu bi dɛdɪkeɪtɪd hɪr tu ðɪ ʌnfɪnɪʃt wɜk hwɪtʃ ðeɪ hu fɔt hɪr
ə ə i ə ə oə ə iə i ə ə
hæv ðʌs fɑ(r) so no(ʊ)blɪ ædvænst. ɪt ɪz ræðɚ fɔr ʌs tu bi hɪr dɛdɪkeɪtɪd
a ɪ i oə ə ɒ ə ɪ
tu ðə greɪt tæsk rimeɪnɪŋ bɪfɔr ʌs ðæt frəm ðiz ɑnəd dɛd wi teɪk ɪnkrist
ə ɒ oə ə ə ə
dɪvo(ʊ)ʃ(ə)n tu ðæt kɔz fɔr hwɪtʃ ðeɪ geɪv ðə læst fʊl mɛʒɚ əv dɪvoʊʃ(ə)n;
ə iə i i ɒ ɒ ə
ðæt wi hɪr haɪlɪ rɪzɔlv ðæt ðiz dɛd ʃæl nɑt hæv daɪd ɪn veɪn; ðæt ðɪs
ə ɒ ɜ (ə) ə ə ɪ
neɪʃən ʌndɚ gɑd ʃæl hæv ə n(j)u bɜθ əv fridəm, (æ)n(d) ðət gʌvɚ(n)mənt
(ə) oə ɒ ə ə ɜ
ʌv ðə pipl̩, baɪ ðə pipl̩, (æ)n(d) fɔr ðə pipl̩, ʃæl nɑt pɛ(r)ɪʃ frʌm ðɪ ɜθ.

i ə æ
gɛtɪzbɚg ədrɛs
baɪ eɪbrəhæm lɪŋkən

II—*Purpose:* To learn the phonetic alphabet.

Method: Practice reading the following disconnected words until you can read them rapidly and accurately:

baʊt, boʊt, bit, bɪt, beɪt, baɪt, bætl̩, bɑtl̩, bɝt, bɔt, bʌt, bʊk, bæt, bɜd, bɪrd, bɔɪl, beɪl, bɛl, bik, bæk, bɔk, bʊk, bɑr, baɪɚ, bɝ, bɪr, dæn, dɑn, dʌn, dɑrt, dɜt, daʊt, dil, dɪl, dɛn, deɪn, daɪn, dun, doʊ, din, dɔn, dɔg, djuk, dʌk, daɪk, dip, dɪp, dɔb, dæb, dɛf, fjuz, ful, fjul, fʌs, fʌz, friz, fraɪz, fɪz, fiz, frɔθ, frɔt, fɝðɚ, fɔɪst, fɜst, faʊl, foʊld, fɝl, fɑrðɚ, fɜmə, fɑrmɚ, fɔt, faɪt, feɪt, fɪr, fɛr, fɑr, fɝ, foə, fɜm, foʊm, form, fjum, fʊl, fɔn, fʌn, faɪn, hjumɪd, haʊl, hɪt, hit, heɪt, hɪl, hɔɪl, hil, hɔl, hoʊl, hʌl, hæt, hɑt, hɜt, hɑrt, hɑrθ, hɑrʃ, hɔrs, hoʊz, haʊs, haʊz, hæz, hɪz, kiz, kɪs, kætʃ, kæʃ, kæts, kaʊtʃ, kæʒʊal, kɔstɪk, kɔz, kɔɪl, kwaɪt, kwaɪət, kwɪt, kwoʊt, kwɔɪt, kɔɪ, kɔt, kaʊɚ, kɜd, kʌd, kʊd, kjuz, kuz, kʌzən, kjut, kɝt, kɑrt, kin, kɪŋ, kwin, kwaɪɚ, kwɪl, skwɜm, lɛðɚ, lɛtə, læðɚ, leɪð, læθ, laɪt, liθl̩, lɛdʒɚ, liʒɚ, ligl̩, lɔŋ, lɔn, loʊn, lɔɪn, laʊndʒ, lɔndrɪ, lɜn, laɪn, lʌŋ, leɪn, krʌtʃ, krʌʃ, kræʃ, klʌtʃ, krʌntʃ, kaʊnt, kɔɪn, kaɪt, kin, kraʊn, mæn, min, mɛn, meɪn, mun, maɪn, mʌðə, mʌtɚ, mɝdɚ, mʌtn̩, mɔθ, maʊθ, maʊð, mʌtʃ, mʌʃ, mʌst, mʌsl̩, mʌzl̩ mju, mɝdʒ, mɑrdʒɪ, mɪdʒɪt, mɛʒɚ, meɪl, meɪdʒə, mɔl, maɪl, mil, mjul, ðɪs, ðɛn, θɪŋk, θɪn, iðə, iθɚ, wɛðə, hwɛðɚ, wɪðɚ, wi, wɪð, wɪθ, mus, θɪðə, θiətɚ, θɪəri, θɔtfl̩, wɪʃ, hwɪtʃ, wɪtʃ, wɪl, hwil, hu, wu, hwaɪ, waɪ, wɒtə, wɒʃ, gərɑʒ, əblaɪdʒ, trɛʒɚ, trɪgə, hwaɪl, waɪld, hwɛt, wɜld, hwɝld, hwɪt, wɪt, hwaɪt, weɪl, hweɪl, gɔrdʒəs, dʒɔrdʒəz, prɛstiʒ, prɛsɚ, prɛʃɚ, liʒə, lɛsɚ, lʌk, beɪʒ, beɪz, bɔɪz, bɔɪs, baɪz, boʊz, bɔs, biz, brɪdʒəz, bidz, zɪŋk, sɪŋk, sil, zil, zɪθə, zɛfɚ, zum, veɪs, feɪs, feɪz, vɑz, vɔlt, vɪgə fɪgjʊr, bɪts, bɪdz, kɑbz, kɑps, fast, vast, vɛst, frɔst, sɪl, vɪɪkl̩, veɪl, feɪl, faɪbɚ, vaɪpɚ, viəmənts, vɛdʒɪtəbl̩, vɜs, faɪnɚɪ, bit, ʃit, sit, ʃʌdə, ʃʌtɚ, ʃɛr, ʃʊr, tʃɛr, tɛrz, ʃeɪz, tʃɪr, tʃɛs, tʃɪrz, ʃʊd, tʃaɪld, ʃud, sud, tʃɔr, dʒɪə, dʒɑr, tʃit, dʒeɪl, kloʊʒɚ, kloʊsə, kloʊz, kloʊðz, klɔθ, plɛdʒ, plɛʒə, pipl̩, pliz, kwɛstʃən, æmətjʊr, jɛs, dʒɛst, joʊk, dʒoʊk, jul, dʒuəl, jʊr, jʊɚ, jɑt, uz, juz, jus, jæp, dʒæp, jist, ist, dʒʌst, baɪts, bɪdz, bidz, kɑrz, kɑrts, mɪsɪz, mɛsɪz, slɛpt, drimd, skritʃɪz, skrætʃɪz, loʊdz, lɑdʒ, stoʊvz, stʌfs, kɪndlɪŋ, rɪŋɚ, lɪŋgə, sɪŋɚz, lɔŋgə, strɔŋgɚ, paɪnts, peɪnts, pɪnz, stɑrz, stɑrts, kæmps, hɔnts, hæmz, peɪnz, hændz, hɛnts, hɪnts, ʃɪp, tʃɪp, sɪp, zɪp, tiə, taʊɚ, tɔɪl, twɪl, twaɪs, twɪst, twɝl, twɪn, twaɪn, tweɪn, kwɪlt, kweɪnt, kwɪkə, ɜn, jɝn, ɜdʒ, ɝd, jiə, jor, jɑrn, jɑ, dʒɑn, dʒɑr, tʃæp, tʃɑp, tʃoʊk, dʒoʊk, tʃɛst, dʒɛst, laɪɚ, tɛə, taɪɚd, tɑrd, dʒɑt gɑt, ɛksɪt, ɛgzæmən, ɛkspɛl, kwɪz, kwɪvɚ, kwɜk, zinɪθ, zɛst, jæm, jæŋki, jɑrd, dʒæm, jɔn, jild, jɑndɚ, ʌgli, ʌpraɪt, ʌʃɚ, jutɪlɪtɪ, weɪst, wɛst, hwiz, hwɛr, wɛə, hwɪp, waɪp, hwɪf, waɪf, hwɪz, waɪz, tədeɪ, dʒin, dʒɪn, geɪn, gʌn, dʒɜk, dʒeɪn, dʒun, dʒoʊn, geɪm, dʒeɪmz, dʒɜmz, dʒɛmz, gæðɚ, geɪt, gɛt, dʒɛt, gɪə, dʒɪr, gɔz dʒɔz, geɪz, dʒoʊz, geɪ, dʒeɪ, gus, dʒus, dʒuz, goʊst, gɪft, dʒɪndʒɚ, gɪŋəm, dʒɪpsɪ greɪt, graʊnd, taʊn, dɪleɪ, haʊl, θɔ, ðæn, θɛft, θim, θisɪs, ðiz, θɪk, θɪmbl̩, θɪŋ, θɜd, θaʊzənd, θɔrn, ðaɪn, ðaʊ, θræʃ, θrɛd, θroʊt, θrʌʃ, ðaɪ, θaɪ, ʃæl, ʃɛl, ʃoʊl, ʃeɪm, ʃik, tʃoz, izɪ, krʊk, dʌz, trʌmp, stænzə, zibrə, əlaʊ, smuð, fɔrən, dəlɪʃəs, ʃu, məʃin, vɪnjard, siʒə, sizɚ, vɪʒən, kənfjuʒən, neɪtʃɚ, tʃɪl, eɪdʒ, hwɪtl̩, gɛsəz, ant, laf, dans, hɒrɪd, lɒftɪ, saɪð, θʊroʊ, θif, tʃuzəz, kæmɪoʊ, ɔtəmoʊbɪl, sʌlfə, vɑrnɪʃ, pjuɚ, sɔrsɚɚ, pətrolɪəm, rɛgjəlɚ, vju, sɪzəz, æksɛs, məskitoʊ, skwɔ, saɪkɑlədʒɪ, dʒinɪælədʒɪ, greʃəs, pɚtʃəs, rɛkwɪzɪt, groʊθ, tʃɪk, ædvɛntʃə, dɪfθɔŋ, trænskraɪb, əbæʃ, æktʃuəl, iklɪps, ɛrɔr, ɛkskjuz, dʒɚnl̩ɪst, sidz, skwɑʃ, ʌnsɪvɪlaɪzd, ʌndʒʌst, juθ, æbdʌkt, igətɪst, ɛskeɪp, ɛksɚsaɪz, dʒʌŋkʃən, siɛstə, ɛkskwɪzɪt, ʌŋkʃəs, ʌnjuʒʊəl, æbhɔrənt, keɪɔs, eɪtin, iθɪrɪəl, ɛksplɔɪt, zɪroʊ, sɪtʃueɪʃən, skwɛltʃ, ʌŋkl̩, ʌnjildɪŋ, hwɪspɚ, æbrʌpt, sɚkjulɚ, ɛloʊkwɛnts, julədʒaɪz, dʒɛntl̩, ʃiθ, slɔtə, skwɛr, ʌnikwəl, vɝdʒ, wɪzdəm, zoʊɑlədʒɪ, ækjumjuleɪʃən, koʊægjuleɪt, gɑsɪp, ʃaʊɚ, slʌgɪʃ, junɪtɪ, vɪʃəs, wɜʃɪp, wɔrʃɪp, ətʃivmənt, kɑgnɪzənts.

III—*Purpose:* To gain practice in using the phonetic alphabet to make exact distinctions in different ways of pronouncing the same words.

Method: Select from the different transcriptions of the following words the pronunciation that you think the best for use in rapid and relatively casual speech:

argument	ɑrgjumɛnt, ɑrgjəmənt, ɑrgəmn̩t
accurate	ækrət, ækjʊrət, ækjureɪt
statistical	stætɪstɪkl̩, stətɪstɪkl̩, stəstɪstɪkəl
medieval	mɛdɪivl̩, midivl̩, midɪivl̩,
experimental	ɛkspɪrmɛntl̩, ɛkspɛrɪmɛntl̩, ɛkspɛrəmɛntl̩
theory	θiərɪ, θɪri, θiəri, θɪrɪ,
practically	præktlɪ, præktɪkəlɪ, præktɪklɪ
association	əsoʃɪeɪʃən, əsosɪeɪʃən, əʃoʊʃɪeɪʃən
conscientious	kɑnʃɪɛnʃəs, kɑntʃɪɛŋktʃəs, kɑnsɪɛntʃəs
hundred	hʌndɚd, hʌndrɛd
picture	pɪtʃɚ, pɪktʃɚ, pɪktʃjʊr
literature	lɪtrətʃʊr, lɪtɚətʃʊr, lɪtɚətjʊr
amateur	æmətʃɚ, æmətʃʊr, æmətjʊr
clothes	kloʊz, kloʊðz, klɔθs
particularly	pɑrtɪkjulɛrli, pɚtɪkjɚlɪ, pɛrtɪkjələ˞lɪ
intellectual	ɪnəlɛkʃuəl, ɪntəlɛktʃuɛl, ɪntəlɛktʃʊəl
gentlemen	dʒɛnl̩mən, dʒɛntl̩mən, dʒɛntɛlmɛn

illegitimately	ɪlɛdʒɪtɪmeɪtlɪ, ɪlədʒɪtəmətlɪ, ɪlədʒɪtɪmɪtli
vegetable	vɛdʒtəbl̩, vɛdʒɪtəbl̩, vɛdʒiteɪbl
representative	rɛprɪzɛnteɪtɪv, rɛprɪzənətɪv, rɛprɪzɛntətɪv
parliament	pɑrləmənt, parlɪəmənt, pɑrliəmɛnt
February	fɛbjuɛrɪ, fɛbruɛrɪ, fɛbjəwɛrɪ
handkerchief	hæŋkɚtʃɪf, hændkɚtʃif, hæŋkɚtʃif
gradually	grædjəlɪ, grædjuəlɪ, grædʒəlɪ
temperature	tɛmpətʃɚ, tɛmpɛrətjʊr, tɛmpɚətʃʊr
deputy	dɛpətɪ, dɛpjutɪ, dɛpjʊtɪ
suggested	sədʒɛstɪd, səgdʒɛstɛd, səgdʒɛstɪd
recognized	rɛkənaɪzd, rɛkəgnaɪzd, rɛkɔgnaɪzd
probably	prɑblɪ, prɑbəbli prɑbəblɪ
identity	aɪdɛnətɪ, aɪdɛntɪti, əɪdɛntətɪ
unfriendly	ənfrɛnlɪ, ʌnfrɛndli, ʌnfrɛndlɪ
language	læŋwɪdʒ læŋgwɪdʒ, læŋguɪdʒ
finally	faɪnlɪ, faɪnæli faɪnəlɪ
popular	pɑplɚ, pɑpjulɚ, pɑpjəlɚ
introduce	ɪntɚdus, ɪntrodjus, ɪntrədus
sophomore	sɑfmɔr, sɑfoʊmoʊr, sɑfəmɔr
perspiration	prɛspɚeʃən, pɜspɚeɪʃən, pɜspɚeɪʃn̩
comfortable	kʌmftəbl̩, kʌmfɔrtəbl̩, kʌmfɚtəbl̩
casualties	kæʒəltɪz, kæʒuəltɪz, kæʒuæltiz
chocolate	tʃɑklɪt, tʃɑkəleɪt, tʃɔkəlɪt

IV—*Purpose:* To learn to represent sounds accurately by means of phonetic transcription.

Method: Transcribe the following words in phonetic symbols:

beat, bid, bait, peg, pack, pass, palm, dog, down, dough, took, tool, touch, curb, keys, kill, game, James, guess, Jess, gather, mamma, Maude, mowed, not, naught, note, wrong, longer, spunk, fight, fate, foul, vogue, vault, think, thou, thimble, thumb, those, they, says, scissors, zinc, sins, since, zebra, hurl, howl, who, ocean, chance, shoe, show, chase, cheat, measure, garage, gauge, beige, look, little, level, wide, white, women, woman, which, witch, own, on, wedge, whale, yellow, yacht, youth, roar, route, really, church, judge, chart, shirt, chin, shin, share, chair, jar, joke, yoke, choke, Jews, juice, chest, chess, jest, just, chilled, jilt, gilt, guild, cherry, Jerry, sherry, surely, Shirley, chuck, chug, jug, shuck, bats, baths, batch, badge, birch, purge, boys, Boyce, bays, base, blight, blithe, bumped, punned, gist, jest, guest, bust, June, Joan, Jane, Jim, about, bowed, paid, pate, bathe, basis, bases, paces, Burt, bird, birth, purred, pert, bias, buys, pious, buy us, meter, middle, metal, medal, could, good, cooed, peel, pill, pale, pal, pull, pool, Paul, pole, hull, hole, haul, who'll, stair, star, store, stir, poor, pore, purr, tired, tarred, towards, toured, dear, dare, door, doer, but, bought, boot, boat, beauty, cure, mute, fuse, fuel, fool, Yale, pretends, pretense, crew, grew, cause, gauze, clock, glow, colon, ground, crowned, bidder, bitter, gadget, cloud, glued, closer, closure, cash, catch, George's, gorgeous, oyster, union, employer, vicious, youngster, thirty-first.

V—*Purpose:* To gain practice in writing phonetic transcription and incidentally to learn to observe accurately sounds in rapid speech.

Method: Transcribe each day a paragraph of fifty words or more (found in this book or elsewhere) until you have succeeded in doing three paragraphs without error.

6.

Ear Training

FOR any speech-improvement effort, the importance of hearing and good auditory judgment can hardly be overemphasized. From the time that an infant begins to make random vocal sounds, his sense of hearing is directly and necessarily involved in the process of learning to control his vocal mechanism; and from the moment that a child uses his first word as a medium of communication, his development of speech effectiveness is strongly influenced by the ability of his listeners to hear and to understand him. The fact that the hearing of both the speaker and the listener is inevitably involved in any speech-improvement program is mentioned or inferred several times in the preceding chapters; but now as attention is to be directed towards the correction of errors in articulation, it seems advisable to consider more carefully the value of ear training in the correction of faulty speech.

Variations in Hearing Efficiency

The human ear is a delicate organ that is normally capable not only of hearing sounds but also of discerning variations in the pitch, force, quality, and timing of sounds. A complete understanding of the physiological operation of the ear as a receptor seems hardly necessary. The ear receives sound-wave impulses and converts them into nerve impulses which are transmitted to a part of the brain where they become conscious sensations of sounds which possess discernible characteristics of force, pitch, quality, and duration or timing.

The sense of hearing of different individuals may vary a great deal, not only in the degree of acuteness but also in the capacity to discern slight variations in the characteristics of sounds. One person, for example, might have an exceptionally keen faculty of hearing in the sense that he can hear many faint sounds that the average person cannot hear, but he may be unable to discern slight differences in quality or pitch that most people can perceive quite easily. Another person might be slightly hard of hearing but able to perceive very slight differences in the pitch and quality of all sounds that are audible to him. Still another person might have average powers of auditory perception except that his ear seems relatively insensitive to high-frequency sounds. As a result, he may be unable to distinguish certain quality differences that result from high-frequency overtones; and he may be unable to hear some distinctive speech sounds such as certain consonants.

The acuteness of a person's hearing and his power to discern slight variations in the different characteristics of sound depend upon two factors:

1. The organic functioning of the ear itself that converts sound waves into nerve impulses.
2. The neural functioning of that part of the brain which converts nerve impulses into conscious sensations of sound.

The organic functioning of the ear as a sound receptor probably cannot be improved by training or practice. Its physical structure determines its relative sensitivity to sound waves or to the sound-wave variations that account for the different characteristics of sound, and no amount of training or practice can improve that structure.

The neural functioning of the auditory area of the brain, on the other hand, does not depend upon a fixed physical structure. The neural patterns in this auditory area, which determine auditory impressions, have been established by past auditory experience and training. And the possibility of improving the neural functioning of the auditory area of the brain through further training and experience is practically unlimited. We are all familiar, for example, with the amazing ability in auditory perception which many people are able to develop after short periods of blindness; and everybody has heard of the phenomenal perceptive powers developed by many symphony orchestra conductors who can detect slight errors made by individual musicians among a hundred or more, all playing simultaneously. Such powers are developed by training or practice which can affect only the neural part of the hearing mechanism.

Speech and the Listeners' Hearing

As indicated in Chapter 1, the effectiveness of communication is partly determined by the perceptive skill of the listeners. For complete communication, a listener must hear speech sounds, recognize words, understand the literal meanings of those words, and appreciate the full significance of their connotative values in context. At any point, this communicative process might break down. A listener might, for example, be unable to hear the speaker's words if the speech sounds are not loud enough or distinct enough in utterance. He may hear words without understanding their individual or combined meanings, if many of the words are unfamiliar or if the structures of the sentences are too complicated. Or he might be able to understand literal meanings without perceiving many of the suggested meanings and without appreciating the full significance or importance of the whole speech, if the speaker's intonation pattern is unexpressive and hence his speech fails to stimulate alert interest.

Listening is greatly diversified because of extreme differences not only in listeners' degrees of willingness or unwillingness to respond favorably to the speaker's influence, but also in listeners' abilities to hear and to understand speech. Consequently, a speaker must adjust his speech clarity to the perceptive powers of his listeners. He may need to increase his clarity of articulation, his clarity of verbal expression, or his clarity of tonal expression inherent in the intonation pattern. Any adjustment of articulation or of tonal expression must be guided by the speaker's own sense of hearing and auditory judgment.

Interdependence of Speech and Hearing

Ear training in the field of music is a direct and standard procedure. Courses in ear training are aimed at increasing the power of auditory observation and improving the critical judgment of young musicians. The musicians then can use this auditory power as a guide in the production of musical sounds. Ear training has the same objectives in the field of speech, but there are three important differences between speech and music in terms of the interrelationships of hearing and sound. These differences may be explained as follows:

1. The improvement of speech is a process of relearning or substituting new habits for old. It is not a process—as music usually is—of relatively new or initial learning.

2. The sounds of speech are symbolic, and the attention of both speaker and listener is centered upon the meanings suggested or symbolized by the sounds rather than upon the sounds themselves, as in music.

3. The sounds of speech are not so consciously or directly controlled, as are the sounds of music. Effective speech results from spontaneous and automatic operation of good speech habits, and is motivated by an active desire to communicate thoughts and feelings. Any direct or conscious control of the speech process can only result in stilted and artificial speech.

A person learns at a very early age to talk and to understand the speech of others; and each year thereafter he acquires experience in speaking and in listening to speech. As the years pass, an individual hears his native language spoken in many divergent manners and dialects, in a great variety of voice qualities, and in widely varied intonation patterns. So he learns to understand speech in spite of variations, and he develops an unconsciousness of, or toleration for, different manners of speaking. If a person can, without difficulty, recognize the words uttered and the meanings intended by different speakers, he may fail to notice rather obvious differences in their manners of speaking.

The average person learns to listen to speech without consciously observing very carefully or accurately the sounds of speech. When, for any reason, vocal, articulatory, or intonating faults develop in his own speech, he might not notice them. Or if he does notice them but carelessly neglects to correct them immediately, his ear becomes accustomed to them and loses its power to detect them as faults. Even gross faults of speech expression might develop slowly, a little at a time, without being noticed because the ear has, by easy stages, gradually developed a tolerance for them. Any error or falsity of speech sound, if repeated often enough will eventually seem correct and true to the ear. Unpleasant or ineffective voice qualities, unconventional or uncultured pronunciations, inaccurate or slovenly enunciations, and false or misleading intonation patterns may be developed as bad habits of speech. When his ear becomes accustomed to such faults and hence the speaker is unable to detect or recognize them as faults, the consequent lack of critical judgment may be called a bad habit or fault in his hearing.

Improvement of Auditory Observation and Judgment

Improvement of one's auditory observation and critical judgment of his own basic voice quality, as indicated in Chapter 4, may require the aid of a specialized teacher and perhaps the help of some means of recording and listening to a reproduction of his own voice. As indicated in Chapter 5, the use of the phonetic alphabet in transcribing the sounds of normal, rapidly flowing speech is especially valuable as ear training because such a process necessitates careful listening and analysis of rapid speech in order to identify all the individual speech sounds used.

Later in Part II of this text, as we turn our attention to the subjective process of composing expressive intonation patterns for tonal communication, the method of improving auditory observation and judgment becomes very complicated because an intonation pattern can be evaluated only in terms of the meaning that it was intended to express. When we say that an intonation pattern is false or artificial, we mean that the meaning expressed by it is not the meaning that the speaker intended to express. A student in a public-speaking class, for example, might deliver an aggressive and dogmatic speech in a wonderfully expressive intonation pattern that reveals clearly how scared, self-conscious, and apologetic he really feels. We say, however, that his intonation pattern is false because it belies the aggressive dogmatism expressed verbally. As another example, a student in a class in oral interpretation reads a selection aloud and members of the class criticize his reading as stilted, artificial, and "phoney." Actually, the intonation pattern used by this student indicated very clearly its actual motivation. The student was not interested in the selection that he attempted to read and he was only vaguely aware of a general outline of its meaning. However, he wanted a good grade for his recitation so he attempted to compensate for his lack of interest and understanding by a forced enthusiasm in his manner of reading. The intonation pattern was as "phoney" as the forced enthusiasm that it expressed; however, as an intonation pattern it was really natural and effective in telling the truth. We call such an intonation pattern false because of its failure to express the meaning that the author of the selection intended and that the reader should have intended.

Expert evaluation of speech intonation patterns depends upon two factors:

1. The ability to perceive accurately all the sound variations that make up speech intonation patterns.
2. The ability to sense any falsity of intonation pattern in terms of the intended meaning.

The first of these factors depends upon actual skill of auditory perception. The simultaneous variations in force, pitch, quality, and timing are often very rapid and extremely subtle so that the ability to perceive all speech variations accurately requires a keen discernment that must be acquired by experience in careful observation. The ability to sense any falsity in a speech intonation pattern depends upon both the ability to sense the intended meaning and an auditory memory image of what the intonation pattern should sound like in terms of that meaning. Such an ability is based upon years of listening experience.

Auditory Memory and Guidance

A person with normal hearing hears his own language spoken from early childhood. He hears ideas verbally expressed in articulate speech and he hears expressive intonation patterns, and he learns to imitate both the articulations and the intonations. He builds up an articulate vocabulary and a repertory of expressive sounds that are closely associated with thoughts and feelings, so that any impulse to communicate familiar thoughts and feelings will automatically motivate words and intonation patterns to express them.

The muscular process of composing expressive speech patterns is guided to some extent by the speaker's auditory sense of the appropriate sounds. This auditory sense has the same relationship to the process of speaking that the sense of sight has to writing. A person with normal hearing rarely if ever has the experience of speaking without being able to hear the sounds of his speech, but nearly everyone has had the experience of trying to write in complete darkness, and they know how dependent they are upon their sense of sight which guides the muscular process of writing. A speaker is even more dependent upon his sense of hearing which guides the muscular process of speaking because speech patterns are infinitely more complex than are the patterns of writing.

The amount of auditory guidance used or needed varies greatly with different kinds of speaking. When a speaker attempts to communicate only his own thoughts and feelings in routine conversation, for example, he uses only a very familiar vocabulary and his usual patterns of speech that are based upon his oldest habits of oral expression and that require only a minimum of auditory guidance. But when a speaker attempts to load his speech with an exceptional degree of significance or meaning, using relatively unfamiliar words, or when he attempts to expand and project his speech for a large audience of comparative strangers, he speaks more carefully and depends to a much greater degree upon auditory guidance of his process of speaking. Perhaps the greatest need for auditory guidance results from an attempt at impersonation or mimicry.

Impersonation and Mimicry

Impersonation or mimicry may vary a great deal—ranging from a mere suggestion of an attitude or mannerism that might suggest a general type of character to a relatively complete representation of a particular person's manner of speaking.

A speaker might, for example, tell a joke or relate an amusing incident involving some dialogue in which he gives the barest suggestion of predominant character attitudes and, occasionally, partial and exaggerated dialects of the characters quoted. Accuracy of impersonation or mimicry is not important in such cases, because the speaker usually attempts to present only rather broad and conventional caricatures of general types of people. Specific caricatures of living people are often attempted by entertainers who present their "impressions" of nationally prominent personalities or attempt to satirize certain local individuals, as might be appropriate at a traditional "gridiron banquet." In such cases, the entertainer usually attempts to caricature the speech of the individual impersonated by giving an exaggerated imitation of a few of his peculiarities or mannerisms of speech. Ability to caricature the speech of others depends upon a keen auditory observation but also upon a knack of selecting the most distinctive mannerisms of a person's speech for exaggeration. It is the same type of knack that a cartoonist uses in drawing recognizable caricatures.

A relatively complete impersonation attempted by an actor or interpreter usually involves the creation of an imaginary but vivid conception of the personality of the character impersonated and a spontaneous reaction to all the attitudes that would motivate the speech of such a character. Usually an impersonator is satisfied if he can give a fairly accurate impression of the distinctive attitudes of the character impersonated without attempting to eliminate his own distinctive manner of speaking. For this reason, most actors are easily recognized in whatever roles they play. Some actors are much more easily recognized than are others because their normal intonation patterns are more uncommon or individualistic than are the patterns of others.

How far an actor or interpreter should go in attempting to disguise his speech through mimicry and the elimination of distinctive or recognizable elements in his own intonation pattern is usually an individual problem. The elimination of any particular mannerisms of speech that result merely from habit and are in no way expressive of meaning is, of course, desirable; but the elimination of distinctive or recognizable elements of one's intonation pattern which are expressive of personal warmth and insight is very undesirable.

It might be possible for an actor or interpreter to develop by means of mimicry an intonation pattern so similar to that of another person that he loses all the recognizable elements of his own speech pattern, but it is improbable that he can motivate such an imitated pattern and produce it spontaneously so that his speech would sound deeply sincere and significant.

The Value of Mimicry and Demonstration

Learning to talk is principally a process of imitation or mimicry; and demonstration and mimicry are essentially a part of any program of ear training. However—paradoxical as it may seem—both demonstration and mimicry are rather popularly believed to be dangerous devices if used in an attempt to develop effective vocal expression. Avoiding the use of demonstration as a teaching device is a stereotyped principle that is followed unquestioningly by many teachers of speech and interpretation, and by many theater directors. This principle is based upon the assumption that any direction by means of the demonstration of an expressive speech intonation pattern results inevitably in parrotlike mimicry unaccompanied by a full realization of the meanings to be communicated. If the attention of the learner is concentrated upon the pattern demonstrated and upon his attempt to reproduce all of its complex variations accurately, rather than upon the thoughts and feelings expressed by such a pattern, the result is certain to be shallow or artificial speech. But when a learner listens to a demonstration of effective vocal expression, his attention is not necessarily centered upon the variations of the intonation pattern. He might center his attention upon the thoughts and feelings that motivate the pattern which are much easier for him to discern. It is also much easier for him to remember the meanings communicated by a speech pattern than it is to retain an auditory image of the complete pattern expressing those meanings. Furthermore, even if a person actually tried to mimic a pattern of speech without understanding its meaning, he must usually have the pattern repeated several times before he can memorize its form. So it seems that the dangers of meaningless mimicry can be avoided merely by never repeating demonstrations often enough to permit memorization of their intonation patterns.

Regardless of the degree of suspicion with which any person might regard demonstration and mimicry when used as aids in the improvement of vocal expression, he should never overlook the basic value of both as methods of ear training. Attempts to reproduce precisely expressive speech intonation patterns requires exact and careful observation of the vocal and articulatory changes. By listening to expressive speech, a person learns to recognize certain speech patterns that express specific thoughts and feelings which he himself might never attempt to communicate. Through experience in listening, a person usually learns to perceive the meanings in many speech intonation patterns which he may be unable to reproduce in his own speech. It is like being able to understand, in the speech of others, the meanings of many words which are not in one's own speaking vocabulary.

If, for example, a very young interpreter is attempting to impersonate a firm but kindly father who is speaking to his son, that interpreter obviously must compose an intonation pattern that is expressive of experience and background that he does not possess. He may understand perfectly that this father should be represented as a mature person who speaks with quiet authority; but, lacking maturity and the background that would motivate authority, he probably has no experience in expressing thoughts and feelings like those of a father. In his initial attempts to speak in a fatherly manner, he should, of course, attempt to assume a fatherly attitude, but his speech must be guided by his recollection of appropriate intonation patterns heard in the past that may be retained as an auditory image in memory. If the interpreter cannot recall an appropriate speech pattern or if his recollection of it is vague or faulty, he will be like a musician playing by ear who forgets the melody he is attempting to play. This interpreter will need to hear an appropriate intonation pattern in order to renew his auditory image of it. He may renew his impression of how an intonation pattern expressing kindly authority should sound either by listening to a good demonstration of it or by seeking out the opportunity to observe a kindly father talking to his son. The demonstration is usually far more convenient.

If a person attempts to learn to speak with a foreign dialect, he must undergo careful ear training by listening to and attempting to mimic authentic models of that dialect. If the average person tries to speak with a particular foreign dialect while depending only upon his memory images of that dialect, the result is usually a hopeless mixture of many imperfectly remembered dialects.

Although repeated demonstrations and mimicry are not to be recommended as the most effective means of developing expressive and spontaneous speech intonation patterns, both demonstration and mimicry are very valuable methods of ear training, which serve to improve the ability to perceive speech sounds accurately and to store up auditory memory images for future use in guiding spontaneous vocal communication.

Summary

The ability of both the speaker and the listener to hear is involved in any process of communication; so a careful consideration of the value and nature of hearing and ear training is in order.

The sense of hearing possessed by different individuals may vary in degree of acuteness and in ability to discern slight changes in force, pitch, quality, and timing. A person's ability to hear depends upon both the organic functioning of the ear itself and the neural functioning of the auditory area of the brain. Although the organic functioning of the ear can be improved very little, if at all, by training or practice, the neural functioning of the auditory area of the brain can be greatly improved, as may be illustrated by the phenomenal auditory discernment often developed by the blind and by experienced conductors of large orchestras.

The effectiveness of communication is partly dependent upon the perceptive skill of one's listeners; so a speaker must adjust his speech to the abilities of the listeners to hear and to understand. Adjustment of one's speech sounds is dependent upon auditory guidance developed from ear training.

Ear training in the field of speech has the same general objective as ear training in music, but in speech the approach is more indirect since speech sounds should not be controlled as consciously as are the sounds of music. Also improvement in the field of speech involves principally relearning rather than initial learning, as in music.

A speech intonation pattern may be evaluated only in terms of how well it expresses the intended meanings and only the intended meanings. So one's skill in auditory observation and the quality of judgment of speech intonation patterns depends not only upon his ability to discern sound variations, but also upon his sense of the appropriateness of the variations to the meanings intended.

Although a speaker's attention is centered upon the thoughts and feelings which he attempts to communicate, his muscular process of speaking is guided by his sense of hearing and his memory of appropriate and expressive intonation patterns. As a person departs from his usual manner of speaking—as for the purpose of impersonation—he is more dependent upon auditory guidance; and his memory of appropriate intonation patterns may need renewal by means of demonstration and mimicry. Although demonstration and mimicry are not generally recommended as methods for teaching effective vocal expression, they are extremely valuable aids in ear training.

Questions

1. Why is ear training so important as part of a program of speech training?
2. Explain the functions of the ear and the auditory area of the brain.
3. Can the physiological function of the ear itself be improved by training?
4. How may hearing be improved by training and practice?
5. In what ways do individuals vary in their hearing abilities?
6. What circumstances might serve to decrease a listener's ability to hear and to understand a speaker?
7. How may a speaker adjust his speech to increase perception and understanding by his listeners?
8. What is meant by the statement that speech sounds are different from musical sounds because they are symbolic?
9. What is meant by the statement that speech improvement is chiefly a matter of relearning?
10. Explain how a person might develop a tolerance for and hence an unconsciousness of speech faults.
11. How is it possible for a speech intonation pattern to be well motivated and expressive but still false or "phoney?"
12. Upon what does a person's ability to evaluate intonation patterns depend?
13. Explain how demonstration might be dangerous as a device for teaching effective vocal expression.
14. If a person should suddenly become deaf, how do you think it would affect his speech?
15. Could you learn to speak a foreign dialect without the help of either demonstration or mimicry?

EXERCISES

I—*Purpose:* To gain practice in observing exact speech sounds in sequence and to test your memory span for such sounds.

Method 1: Have someone read the following groups of vowel sounds aloud, reading each group rapidly and then pausing long enough to give you time to transcribe the vowels you heard into phonetic symbols. Try to transcribe all the vowels in each group after hearing them only once. Otherwise practice until you can transcribe all sounds after only one rapid reading, or until you are convinced that you have reached the limit of your memory span.

1. i—æ—u
2. ʊ—ɑ—ɛ
3. ɪ—oʊ—ʌ
4. eɪ—ɝ—ɔ
5. aɪ—ju—oʊ
6. ɛ—aʊ—ɔɪ
7. ɜ—ɔ—eɪ
8. ʊ—ə—a
9. ju—ʌ—ɒ
10. æ—i—ɛ
11. oʊ—ɑ—ɝ
12. u—ɪ—ɔ

1. æ—i—ɔ—u
2. ɑ—ʊ—oʊ—aɪ
3. ɪ—æ—ɔ—eɪ
4. ɛ—u—ʌ—ɝ
5. a—æ—ɑ—ɒ
6. ɔ—ɒ—oʊ—ʊ
7. ɚ—ɜ—ʌ—ə
8. oʊ—ɔɪ—aʊ—ʌ
9. i—u—ɑ—ɔ

1. æ—ɑ—oʊ—i—ɪ
2. u—aɪ—eɪ—oʊ—aʊ
3. ɝ—ə—æ—ʊ—ɔɪ
4. eɪ—ʌ—ʊ—u—ɛ
5. ju—u—ʊ—ʌ—ɚ
6. i—æ—ɛ—ɜ—ɪ
7. ə—ɔ—oʊ—ɑ—ɔɪ
8. ɪ—ɛ—ɑ—eɪ—ɔɪ

1. i—æ—u—ʊ—ɑ—ɛ
2. ɪ—ɑʊ—ʌ—eɪ—ɚ—ɔ
3. aɪ—ju—oʊ—ɛ—aʊ—ɔɪ
4. ɜ—ɔ—eɪ—ʊ—ə—a
5. ju—ɑ—ɒ—æ—i—ɛ
6. oʊ—ʌ—ɝ—u—ɪ—ɔ

1. æ—i—ɔ—u—ɑ—ʊ—oʊ
2. aɪ—ɪ—æ—ɔ—eɪ—ɛ—u
3. ʌ—ɝ—a—æ—ɑ—ɒ—ɔ
4. ɒ—oʊ—ʊ—ɝ—ɜ—ʌ—ə

1. oʊ—ɔɪ—aɪ—ʌ—ɪ—u—ɑ—ɔ
2. æ—ɑ—oʊ—i—u—aɪ—ɪ—eɪ

Method 2: Have someone read aloud to you the following groups of nonsense syllables. First mimic, then transcribe each group, and correct your transcriptions as a means of checking your perception.

1. pun—ðɛk—waɪ
2. bʊm—lʌd—zoʊk
3. tɪ—gɛ—jə
4. dæ—θi—nɑ
5. kaɪ—ʃʌ—vɪ
6. ʒu—rɑ—kɚ

7. sɔɪ—jɪ—zaʊ
8. tʃaɪ—vu—hɔ
9. lɛn—lɚ—dʒik
10. waɪg—zɑt—zʊŋ
11. ðu—ʃaɪb—hwɔl
12. hɔn—goʊ—zʌŋ

1. pun—tɛk—vidʒ—bɑk
2. beɪ—θɪg—tʃɚ—foʊd
3. tɔn—joʊ—hʊl—sus
4. dik—rɑl—naɪ—fɔʃ
5. kɪb—jə—meɪp—ʒən
6. goʊm—ɜt—hʌf—ʃɛn
7. maʊd—tʃi—kɔɪd—feɪg
8. noʊk—saɪm—vɔl—ðiŋ

1. hjə—tɛk—lə—fjɑ—gəl
2. æʒ—loʊ—zɑ—dʒig—lɪ
3. ʃim—joʊ—bɔm—fin—ɪɛk
4. hwæt—vɜ—gʌv—θil—ək
5. ðeɪl—bæ—lɔɪt—ʒən—ɑk

1. pɒtʃ—lʌn—hɑr—biŋ—gɛf—lɚ
2. brɪ—tæl—mə—ʃikt—loʊl—dʒɔn
3. frɪ—θɔm—rəd—lutʃ—məib—foʊt
4. neɪk—laɪg—ʃum—zʊŋ—tʃi—rɔɪf
5. hwɪn—dʒaɪ—fɔŋ—suk—keɪd—zɑb

Method 3: Have someone read aloud to you the following paired transcriptions. Each pair indicates different ways of articulating the same words. Mimic both pronunciations, then indicate the one which you prefer.

1. pəlis—plis
2. præktlɪ—præktɪkəlɪ
3. dʒulz—dʒuəlz
4. sɛntəmɛntl̩—sɛnəmɛntl̩
5. poʊm—poʊəm
6. prɑbəblɪ—prɑblɪ
7. rɪəlɪ—rilɪ
8. rɛkənaɪzd—rɛkəgnaɪzd
9. sɛkn̩t—sɛkənd
10. ækrət—ækjʊrət
11. kʌmpnɪ—kʌmpənɪ
12. dɪdn̩t—dɪnt
13. ɪntrəsts—ɪntɚɛsts
14. frɛnlɪ—frɛndlɪ
15. ɑrgəmənt—ɑrgjəmənt
16. reɪʃɪəl—reɪʃəl
17. dɪfrənsɪz—dɪfɚəntsəs
18. sədʒɛst—səgdʒɛst
19. supɜfluəs—supɜfʊləs
20. pɑpjəlɚ—pɑpəlɚ
21. fæmɪljʊr—fəmɪlɚ
22. ɛnvaɪɚmənt—ɛnvaɪrənmənt
23. fæmlɪ—fæmɪlɪ
24. dɛpətɪ—dɛpjʊtɪ
25. ɪnɔgjʊreɪt—ɪnɔgɚeɪt
26. progrəm—progræm
27. sændwɪtʃ—sænwɪtʃ
28. vɛdʒɪtəbl̩—vɛdʒtəbl̩
29. sɪŋgəlɚ—sɪŋgjəlɚ
30. ædʒətɪv—ædʒɛktɪv
31. dʒɛntl̩mən—dʒɛnəlmən
32. mɑdɚn—mɑɚn̩
33. krɛdəbl̩—krɛdɪtəbl̩
34. pɚtɪkələlɪ—pɚrtɪkjulɚlɪ
35. ɪnstrəmənt—ɪnstɚmənt
36. əsoʊsɪeɪʃən—æsoʊʃɪeɪʃən

37. prɛspɚeɪʃən—pɚspɚeɪʃən
38. pʌmpkɪn—pʌŋkɪn
39. stətɪstɪks—stæstɪstɪks
40. lɪtɚətjʊr—lɪtrətʃɚ
41. kɑnʃɪɛnʃəs—kɑnsɪɛŋtʃəs
42. ɪntəlɛktʃʊəl—ɪnəlɛktʃəl
43. vɛtɚnɛrɪən—vɛtɚɪnɛrɪən
44. ɪkspɪrmənt—ɛkspɛrɪmənt
45. pɑrlɪəmənt—pɑrləmənt
46. fɛbjəwɛrɪ—fɛbruɛrɪ
47. læŋgwɪdʒ—læŋwɪdʒ
48. æktjuəlɪ—æktʃəlɪ
49. kæʒuəlɪ—kæʒəlɪ
50. əkeɪʒənəlɪ—əkeɪʒənlɪ
51. krɪmɪnl̩—krɪmnl̩
52. baʊndrɪ—baʊndɚɪ
53. maʊntn̩—maʊtən
54. dʒɛnjuɪn—dʒɛnjuwaɪn
55. djʊrɪŋ—dɝɪŋ
56. poʊr—pʊr
57. ɛvɝbədɪ—ɛvrɪbədɪ
58. faʊntən—faʊtən
59. prɪvlɪdʒ—prɪvəlɪdʒ
60. kruəl—krul
61. gɑrdnɚ—gɑrdənɚ
62. gærjələs—gærələs
63. ɪntrədjus—ɪntɚdus
64. aɪdɛnəkl̩—aɪdɛntəkl̩
65. rɛprɪzɛntətɪv—rɛpɚzɛnətɪv
66. hʌndɚd—hʌndrəd

II—*Purpose:* To gain practice in observing and distinguishing different time patterns.

Method 1: Have someone make the following patterns audible either by tapping on a table or wall or by vocalizing such syllables as "də" and "da"—the "də" representing the subordinate dots and the "da" representing the emphatic dashes. In each group three patterns are alike and one is different. Listen to the four patterns in a single group; then pick the one that is different.

1. ...-, ...-, .-.., ...-
2. .-.., .-.., .-.., ...-
3. -..., ..-., -..., -...
4. ..-., .-.., .-.., .-..
5. .-.-, .-.-, .-.-, ...-
6. ..--, .-.-, ..--, ..--
7. -..-, -.-., -..-, -..-
8. --.., --.., --.., -..-
9. .--., ..-., ..-., ..-.
10. .---, .--., .--., .--.

Method 2: Have someone read aloud the following groups of words. Listen to each group; then try to pick the one word that differs from the others in time and accent pattern.

1. association, practically, suicidal, amicable
2. advocacy, experiences, literature, creditable
3. chrysanthemum, benevolence, distributed, eccentuated
4. humiliated, anonymous, particularly, experiences
5. habitual, unfathomable, authoritative, incorrigible
6. representative, inexplicable, constitutional, animosity
7. unexpectedly, insignificant, opinionated, excentricities
8. consolidation, communication, dissemination, inexhaustible

9. metropolitan, supplementary, intellectual, characteristic
10. conglomeration, manufacturing, consolidation, experimental
11. opportunity, information, sentimental, bureaucratic
12. effervescent, calculation, mathematical, computation
13. enumeration, contemporaneous, incomprehensible, paraphrenalia
14. epigrammatical, unconstitutional, autobiography, negligible
15. illegitimately, dissimilarity, unimaginative, revolutionary
16. impracticability, authenticated, objectionable, contaminated

III—*Purpose:* To gain practice in distinguishing similar-sounding words.

Method: Have someone read aloud to you the following word groups. Ask the reader to make no attempt to exaggerate the differences between the word sounds. If you cannot differentiate all the words in any group, ask that they be repeated until you can. Avoid lip-reading by not looking at the reader.

1. main, maim, name
2. made, neighed, mate, nape
3. meet her, meter, neater, neither
4. mind, mine, nine, mime
5. sues, shoes, Jews, juice
6. wish, which, witch, wished
7. whit, wit, width, with
8. wealth, weld, welt, well

Additional similar-sounding word groups may be found at the end of Chapter 7.

IV—*Purpose:* To practice auditory observation by attempting to mimic certain pitch changes.

Method 1: Ask someone to sing at random a number of different pitches (or to strike at random different pitches on a piano) first in groups of four different pitches, then five, then six, etc. Attempt to mimic each group exactly. Continue until you reach the limit of your memory span for consecutive pitches. Repeat often to see if you can extend your memory span.

Method 2: Have someone utter groups of inflected syllables—each syllable being the same except that the pitch inflections are varied. Attempt to mimic each group by reproducing all inflections accurately. Gradually increase the size of the groups until you reach the limit of your memory span.

V—*Purpose:* To develop the accuracy of your auditory observation of speech sounds and intonation patterns

Method 1: Practice various foreign dialects by means of mimicry. Listen to a demonstration, preferably one that is recorded. Write down the lines spoken; then, after listening to the dialect several times, try to mimic it while reading the lines. Repeat your attempts until you are satisfied that you can give an accurate reproduction of the dialect. Then attempt to speak other lines using the same dialect.

Method 2: Practice mimicking the intonation pattern of someone else. It is preferable to have that person record a few lines so that you may hear the identical pattern many times before attempting to imitate it.

VI—*Purpose:* To develop accurate observation of your own intonation patterns.

Method: Record or repeat a short selection many times until you are very familiar with it. Then substitute "da" and "də" for the accented and subordinate syllables respectively, and reproduce the entire intonation pattern as completely as you can. Practice until you are satisfied that you can mimic your intonation pattern accurately without speaking the words.

7.

Enunciation and Projection

IN TERMS of sound, speech may be subdivided into a number of elements or units. The smallest of these subdivisions is the phonetic unit that is most accurately represented by a symbol of the phonetic alphabet. The next larger subdivision is the syllable that consists of one or more phonetic units in continuous sequence. The syllable is set apart by slight breaks in sound continuity, and it may be called the smallest uninterrupted unit of utterance. Next, in order of size, comes the word that consists of one or more syllables and may be called the smallest unit of language. In rapidly flowing speech, words are usually separated no more definitely than are syllables; and, consequently, only those listeners who are very familiar with the language can easily distinguish its words from one another in rapidly flowing speech. The next larger subdivision is the phrase that is made up of one or more words and comprises a sense unit or an element of thought as determined by expression. Phrases are divided from each other by pauses that are distinctly longer than the slight breaks in sound continuity that separate syllables and words within a phrase. Finally comes the sentence that consists of one or more phrases and expresses a complete thought. The pauses that separate sentences are not necessarily any longer than those separating phrases within a sentence.

All of these speech subdivisions blend together into a

rhythmic pattern of sound that should be conventional enough to permit easy recognition of words by a listener, in spite of any individual speech characteristics that are peculiar to the speaker. Spoken words and combinations of words are most easily understandable when their sounds are most familiar, or when these sounds are most nearly identical to word sounds previously heard.

Pronunciation and Enunciation Defined

The kind of conventionalization of spoken language that makes it clearly understandable is called pronunciation and enunciation. Good oral diction involves both.

Pronunciation is the auditory form of a single word. It refers to the combination of sounds that make up the recognizable word. To any listener the best pronunciation of a word is the one that is most familiar to him. Good or acceptable pronunciations are hence established by usage. Any so-called "mispronunciation" of a word usually results from a mistaken impression of the sound pattern of that word that the speaker believes is most commonly used by other speakers.

Enunciation, on the other hand, refers to the precision or exactness of the articulation of a word or a group of words uttered in rapid sequence. It is concerned more with the clarity of speech in general than with the conventional accuracy of a single word. When a speaker combines several words into phrase units that must flow rapidly, he often has to make some sound combinations that are relatively difficult to articulate in rapid sequence. In such cases, he may either slow up his speech enough to articulate these combinations exactly—as though each word were a separate unit—or he may modify some of the phonetic units and omit others to permit rapid articulation with a degree of ease. The latter alternative is commonly chosen. Enough omissions and modifications of phonetic units to permit an easy and smooth flow of speech is in good taste and is far preferable to the labored and jerky delivery that would result from an effort to avoid any sound distortions in the process of easing articulation. Any sound omissions or distortions that are customary and in good taste are established by usage just as the best pronunciations are established.

It should be remembered that when a person speaks, the process of pronouncing words and of enunciating his speech are dependent upon deep-seated habits. These habits are based upon two kinds of memory images—auditory images of words as he usually hears them, and muscular images of words or word combinations as he usually speaks them. One's auditory images which determine his sense of the proper pronunciation of words are originated usually as a result of listening and hearing certain pronunciations more frequently than others. One's muscular images, which determine the degree of exactness and precision of his articulatory movements and the clarity of his enunciation, are formed by his experience in talking at the time when his muscular habits of speech were being formed. Good pronunciation is a matter of knowledge, while good enunciation is a matter of skill.

Clarity of speech as it is heard across any distance depends upon the audibility of all distinctive speech sounds that make words recognizable. Each spoken word, with few exceptions, is a combination of a number of speech sounds including both vowel and consonant sounds. All vowel sounds are clear vocal tones that are voiced through a precisely shaped but relatively open mouth passage. A distinctive or easily recognized vowel sound results from an exact adjustment in the size and shape of the mouth cavity, so that the sound produced may be described as being at the exact phonetic center of its phoneme, and, consequently, as distinctly different as possible from similar-sounding vowels that are adjacent to it on the vowel-placement quadrangle (see Figure 6). Consonant sounds, on the other hand, are seldom clear vocal tones. Most of them are exploded, frictional, or muffled noises that have no discernible tonal qualities. The distinctive sounds of the great majority of consonants depend upon the precision and vigor of articulation and an adequate degree of breath pressure.

In enunciating a rapid flow of words, the articulatory movements, including the adjustment of breath pressures, are subconsciously made and are extremely swift; they depend upon habits most of which date back to one's cradle days. Such habits are both muscular and auditory, and any faulty enunciation of speech might result, therefore, from a muscular failure to articulate all speech sounds with sufficient vigor and precision or from an auditory failure to recognize faulty sounds that are uttered and the consequent lack of any effort to correct them.

Quality and Modes of Enunciation

Good enunciation is not easy to describe because the evaluation of enunciation in any particular case depends to a great extent upon the occasion for speaking and the degree of care in articulation that the specific listeners expect upon such an occasion.

There are many modes of enunciation that vary with the training of the speaker and with the degree of care that he uses in speaking. At one extreme one might find the uncultured and carelessly casual speech of small boys on the playground and at the other extreme is the careful, highly cultured, and reverent or formal speech that might characterize the reading of the scriptural lesson in church before a highly cultured congregation. The difference results partly from the difference in the general cultural levels and articulatory skills of the speakers and partly from the degrees of care that are expected by the different listeners. Various occasions or types of listeners demand varying degrees of care in speaking and hence different modes of enunciation. A careful, highly cultured, and formal type of enunciation, for example, used before a group of class-conscious and unskilled laborers would probably seem affected or even effeminate and might stimulate in this particular audience a reaction of distrust or suspicion towards the speaker. On the other hand, an uncultured and carelessly casual mode of reading a passage from the Bible before a cultured church congregation would seem shockingly out of place.

No one except an actor or interpretative reader is expected to be able to make radical changes in his mode of enunciating speech; and actors or readers need to be able to make such changes only for the purpose of characterization. The average person, who needs to speak only as himself, will wish to change his mode of enunciation only a little as he adapts his speech to different occasions and different listeners. Anyone interested in effective speech should develop a habitual mode of enunciation that is appropriate to the kinds of occasions and listeners that he might expect to meet most often. Most of us expect to speak most frequently upon informal occasions before cultured listeners; therefore, our most appropriate mode of enunciation might be described as a cultured conversational quality or "the style of well-bred ease." Such a mode of enunciation results in easy, smooth-flowing, but distinct speech that is both effective and pleasing to the listener.

Poor or slovenly enunciation is usually associated with a lack of culture and a lazy carelessness. However, there are several contributing factors which might account for relatively rough and inaccurate enunciation. Such factors are:

1. Initial imitation of poorly enunciated speech—an uncultured background.

2. Inaccurate perception of rapidly flowing speech sounds and hence the formation of only vague and inexact memory images of such sounds.

3. A complacent acceptance of imperfect enunciation as an ideal indicative of one's social class and of his freedom from cultural patterns.

4. Lack of muscular coordination or the skill necessary for rapid and accurate articulation.

5. Lazy indifference toward one's effectiveness of communication, and a consequently unanimated and careless manner of speaking.

An examination of the above factors shows that cultural background, skill, and speech motivation are all involved in determining the quality of enunciation. The first and third items above refer to the effects of cultural background—both the kind of speech one hears and learns to imitate, and the kind of speech one wishes to learn. The second and fourth factors refer to the auditory and muscular skill involved in learning. And the last item refers to the rather fundamental problem of the speech personality or the degree to which the speaker has an active desire to communicate to or influence his listeners—the desire to communicate and influence being dependent upon the speaker's appreciation of the significance of the material to be communicated and the importance of the listeners' response.

A cultured, conversational style of enunciation is distinct, rapid, and unlabored; hence it involves an inevitable three-way compromise between speed, exactness, and ease. An extreme in exactness with a consequent lack of ease might be illustrated by the kind of speaker who seems to assume that the spoken language is derived from the written language rather than vice versa; so he attempts to avoid all qualitative changes of speech sounds even when speaking rapidly and informally. He tries to give full and precise utterance to the speech sounds represented by every letter in unaccented syllables and subordinate words exactly the same as he would if these syllables and words were accented and emphasized; and he tries to avoid all natural modifications of speech sounds that result from the influence of adjacent sounds. Such a speaker seems to expend an excessive effort in speaking and his speech seems affected, overly precise, and pedantic. Illustrating the other extreme is the casual and careless speaker who pays no attention to the exactness of his articulation. He mumbles and slurs his speech sounds because he fails to articulate them vigorously enough. He omits some sounds entirely, weakens others to the point that they are virtually inaudible, distorts some sounds, changes the order of others, and occasionally adds extraneous sounds. Such a speaker usually seems to lack vitality, and his speech seems dispirited and indistinct as well as uncultured.

Somewhere between these two extremes there is an easy but distinct manner of speaking that may be rather vaguely defined as good enunciation. It is articulated clearly and distinctly enough to minimize the effort of the listener to understand; yet it flows smoothly and spontaneously without apparent effort on the part of the speaker. Good enunciation cannot be exactly described in terms of the pronunciation of words because the sounds of individual words change as a result of speed of utterance, degree of accent or subordination, and the influence of other sounds immediately preceding or following. The development of good enunciation can be guided only by good taste; and good taste may be developed through unbiased observation of the speech of cultured speakers speaking rapidly. An ability to discern the individual speech sounds that make up a continuous flow of rapid speech may be acquired gradually by careful observation, which may be greatly aided by a discriminating use of the phonetic alphabet.

Poor Enunciation

Types of poor enunciation may be classified under four headings—distortions, substitutions, omissions, and additions. Any particular tendency towards faulty enunciation may be distributed generally among speakers of the whole country, or it might be confined to one area of the country and therefore be called a localism.

Distortions may be in the nature of unpleasant vocal qualities or slurred and indistinct speech sounds. A harsh and tense nasality, being an unpleasant vocal quality, occurs most frequently on certain vowels and diphthongs—most commonly on the "æ" "ɛ," "eɪ," and "aʊ"—when they are preceded or followed by one of the nasal consonants—"m," "n," and "ŋ." A tendency towards a nasal twang is distributed fairly generally among all Americans. A harsh and tense "ɝ" sound, caused by holding the tongue too high and too tense, on the other hand, is limited only to a certain number of the users of the general American standard of speech (see the next chapter for identification of speech standards), and hence this fault may be called a localism. Other distortions might include thick or slurred consonant sounds such as might occur occasionally in the articulation of such sounds as "s," "z," "θ," "ð," and "ʃ."

Substitutions are quite common. A lisp, for example, is a substitution of one consonant sound for another. Many foreign dialectual influences and regional conventions result in sound substitutions both in consonant and in vowels—"v" for "w" and "ɪ" for "ɛ," for example. And some substitutions like in "gɪt" for "gɛt," "dʒɪst" for "dʒʌst," and "goʊɪn" for "goʊɪŋ" are common among all Americans.

Omissions of sounds or even syllables from certain words is a very common fault that is widely spread among all English-speaking peoples. Examples are such words as: gentlemen, modern, probably, regular, language, recognize, vegetable, and popular, which might be enunciated to sound like "dʒɛnəlmən," "mɑɚn," "prɑblɪ," "læŋwɪdʒ," "rɛkənaɪz," "vɛdʒtəbl," and "pɑpəlɚ."

Additions of single speech sounds or extra syllables are not very numerous. Most additions seem to be localisms especially of southern speech resulting from a relatively slow and drawling delivery. In an extremely broad Southern speech, for example, the word "man" might be enunciated as "mærɪjən." Other additions seem to be no more than conventional errors that have no apparent explanation in terms of origin. Some words to which extraneous sounds are often added include: film, elm, grievous, and idea, which may be enunciated "fɪləm," "ɛləm," "grivɪəs," and "aɪdɪr."

The Projection of Speech

There is a general tendency to confuse the projection of speech with the loudness of voice when speaking. If a listener says, "I can't hear you," a speaker usually responds by talking louder. However, when a person increases the loudness of his voice, although the sound of his voice will carry farther, it does not follow necessarily that his words can be understood at a greater distance.

A spoken word is usually a combination of vowel and consonant sounds. The projection of spoken words will depend upon the carrying power of a sufficient number of speech sounds to make the words recognizable at a distance in spite of any possible noise or interference present in the environment. A vowel sound is a clear vocal tone and its projection depends upon its loudness. But the projection of consonant sounds is quite another matter. Some consonant sounds are voiceless, and nearly all of them result from momentarily closing or nearly closing the mouth passage in some particular way, so that even the voiced sounds are too muffled to carry any distance as discernible vocal tones. Consequently, most consonant sounds must be projected by the precision and vigor of the articulatory movements and the degree of breath pressure behind any complete or partial closure of the mouth or throat passage. The loudness of the voice has virtually no effect upon the projection of most consonant sounds, since even in voiced consonant sounds, such as "b" and "v," the voice is too muffled to have carrying power.

The relative importance of vowel and consonant sounds in

making words understandable cannot be exactly determined, but there are nearly twice as many consonant sounds; and consonant sounds occur in the spoken language almost twice as frequently as do vowel sounds. There are also many more sound similarities among the consonants, and it is usually quite difficult to project similar-sounding consonants so as to make them distinguishable at a distance. For example, it is more difficult to make the words "pat," "bat," "pad," and "bad" sound distinctly different at a distance than it is to make the words "bit," "bet," "bat," and "bait" distinguishable across the same distance.

The importance of consonant sounds in projecting words is demonstrated rather unwittingly by singers who succeed in projecting a series of beautiful vowel tones but leave their audiences in complete ignorance as to the words of their songs. A singer is naturally more concerned with the strength and quality of his vowel tones than with the vigor of his unmusical consonant noises. A speaker, on the other hand, should be primarily concerned with the projection of his words, which means that he should be especially careful to strengthen those sounds that are normally the weakest and often the most distinctive. These are the consonant sounds.

Projection of speech across unusual distances is generally accomplished partly by increased volume of voice but principally by precise and vigorous articulation (including adequate breath pressures), especially of the consonant sounds. Occasionally projection may be needed, not because of distance but because of poor acoustics or the interference of noise or reverberation. In such cases, precise and vigorous articulation always helps, but sometimes a slower or more deliberate than normal rate of speaking is necessary. If, for example, the echo of one syllable coincides with and hence interferes with the perception of the next syllable, a change of timing will result in avoiding such interference. A speaker who faces an unusually difficult problem in projection usually needs to experiment by trying out various adjustments of speech in order to find the best one.

Improvement of Enunciation and Projection

Good enunciation must be based upon good, subconscious habits of precise, vigorous, and easy articulation, including good breath control. The difficulty to be encountered by any individual in attempting to establish such habits will depend upon the quality of the habits he has already established. In practicing for the improvement of enunciation, two steps are probably advisable. The objective of the first step is to increase the strength and precision of articulatory movements and breath control. This involves practice or drill in slow, careful, and vigorous articulation with a conscious exaggeration of individual speech sounds, particularly of consonant sounds. This should be accompanied, of course, by careful listening, which tends to develop a consciousness of the exact nature of individual speech sounds as they are carefully articulated. Such a consciousness serves to make a person aware of his slightest errors when speaking rapidly. The second step in improving enunciation consists of drills in fast articulation while attempting to avoid, as much as is consistent with smoothness of speech, the omitting, slurring, or weakening of individual speech sounds. The ultimate objective of both steps is to develop habits of smooth and relatively vigorous articulation in rapid speech which will require no conscious attention on the process of speaking, and which will give the impression of smooth and effortless but distinct speech across whatever distance may separate speaker from listener.

Skill in projection may require additional practice in projecting speech in a variety of situations representing different acoustical difficulties such as distance, noise, reverberation, and bad acoustics of undetermined causes.

Summary

Enunciation is the process of articulating a series of words in connected speech. If the words are uttered with ease and distinctness so that they are easily understood, the enunciation is good. But if the words are muddled or indistinct and hence unrecognizable, the enunciation is poor. Projection is the oral transmission of speech sounds so that words are recognizable in spite of distance or any kind of interference, such as noise or reverberation, that may intervene between the speaker and the listener.

The effectiveness of both enunciation and projection depends upon the audibility of distinctive vowel and consonant sounds that make words recognizable. Vowel sounds are vocal tones that are distinctive when properly formed by a precise mouth adjustment, and their power of projection is directly proportional to the loudness of the voice. By way of contrast, consonant sounds seldom consist of distinctive or projectable vocal tones. They are usually articulatory noises that can be projected only by precision and vigor of utterance that is supported by strong breath pressures.

The mode of enunciation varies with the degree of care used in articulation, depending upon the listeners and the occasion. For general use, a cultured conversational mode of enunciation seems desirable. Such a mode involves a three-way compromise between speed, exactness, and ease of utterance which can be guided only by good taste.

Projection of speech is commonly confused with the loudness of the voice when speaking; however, only vowel sounds may be projected by the loudness of the voice. The consonant sounds, which are often more effective than vowel sounds in making words recognizable, can be projected only by precise and vigorous articulation aided by sufficiently strong breath pressures.

Special problems in projection resulting from various kinds

of poor acoustics may require a change in timing of speech as well as precise and vigorous articulation, and occasionally projection may be improved by decreasing rather than increasing the loudness of vowel sounds.

Any drill program for the improvement of enunciation should usually involve two steps—one, to develop strength and precision in articulating speech sounds and an auditory consciousness of speech sounds that are properly articulated; and two, to develop muscular skill in fast and easy articulation. Good enunciation can be developed only by establishing it as a subconscious habit of speech.

Use of Enunciation Exercises

The many and varied exercises at the end of this and other chapters obviously need to be distributed over much more time than that needed for the study of any single chapter. Naturally some of these exercises will be of much greater value to some individuals than to others. In fact, many exercises aimed at eliminating specific faults are of no value to speakers whose speech is comparatively free of such faults.

Full benefit of the exercises can be obtained by any individual only through systematic repetition of those drills which are best adapted to his particular needs. And such repetitions should be distributed over many weeks, months, or as long as further improvement is still possible.

Questions

1. Name and explain the five elements of oral speech.
2. Define enunciation of speech.
3. How does enunciation differ from pronunciation?
4. Why does a conscious effort to articulate carefully and distinctly usually fail to produce good enunciation of speech?
5. Define projection of speech and differentiate it from intelligibility.
6. What kinds of speech sounds are usually most difficult to project?

7. What accounts for variations in mode of enunciation?
8. What mode of enunciation is usually most effective for general use?
9. Good enunciation results from what inevitable compromise?
10. How may an individual learn to make such a compromise intelligently?
11. Why does speaking louder sometimes fail to improve projection of speech?
12. How should a person go about improving his enunciation?
13. How do you think that you could best project your speech in an auditorium having excessive reverberation?

EXERCISES

I—*Purpose:* To improve habits of enunciation by gaining vigor, precision, and speed of articulation and breath control, and by developing an auditory consciousness of precisely articulated speech sounds.

Method: Practice reading the following selections for clarity and speed while listening carefully to resulting sounds. First, read very slowly while exaggerating as vigorously as possible every consonant sound. Next speed up your reading and repeat until you have developed your maximum speed without omitting or unduly weakening any of the consonant sounds.

1. My object all sublime
I shall achieve in time,
To let the punishment fit the crime
The punishment fit the crime;
And make each prisoner pent
Unwillingly represent
A source of innocent merriment!

W. S. Gilbert

2. I seized him by his little pig-tail,
And on his knees fell he,
As he squirmed and struggled,
And gurgled and guggled,
I drew my snickersnee
My snickersnee.
Oh, ne'er shall I forget the cry,
Or the shriek that shrieked he,

As I gnashed my teeth
When from its sheath I drew
My snickersnee!

W. S. Gilbert

3. In other professions in which men engage
(Said I to myself, said I),
The Army, the Navy, the Church and the Stage
(Said I to myself, said I),
Professional license, if carried too far,
Your chance of promotion will certainly mar,
And I fancy the rule might apply to the Bar
(Said I to myself, said I).

W. S. Gilbert

4. I am the very model of a modern Major-General;
I've information vegetable, animal, and mineral;
I know the Kings of England, and I quote the fights historical,
From Marathon to Waterloo, in order categorical,
I'm well acquainted too with matters mathematical,
I understand equations, both simple and quadratical;

W. S. Gilbert

5. Then a glance may be timid or free,
It will vary in mighty degree,
From an impudent stare
To a look of despair
That no maid without pity can see;
A glance of despair is no guide,
It may have its ridiculous side;
It may draw you a tear
Or a box on the ear;
You can never be sure till you've tried!

W. S. Gilbert

6. If any well-bred youth I knew
Polite and gentle, neat and trim,
Then I would hint as much to you,
And you could hint as much to him.
But here it says in plainest print,
It's most unlady-like to hint,
You may not hint, you must not hint,
It says you mustn't hint, in print!

W. S. Gilbert

7. As I go out the door
Of damozels a score
All sighing and burning,
And clinging and yearning
Will follow me as before.
A most intense young man,
A soulful eyed young man,
An ultra-poetical, super aesthetical,
Out-of-the-way young man.
Conceive me, if you can,
A matter-of-fact young man,
An alphabetical, arithmetical,
Everyday young man.

W. S. Gilbert

8. A magnet hung in a hard-ware shop,
All around was a loving crop
Of scissors and needles, nails and knives,
Offering love for all their lives;
But for iron the magnet felt no whim,
Though he charmed Iron, it charmed not him,
From needles and nails and knives he'd turn
For he'd set his love on a silver churn.

His most aesthetic very magnetic fancy took this turn
"If I can wheedle a knife or a needle, why not a silver churn?"

And iron and steel expressed surprise,
The needles opened their well drilled eyes,
The pen-knives felt "shut up" no doubt,
The scissors declared themselves "cut out";
The kettles they boiled with rage 'tis said,
While every nail went off its head,
And hither and thither began to roam
Till a hammer came up and drove them home.

While this magnetic, peripatetic lover he lived to learn,
By no endeavor can magnet ever attract a Silver Churn.

W. S. Gilbert

II—*Purpose:* To gain practice in clear articulation and projection. *Method:* Practice reading the following word groups, making them as clearly distinguishable from each other as possible. Then test your clarity of reading before groups of listeners across various distances and under various difficult acoustical conditions and check in some way the effectiveness of your articulation in terms of what your listeners hear

sense, thence, tense, fence
broth, brought, bossed, tossed
froth, frost, frought, broth
Weiss, wise, wives, wife's
beeves, bees, beets, beast
buffs, bus, busts, puffs
dose, doze, dotes, pose, post
thieves, these, thief's, tease
griefs, grease, greets, creased
lease, leaf, leaves, leased
life's, lies, lice, lithe
left, laughs, lass, lasts
lives, lists, Liz, lifts
muffed, must, muss, mutts
mouse, mouth, mouthes, mows
neath, niece, knees, neat
knife's, nice, knives, nights
paves, pays, pace, pates
roofs, ruse, roots, Ruth's
mit, knit, nib, nip, mid
knob, mob, mop, not, nod
main, maim, name
line, lime, lying
lane, lame, laying
have, half, aft, halved
made, neighed, mate, nape
meet, neat, need, mead
mine, mind, nine, mime
Nome, known, moan, home
mode, node, moat, note
mum, none, numb, 'mong
mad, Mack, nag, knack, mat
ooz, use, whose, hues
wish, which, witch, wished
wig, whig, wick, wit, with
wed, wet, whet, web, wept

weather, whether, wetter
wealth, welt, weld, well
ways, waves, waits, waif's
baths, bats, bass, pads, paths
Beth, Bess, best, bets
both, boast, boats, boasts
booth, boots, boost, boosts
breath, breast, breaths, breasts
burst, berth, berths, Burt's
fence, vents, fends, fens
sane, same, saying, shame
shams, jams, Jan's, chance
single, jingle, shingle
shoe, Jew, chew, sue
shows, chose, Joe's, sews
at, hat, add, had, apt
intends, intense, indents
hiss, is, his, hits, its
hand, and, ant, aunt
eyed, hide, height
eight, aid, hate, hayed
hedge, edge, etch, Ed's
other, utter, udder, hover
odd, hod, hot, awed, ought
riding, writing, writhing
rapid, rabid, rabbit, wrap it
dig, Dick, deck, tick, did
dame, Dane, tame, taint
dart, tart, tarred, tired
taunt, daunt, dawned
team, theme, dean, deem
drays, trays, trace, grace
twos, dues, deuce, tooth's
dams, dance, Dan's, tans
ties, dies, dice, guys
fat, vat, fad, fact, fagged

dust, does, doth, puffed, puffs
deaf, death, debts, deaths
faith, fates, face, faced, vase
fits, fists, fifths, fist
has, hath, hats, halves
hearts, harsh, hearths
lengths, lends, length
lass, laths, last, laugh
Luther, lose her, looser
miss, myths, mists, myth
path, pass, past, paths
sheath, she's, sheets, sheaths
mass, math, mast, mats
moss, moth, mossed
youth, used, youths, use
bathes, bays, base, baste
worth, worse, worst
heaves, he's, heaths, heats
loft, lost, laws, loss
race, Ray's, raves
own, ohm, known, home
taught, thought, thawed
drayed, trade, trait, great
drew, true, through, grew
tints, tins, dins, dims
dumps, dunce, duns
fame, vain, feign, pain
vigor, figure, vicar, bigger
sorts, source, swords, shorts
sheep, cheap, jeep
ship, jip, chip, jib
shops, jobs, chops, shots
sights, sides, size
sins, since, sense, sends
slice, slights, slides
call, called, galled, gall
case, Kay's, gaze, gaits
chap, Jap, jab, chad, chat
chin, shin, gin, Jim
cherry, Jerry, sherry, jury,
coat, goat, code, goad

gourd, cord, court
creed, greed, greet, Crete
came, gain, cane, game
gash, catch, cash, cashed
giddy, kiddie, kitty
gist, jest, guest, just
rife, rice, rights, rides,
roves, rose, roast, roasts
ruffs, rust, ruts, rusts
sieve, sis, sifts, sieves
surf, serves, sirs
solves, salts, saws, thaws
see, thee, sees, these
beg, back, peck, peg, bag, pig
blithe, blight, plied, plight
blotter, plodder, plotter
sings, singe, sins, since
cast, gassed, cashed, gashed
choice, Joyce, joys
chuck, chug, jug, shuck
chums, shuns, shunts, chunks
shoot, chewed, jute, juiced
gloats, clothes, glows, close
cod, cot, got, caught, cawed
gird, curt, curd, girth
glance, glands, clans, chance
chard, jarred, chart, sharp
chock, Jock, shock, Jacques
crate, great, grade, drayed, trait
breast, pressed, breaths, breadth
briefed, breed, breathe, breathed
boil, ball, pall, toil, tall
batch, patch, badge, bash
crone, chrome, grown, Joan
crows, grows, gross, Joe's
crumble, grumble, crumple
brute, brewed, prude, crude
board, port, poured, cord
bear, Bayer, pair, pay her
bans, pans, bands, pants
pleat, bleed, bleat, plead

hull, hole, haul, who'll
poor, pore, purr, peer
cheer, chair, chore, char
fear, fair, far, for
men, man, mean, main
Bret, bread, breadth, breath
bought, brought, broth, pawed
basis, bases, paces, pays us
bias, buys, by us, pious
bold, poled, bolt, bowl, pole
palm, bond, bomb, pond
peer, bear, beer, pair
peel, pill, pale, pal
pull, pool, Paul, pole
stair, star, store, stir
tired, tarred, toward, toured
dull, duel, doll, dole
beat, bet, bit, bat, bait
fate, fight, fat, foot
birch, perch, purge, dirge
boys, poise, Boyce, toys
bows, pose, boast, posed, post
boot, booed, booth, tooth
bending, penning, pending
bane, pain, paying, baying
panned, band, pant, tanned
neither, meter, neater, meet her
moos, muse, news, moose, noose
wonder, wander, under, want her
hurt, erred, heard, third, irk
art, heart, hearth, hard, yard
reference, reverence, reverend's
recent, resent, re-sent, re-send

chard, jarred, chart, sharp
chest, chess, jest, jess, just
chilled, jilt, gilt, guild, killed
base, baits, pace, pates, pays, beige
bumped, bunt, pumped, punt, punned
tide, tight, died, tithe, dived
dine, dime, time, tine, thine
dose, toes, doze, toast, those
debt, death, deaf, deft, dead
dense, tense, dens, tens, tends, tenths
seats, sheets, cheats, seeds, chief's
she's, cheese, sheaths, cease, seize
it's early, it's surely, it's Shirley
gem, Jim, jam, Jean, Jan
let, late, lit, light
leg, lag, log, league
neat, nick, knack, knock
Ben's, bends, pens, pence, dense
Pete's, peace, beats, peas, bees
Brice, price, prize, tries, dries
games, shames, James, chains, Jane's
bounds, bounce, pounds, pounce, bouts
brazen, praising, bracing, tracing
bits, bets, pits, pets, bids, beds
boor, purr, bore, poor, burr, pure
bland, planned, plant, band, panned
bright, bride, pride, tried, dries

III—*Purpose:* To improve the clarity of your articulation.

Explanatory Note: Many of the words we use daily are very similar in sound. However, most of the words having similar sounds have very different meanings. Therefore, even when we hear words articulated so that they sound like other words, we recognize the words that are intended merely because we understand the general context of what we hear. In fact, most of us are so proficient in our ability to fill in, from general contexts, the word-gaps in what we actually hear, that we are seldom conscious of the number of individual words that we fail to recognize from sound alone.

The fact that most of those to whom we usually speak have this ability to fill in word-gaps tends to make us careless in our habits of articulation. It seems reasonable to suppose that we can give greater pleasure to others by means of our speech if we articulate all our words clearly enough to save them the mental effort of having to fill in from context the gaps in what they actually hear.

Method: Read the following sentences or phrases to one or more listeners at some distance; then check upon what they heard. Practice and try again, but always read at a normal tempo of speaking and turn away from your listeners so that they do not read your lips.

1. *Gin* passed freely among his merry *jests*. (Jim, guests)
2. The *kiddie* played with the rubber ball. (kitty)
3. He painted his *vase* a bright yellow. (face)
4. A Hallowe'en *which* had passed (witch)
5. The horse was *shot*. (shod)
6. He fell on his *vase* and *mashed* his teeth. (face, gnashed)
7. A cow *crazed* in the sun (grazed)
8. He raced for the *ticket*. (thicket)
9. He won the *price*. (prize)
10. She *sewed* her skirt. (showed)
11. It was *backed* with cotton. (packed)
12. It fell in the *ditch* full of water. (dish)
13. He *wrote* away in a rubber raft slowly *singing*. (rowed, sinking)
14. She *mothered* strange things. (muttered)
15. He worked with a *cold mind*. (coal, gold, mine)
16. It was made of *vine* grapes. (fine)
17. She was *neater*. (neither)
18. The *vat* was in the fire. (fat)
19. The dog was stoutly *muscled*. (muzzled)
20. She was acting *catty* on the golf course. (caddy)
21. *tears* his shirt (there's)
22. *weather* or not (whether)
23. *watch games* (wash James, gains)
24. He took his Saturday night *path*. (bath)
25. He had no *share*. (chair)
26. Hitler hated the *juice*. (Jews)
27. It was a melancholy *tomb*. (tune)
28. The hunter was *cunning*. (coming, gunning)
29. He picked up his *goat*. (coat, code)

30. *Bonds* won the war. (bombs)
31. The *debt* of his father was quite a shock. (death)
32. *Tread* your way carefully. (thread)
33. The English *team* was very amusing. (theme, dean)
34. He did not *heed* it. (heat, eat)
35. sail *both* out in the bay (boat)
36. She wore a *white* hat. (wide)
37. The sheep were *bleeding* pitifully. (bleating)
38. The cloth was ready to be *tied.* (dyed)
39. It was *home aid.* (home made)
40. We need *more rice.* (more ice)

IV—*Purpose:* To improve one's taste for good enunciation.

Method: In the following sentences are many words that are commonly slurred in rapid utterance. Practice reading these sentences as rapid speech. Then transcribe them in phonetic symbols using what you believe is your exact utterance in rapid speech. Compare your transcriptions with those of others. Discuss differences in transcription, thus attempting to arrive at an ideal compromise between speed, exactness, and ease for rapid, cultured speech.

1. The police recovered practically all the jewels.
2. It was just a sentimental poem written by an amateur.
3. It was really wintry when the temperature dropped.
4. A popular theory held that the gentlemen were partners.
5. It was probably a one hundred and fifty piece orchestra.
6. The foreign representative of our government was a woman.
7. The children's theater director recognized her talent.
8. The second experiment yielded accurate statistical data.
9. Then why do you get such thoroughly aggravating films?
10. It was just a friendly argument about racial differences.
11. He suggested that electrical illumination was superfluous.
12. It was because the company didn't understand your unusual interests.
13. An athletic figure in overalls was popular with the children.
14. It was the usual and familiar family environment.
15. The new deputy inaugurated a progressive program.
16. Will you accept a sandwich and a few vegetables?
17. Why don't you just put on a new roof?
18. No singular adjective could describe her.
19. I just introduced your languishing librarian to a handsome bachelor.

20. His lectures are generally educational but usually of great length and of little breadth.

21. The modern cement chimney collapsed again against the roof.

22. The auxiliary association directed the old clothes drive with enthusiasm.

23. Hundreds of foreign families came across the ocean every month.

24. His employer emphasized a need for general education especially in foreign languages.

25. He was not actually a candidate but he probably wanted an invitation to accept the nomination.

26. They escaped during the attack, and with the cooperation of picturesque and friendly mountaineers, they found their way back to allied lines.

27. The cruelty of a barbarous amateur criminal is far worse than that of any professional.

28. They were beginning an argument about the hygienic effects of cold baths, having neither facts nor figures to support either the affirmative or the negative side.

29. It was a casual evening conference concerned with no particular issue.

30. Water consumption by the fountain constituted a genuine grievance.

31. The cavalry captain was a familiar military caricature recognized by everybody.

32. Gaining the friendship of his fraternity brothers was no problem so long as he retained his family's automobile, a Chevrolet convertible.

33. He had the dubious distinction of being unquestionably the most unsociable and unfriendly person in his dormitory.

34. The wistful youths wandered quietly around the reservoir wondering which would prove the most ineffectual.

35. It was a modern poem concerning the privileges and prohibitions of humanity.

36. To the child, adoption meant deliverance from a cruel giant.

37. He was a conscientious student of educational agriculture who was working as a gardener.

38. The gentlemen masked their faces with handkerchiefs to hide their identities.

39. His most conspicuous characteristic was his catholic discernment.

40. The governor's inaugural address was misrepresented journalistically.

41. Such an hypothesis is inevitably misinterpreted or is inexactly perceived.

42. The persistent introduction of such legislation proved impracticable.

43. It was identical to a rural medieval nuptial ceremony.

44. The bridegroom knew only a pictorial representation of his bride.

45. Such procedure is not really or necessarily impracticable.

46. His secretary recognized his literary hypocrisy.

47. The actual number of casualties will eventually be reported.

48. Sophomores make a specialty of manufacturing contradictory ideas.

49. The deputy suggested that the boundary line one mile in width should be satisfactory and effectual.

50. Gradually the theater temperature fell until the boisterous audience finally cooled into an uncomfortable silence.

V—*Purpose:* To improve taste, judgment, and accuracy in the matter of assimilation of speech sounds in adjoining words, determining to what extent a speaker might properly omit or modify sounds when difficult combinations occur.

Method: Transcribe phonetically what you consider to be an acceptable enunciation of the following word combinations in rapid speech. Compare with others and practice generally accepted enunciations.

How do you do?	drop below	horse show
ten nice sets	deep black	brush salt off
Does she?	always safe	fresh smear
She is here	about day break	wish some
Thank you, Sir.	abrupt decision	catch sight of
Don't permit it.	act disgusted	cause smoke
Transcribe them.	adjust data	ease suffering
It can't be done.	arrest decay	cloth tent
What do you want?	masked girl	descend now
find difficult	brisk game	desk stand
red door	break ground	dialect can't
saw all	big kiss	digest safely
be even	enough variety	chest size
some more	tough veneer	dishonest storekeeper

absorb paint	brief venture	district court
club personnel	dress shoe	drift far
earth thrift	shield discs	nymphs' friends
efficient new	succinct truths	clothes thefts
oldest son	asks hosts of	masks shifts
end now	suggests texts	arched chests
established shop	tests subjects	artists' tasks
second note	attempts projects	expects costs
select cast	attacks tastes	averts shifts
shift to	resists association	contradicts dramatists
neglect case	assists suspects	bewitched guests
suggests some	amidst pests	requests contracts
invest some	youth's thirsts	loathes egotists
best school	yields districts	crisped crusts

VI—*Purpose:* To improve flexibility and precision in making articulatory movements.

Method: Practice articulating with vigor, speed, and accuracy the speech sounds indicated and in the manners indicated below. Practice periods for this type of exercise should be short but frequent.

1. Repeat rapidly and according to an improvised telegraphic rhythm (like the rhythms of telegraphic code messages) syllables made up of one or more consonant sounds and one vowel or diphthong sound (for example, beep, beep, beep, etc.). Vary the syllable used until you have used every consonant sound with every vowel or diphthong. Note and repeat often any difficult combinations that you may find. Work for maximum speed of repetition, but be sure that all sounds are accurately articulated.

2. Repeat rapidly and often the paired syllables below that contain speech sounds that are similar and hence difficult to distinguish in rapid speech. In repeating alternately such sounds, work for maximum speed but stress the accuracy and hence the distinctive nature of the sounds. Examples are:

bi—bɪ	bʊ—bʌ	ðі—θi	tʃu—dʒu
bɪ—bɛ	bʌ—bɝ	ðoʊ—soʊ	reɪ—leɪ
bɛ—bæ	bʌ—bɜ	si—zi	hweɪ—weɪ
bæ—bɑ	bæ—ba	ʃi—ʒi	weɪ—jeɪ
bɛ—beɪ	bɒ—bɑ	tʃi—dʒi	ðoʊ—θoʊ
bɑ—bɔ	pi—bi	mi—ni	θi—si
bɔ—bʊ	ti—ði	ɪn—ɪŋ	θi—ti
bɔ—boʊ	ki—gi	ʃi—zi	ði—di
bʊ—bu	fi—vi	faɪ—daɪ	θu—fu

3. Repeat rapidly and many times alternate syllables made up of strongly contrasting sounds and exaggerate the differences, thus working the articulators for flexibility of movements. One might also repeat the movements many times silently just as movements. Examples of such syllables are:

bi—ju	ji—wu	θɔ—gi
pi—woʊ	mi—hu	ʃu—ji
tɛ—hwɔ	ðeɪ—ku	ʒaɪ—toʊ

4. Whisper, repeating many times very rapidly with exaggerated articulatory movements for the sake of muscular flexibility such syllables as the following:

pɑ	wi	θi	faʊ
doʊ	jæ	ðɔ	veɪ
ku	lɪ	ʒæ	ʒɔɪ
lɑ	ʃɛ	tʃu	maʊ
reɪ	hwaɪ	dʒɪ	mɔɪ

VII—*Purpose:* To gain practice in difficult enunciation of many polysyllabic words that might commonly cause one to stumble.

Method: Practice reading the following sentences until you can read them rapidly and smoothly while enunciating clearly.

1. The Athletic Department's argument collapsed for want of accurate statistical data, but he persisted in the theory that baths in wintry temperatures are practically suicidal.
2. His partner coaxed friends of the family not to recognize the association just yet because from four-fifths to seven-eighths of its membership didn't understand the principles of representative government.
3. Did you know that I can go just as soon as she asks me?
4. Miss Shaw insists that she didn't have a good time at the Saturday night horse show.
5. They pretty nearly escaped in a Massachusetts Chevrolet.
6. He boasts that he had more than a hundred screen tests for the pictures.
7. I missed you. Sit down, just so. I must show you something.
8. Don't you think she used to last year? She must have known that perspiration ruins clothes.
9. Grandma makes the best pumpkin pie crusts in the state of Mississippi.

10. An unprecedented constitutional consolidation was negotiated illegitimately by unimaginative administrative representatives.

11. His lackadaisical procrastination and systematic impracticability exasperated the meticulously indefatigable gubernatorial staff.

12. The conscientious statistician underestimated the effects of homogeneity and departmentalization upon the association.

13. The uninhibitable communicativeness of such a sentimental conversationalist exasperated the jurors so that they unanimously repudiated their previous magnanimity.

14. Such ignominious animosity unexpectedly accentuated the incompatibility of the omnipotent bureaucratic instrumentalities.

15. The amicable advocacy of the revolutionary party for all contemporaneous dissemination of subversive literature humiliated the superannuated conservative citizenry.

16. Such a negligible protuberance is almost indistinguishable and indisputably insignificant but, nevertheless, it is particularly characteristic of the chrysanthemum.

17. Such creditable benevolence is attributable to the aggrandizement of incomprehensible transcendentalism.

18. The astonishing eccentricities of the inexhaustible prestidigitator fascinated an effervescent metropolitan audience.

19. The whole conglomeration of extraneous supplementary paraphernalia was distributed philanthropically.

20. The applicability and intelligibility of the classification were substantiated by uncontrovertible experiences.

21. The unfathomable specifications seemed self-contradictory and epigrammatical but indubitably authoritative.

22. He was an incorrigible hypochondriac characterized by avaricious covetousness, malevolent meddlesomeness, and intellectual impermeability.

23. The Aluminum Corporation negotiated an unprecedented and seemingly unconstitutional consolidation of several undistinguished metallurgical manufacturing concerns.

24. A statistician must handle all sorts of experimental statistics and attempt to understand the incomprehensible and explain the inexplicable.

25. It was an anonymous autobiography of a boisterous but bewildered blusterer who was accomplished in self-aggrandizement and chivalrous circumlocution.

26. Their dissimilarities—his idiosyncracies and her frivolity—led

to disorganization, desertion, reconciliation, and finally a schizophrenic pacification that became habitual.

27. He was a loquacious and opinionated mathematician who spouted calculations, computations, enumerations, and commensurate statistical apportionments at every opportunity.

28. Motivated by popular acclamation, his benevolence, philanthropy, and promiscuous prodigality brought on bankruptcy, loneliness, and humiliation.

29. His perspicacious pertinacity brought about legislative reverberations, the recapitulation of contradictory ramifications in reactionary argumentation, and finally the ratification of the conciliatory legislation.

30. The veterinarian accomplished resuscitation by means of refrigeration, then slow recuperation and rejuvenation—but all without remuneration.

31. It is difficult to particularize a description with any degree of specificity when such multifarious and heterogeneous inconsistencies of phenomena make accurate perception impossible.

32. In spite of his asceticism and fastidiousness, he had an adolescent personaltiy characterized by talkativeness, credulousness, and susceptibility to every subversive influence.

33. He had the unmitigated officiousness to submit simultaneously both his resignation and a request for a spontaneous recommendation for authorization to retain a company automobile.

34. It was a case of unpremeditated misrepresentation of Mohammedanism caused by an insignificant misinterpretation rather than by disapprobation or malevolent condemnation.

35. The melancholy librarian sent out announcements of her sister's anniversary celebration that would be particularly loathsome to her because of the consequent flood of congratulatory effervescence that would reopen old wounds.

36. The absurdity and even ridiculousness of some polysyllabic terminology and lengthy nomenclature may be counteracted by the value received in articulatory exercise.

37. American colonial aeronautical development suggests either an anachronism or an unintelligible ambiguity.

38. He had a persistent hallucination, making him belief that he was a hereditary executioner of insects and mosquitoes and that assassination to the point of annihilation or extermination of all pests was his primary function.

39. Being a legitimate instrumentality is sufficient justification for individual provocation by indiscrimination.

40. His asymmetrical lineaments were manifestations of alcoholic deterioration or corporeal retrogradation.

41. As a candidate for the legislature, he abandoned a competitive brokerage business and started an agricultural apprenticeship, hoping that the farmers' vote might compensate for his political colorlessness.

42. The musical accompaniment, although creditable, was a blasphemous violation of ecclesiastical conventionality.

43. The impracticability of any attempt to rehabilitate such temperamental and obstreperous barbarians seems unmistakably apparent but some discriminating plan for their liberation and enfranchisement seems necessary.

44. Guilessness, gullibility, frivolousness, loquaciousness, effervescence, and changeableness are alleged to be fundamentally feminine characteristics, but the allegation is questionable.

45. Their paraphernalia was particularly impracticable, which virtually eliminated them from competitive participation.

46. It was a preposterous and enigmatical fabrication, an inappropriate improbability, an incomprehensible and manufactured prevarication—in short, it wasn't true.

47. The impossibility of disentangling subjectivity from externalization resulted in the semantic confusions of such perfunctory parallelisms and diversified but authenticated synonyms.

48. He achieved a satisfactory recuperation in the punctilious tranquility of the environment in his impenetrable habitation—the state penitentiary.

49. A particularly objectionable brand of nonconformity contaminated the confederacy, tending to neutralize bureaucratic actions, thus promoting procrastination and rendering all purposive progress problematical.

Elimination of Common Faults in Enunciation

It is obviously impossible to consider here all the errors that might have become fairly common in all the varoius areas of America. The following list seems to include those faults that are common in fairly wide-spread areas. The general purpose of the following exercises is to improve the vocalization or articulation of certain sounds that may be recognized as either unpleasant or inaccurate. The general method of eliminating such faults has three steps:

1. To develop an auditory consciousness of the fault,
2. To discover a means of avoiding or correcting the fault,
3. To practice such avoidance or correction until a new habit is formed that may be substituted for the old faulty habit.

Distortions

Nasality: Although nasality (as a vocal fault) may show up on any vowel or diphthong sound, there is a distinct tendency for nasality to occur most frequently and most noticeably in the utterance of front vowels, especially when those vowel sounds precede or follow one of the three nasal consonants, "m," "n," or "ŋ." In the following word-pairs, for example, there is a much stronger tendency to nasalize the vowel or diphthong sound in the first word than in the second.

Method 1: Compare carefully your normal vocalization of the following paired words. With the help of others (and perhaps a tape recorder) try to determine if you have any tendency to nasalize the vowel or diphthong sounds in the first word of each pair. If so, practice vocalizing the first word as nearly like the second word as possible, using as nearly the same "placement" or basic quality as possible and the same degree of ease or relaxation.

man—Munn	ran—Ron	hanger—hunger	bean—bone
mound—moaned	fame—foam	main—moan	jangle—jungle
mine—moon	fanned—fund	nine—noon	Jane—Joan
mam—mom	found—fawned	noun—numb	Jean—June
Nan—none	game—gum	bang—bong	ram—roam
lamp—lump	gown—gone	bank—bunk	clang—clung
lane—loan	lean—lawn	found—fund	tame—Tom
can—cone	mine—moan	gang—gong	sign—sum
cain—coon	pan—pun	gown—gaunt	wine—one
Dan—Don	ping—pong	hang—hung	ban—bun
down—dawn	pink—punk	land—loaned	ham—home
fan—fun	pounce—punts	sank—sunk	Anne—on
sang—sung	pound—punned	tan—tone	angry—hunger
name—Nome	fame—foam	town—tune	clam—calm

Method 2: Practice reading the following sentences, being especially careful to eliminate nasality.

1. The anvils rang, and the hammers beat.

2. A jungle of bamboo and tangled vines hampered the team's flight down the mountainside.

3. Nancy's Aunt Janet finally danced with the famous Count.

4. The Master's name is James, his man's name is Dan.

5. A lantern hanging on the main mast was their answer.

6. The angry wrangling gangsters are now hanging around town.

7. Down South, out West, or back East, anyone may have a nasal twang.

8. The clanging links of the dangling chain aroused Ann from a sound nap.

9. With bell jangling, the train ground to a stop and a lanky masked bandit leaped down from the baggage car.

10. The command to hang the whole gang rang out like the bang of a cannon.

11. They found the hound out in the rain playing games with a great Dane.

12. The singer sang with the same quaint anguish that made her famous.

13. Bank rhymes with thank, hand with grand, candle with handle, and anguish with languish.

14. No doubt the Count will sanction a fancy and roudy banquet of some kind.

15. He was a dandy in fancy dress, a ranting ham bowing elaborately for scant applause—in short, a rank amateur.

Harsh "ɝ" Sound: A general American localism.

Method 1: Read the following word-pairs and compare the "ɝ" sound in the first word of each pair with the vowel sound in the second. If the "ɝ" sound is any more tense and harsh than the other vowel sound, repeat until you are able to vocalize the "ɝ" sound in a manner that is just as relaxed and pleasing to a listener as the other vowel sounds. Expert judgment of a specialist and a tape recorder will help this process.

bird—bud
berg—bug
burn—bone
curt—cut
curb—cub
curl—coal
curve—cove
dirt—dove
dirge—dodge
first—fast
furl—full
firm—foam
fern—phone
girl—gull
gird—good
hurt—hoot
heard—hood
hurl—who'll
jerk—joke
learn—loan
nurse—noose
pert—put
pearl—pool
turn—ton
Turk—took
turf—tough
term—tomb
terse—toss
word—wood
shirt—shoot
skirt—scoot
work—walk

Method 2: Practice reading the following sentences, being careful to avoid any tenseness or harshness in vocalizing the "ɝ" sounds. Practice such reading often until you can avoid such harshness very easily.

1. The earth along the curb was covered with burning turf.
2. She urged her horse into a surge of speed around the curve of the first turn.
3. While in church, Burt heard the bird chirp as it hunted worms in the newly turned dirt.
4. Sir Herbert served his term with the Turkish firm.
5. Shirley's nurse, looking absurd in fur turban, turtle-necked jersey, and purple skirt, took her place as a juror.
6. The versatile German surgeon and his nervous nurse were certain that it was a case of murder.
7. He was irked to learn of the permanent merger of their firm with a rural concern.
8. It takes courage or nerve to wear such an absurd bird on one's hat.
9. He imagined that something worse was lurking around every murky curve.
10. Herman turned the firm turf in regular vertical furrows.

Faulty Fricative Consonant Sounds: Because of slightly misshapen jaw or tooth formations or slight misplacement of the tongue, many speakers tend to thicken or slurr the "s," "z," "θ," "ð," and "ʃ" sounds. Some speakers tend to lisp by substituting one fricative for another. Some speakers tend to wheeze or whistle some of their fricative sounds, while others can make such sounds barely audible even at close range.

Faulty "s" *Sounds:* The "s" sound is subject to several faults—a lisp (usually resulting in the substitution of a "θ" sound), a distinct whistling effect, or a weak and barely audible sound thickened by an inept tongue adjustment.

Method 1: Practice hissing until you can make a clear and strong "s" sound that is distinctly different from a "θ" sound and has no tendency towards a whistle.

Method 2: Practice reading the following paired words while working for a proper contrast in sounds:

sense—thence	knife—nice	math—mass	sin—thin
these—seize	bath—bass	youth—use	lice—lithe

griefs—grease	burst—berth	worth—worse	race—wraith
moth—moss	face—faith	writhe—rice	ruse—Ruth's
mouth—mouse	myth—miss	that—sat	sigh—thigh
neath—niece	pass—path	thumb—some	thick—sick
thaw—saw	seem—theme	Norse—north	song—thong
they—say	loft—lost	goofs—goose	lath—lass
sheets—sheaths	ruse—roofs	dust—doth	think—sink
sank—thank	thought—sought	Bess—Beth	fates—face

Method 3: Practice reading the following sentences while being especially careful in uttering the "s" sounds. Try projecting these same sentences across some distance to one or more listeners and ask for criticisms.

1. The theme on sin seems so thin and frothy that, if it were in water, I don't think it would sink.
2. They say that debts caused his death, but his wife's wise, youthful, and useful niece helped her face the future fates with face-saving faith.
3. Both Bess and Beth know best that these thieves left less, although they did leave at least two nice knives.
4. A thick and sick-looking growth of gross weeds overran the paths that ran past Ruth's bird roosts.
5. Not being a lisper, I can make "thank" and "sank," "saw" and "thaw," "Norse" and "north," as well as "sigh" and "thigh" sound distinctly different from each other.
6. Six, silly susceptible spinster sisters secretly solicited the sympathy of a single defenseless swain.
7. She successfully substituted a standardized system supposed to force subservient submission.
8. A special species of slick, self-assertive salesmen sought by successive sensations to sustain suspense.
9. The supposedly sophisticated society assembled secretly for senseless sessions of superficial, sophomoric sophistry supervised by a sinister sorcerer.
10. Susan scraped up sufficient funds by composing silly sketches of surprising sweetness and a series of slick, short stores of suspense and suicide.

Faulty "ʃ" *Sounds:* Often thick or whistled.

Method 1: Practice reading the following paired words, while uttering the sounds that make them different as distinctly as possible.

Record if possible, and notice whether or not the "ʃ" sounds seem clear.

she—see	shake—sake	suit—shoot	shows—those
shell—sell	shine—sign	sun—shun	shear—sear
seek—shiek	sin—shin	sour—shower	sheet—seat
seen—sheen	sad—shad	thank—shank	she's—cheese
sip—ship	sod—shod	thigh—shy	thin—shin
said—shed	show—so	third—shirred	shorn—thorn
sale—shale	sore—shore	shore—Thor	through—shrew
same—shame	soul—shoal	they—chaise	though—show
shack—sack	sue—shoe	chop—shop	shread—thread
sag—shag	thee—she	chip—ship	thrill—shrill
shied—side	shaw—thaw	cheap—sheep	thrive—shrive
sock—shock	their—share	chic—cheek	thus—shush

Method 2: Practice reading the following sentences aloud while being especially careful to articulate the "ʃ" and "s" sounds precisely and distinctly. Record your reading if possible and study the results.

1. A shot from the sharpshooter's shell shattered the shaft and ricocheted with a short, shrill shriek.
2. After shearing, the shortsighted sheep shunned the sunshine for the shade of the shack, only to shiver and shake from chill.
3. It's a shame that such a shy child should be shining shoes in a shabby shoe shop a short step from the station.
4. A shrill, childish screech shattered the Bishop's last chance of finishing the chapter in peace at this session of the association.
5. With a splashing, swishing swirl, a small swordfish flashed past the shoal chased by a ferocious shark.
6. The shabby chef made hash of a dish of fresh shellfish, then he dashed out and fell over the little shaver's shoeshine stand.
7. A conscientious shepherd should shield his sheep from gushing or splashing water and falling shale.
8. She "swished on" a slick sheet of shellac over the sash, giving it a "lush," shimmering sheen.
9. The sheriff bashed in the shop shutter to flush out the brash thieves into the open.
10. A single shingle is sure to shield the fresh gash from splashing rain.

Faulty "θ" and "ð" Sounds: Often thick, slurred, or weak.

Method 1: Practice reading the following sentences aloud while being particularly careful to articulate the so-called "th" sounds clearly and easily. Record if possible and study the results.

1. They thought that either ether or some other anesthetic running through the feathery froth would further smother the mother moth.
2. Whither goeth thou, Father, in this withering weather? To soothe thy fifth brother in the depths of despair.
3. The three thieves thrashed hither and thither through the thick, thorny thicket threatening to throttle each other.
4. The athletes' bathhouse had three pathetically thin, tin tubs and very little warmth.
5. The fourth booth of lath, covered with a thin cloth, was further north than they had thought.
6. I thought they taught them how to tie a throbbing thigh with a leather thong.
7. Through thick and thin they continued to follow that uncouth good-for-nothing thief.
8. Then and there three thousand youthful throats let forth a mammoth shout of enthusiasm.
9. They thought that a thick growth of hawthorn would screen their stealthy approach along the path.
10. A kind of loathing seethed within him so that his teeth seemed to be projected in a threatening manner by every breath he breathed.

Faulty "z" *Sounds:* Often thick, slurred, or weak.

Method 1: Practice reading aloud the following sentences, being especially careful to articulate the "z" sounds precisely. Record if possible and study the results.

1. The zig-zagged zipper does buzz as the breezes blow.
2. Joe's quiz-kids, wearing fuzzy, azure fezes, dazzled the audience with sizzling zither music.
3. The blazing Zeppelin zoomed through fleecy and fuzzy clouds over the zoo.
4. To advertise his zinc business, he offered a Zulu zebra as a zany prize.
5. Can you hear the difference between "sue" and "zoo," "price" and "prize," "advise" and "advice," "sink" and "zinc," "bus" and "buzz," "fussy" and "fuzzy," and between "zoot" and "suit?"
6. The final "s" in words like "plays," "bees," "beads," "dogs," "fans," and "bows" is uttered as a "z" sound because of the preceding voiced consonant.

7. The boys played jazz and blues numbers to please the zestful zanies.

8. In spite of their zeal, their zither act fell from the zenith to zero.

9. Elizabeth and Ezekiel zealously studied the signs of the zodiac.

10. It was not a lazy or dizzy limousine, but a busy "lizzie" named Zephyr after the west breeze.

Substitutions

Substitutions of one speech sound for another (usually resulting from some foreign or domestic dialect influence) are quite numerous. Only those that seem most common are included here.

The Substitution of "ɪ" for "ɛ" (and sometimes vice versa): a localism principally of the South and the Southwest.

Method 1: Practice reading the following paired words while working for a distinctive contrast between the "ɪ" and "ɛ" sounds.

neck—Nick	ten—tin	six—sex
dipped—depth	rents—rinse	letter—litter
Ben—been	whither—whether	medal—middle
left—lift	pit—pet	peer—pair
leer—lair	bed—bid	trick—trek
him—hem	bit—bet	beer—bear
tents—tints	many—Minnie	killer—Keller
hints—hence	sense—since	hymns—hems
dead—did	evince—events	led—lid
pin—pen	dent—dint	let—lit

Method 2: Practice reading the following sentences rapidly, being especially careful to utter every "ɪ" and "ɛ" sound clearly.

1. Since I can't make sense of the story of how he sinned, I'll send it to you.

2. Being pretty, it's a pity that she's petty, but that's better than being bitter.

3. Ten tin soldiers were placed in tents that were colored with a rinse; ten real soldiers paid high rents because they had no tents.

4. Feminine representatives at the Democratic convention felt the temptation to rebel against the inexcusably bitter reflection upon their sex uttered by six of the television network commentators.

5. The Denver delegation presented a letter from a local dentist energetically pressing charges against the secretary of the ex-president.

6. An unfriendly senator testified against them whenever they attempted to gain a separate settlement; so they went to the editor of the friendly press and asked him to present the entire episode objectively to the public.

7. Even intellectual men may remember when some sensational event had temporarily paralyzed their sense of right and wrong.

8. Six of the ten members of the reception committee surrendered themselves to the steady task of penning names of delegates upon slips of paper and pinning them to their respective owners.

9. He didn't get the gist of the jest. Did he just miss the gist or did the jester just mess the jest.

10. His desk was a litter of letters, class pins, fountain pens, pencils, and textbooks, with a messy metal ash tray in the middle.

Substitution of the "ɔɪ" *for the* "ɝ" or "ɜ" *Sounds:* a localism that is usually associated with Brooklyn, New York.

Method 1: Practice reading the following word pairs aloud, being careful to make a very clear distinction in sound between the words of each pair:

voice—verse	Hoyle—hurl	boys—burrs
learn—loin	rural—royal	curl—coil
Earl—oil	purrs—poise	avoid—averred
foil—furl	bird—Boyd	first—foist
Hoyt—hurt	quirt—quoit	dirt—doit

Method 2: Practice reading aloud the following sentences, while being especially careful to distinguish clearly between the "ɔɪ" and the "ɝ" or "ɜ" sounds. Other appropriate sentences for practice are on page 201.

1. Colonel Boyd in boiled shirt and derby hat attended the thirty-first anniversary of his lawyer's birth.

2. When the dirt abounds with earth worms and is covered with tall ferns or a firm turf, the soil is good and seldom thirsty.

3. Lloyd first tried to foist the worthless coin upon Joyce and she in turn had the nerve to turn it over to her nurse.

4. Loyal and worthy members of the firm learn to serve their terms without shirking.

5. Joyce joined her girl friend in a "joint" on Thirty-third street.

6. Amid the noise and turmoil some annoying person hoisted a moist and soiled flag.

7. Mr. Doyle was an oily "bird" who wanted to adjourn early.

8. Looking pert in her new skirt, she enjoyed being coy and flirting a little with another boy.

9. They tried to avoid the curved oyster-shell drive and struck soft dirt.

10. They adjourned the first meeting in an adjoining room.

Substitution of "ɛu" *or* "æu" *for the* "aʊ" *Diphthong:* a common Southern localism, but not entirely uncommon in other areas.

Method 1: Practice the individual sounds that make up the preferred diphthong—"a" and "ʊ"—alternately, gradually speeding up the sequence until you glide smoothly from one to the other. Then carefully practice such phrases as "down town," "brown cow," and "clown around" until you can utter them easily without prolonging or broadening out the diphthong sounds.

Method 2: Read aloud the following sentences while being especially careful to utter the "aʊ" diphthongs in an approved manner:

1. The scout opened his mouth to shout but no sound came out.

2. When the clown bowed down to the ground he found a pretty round crown.

3. How about going down town to the county court house?

4. The cowardly hound bounded into the fountain and was drowned.

5. They ran around the brown tower of the power house.

6. A lazy lout lounged about the town tower until his cow was found.

7. The rowdy crowd shouted and howled down some clown from the Town House.

8. Now there is little doubt about the power of the vowel sounds.

9. A cloud to the south shaded the mouth of the little canyon gouged out of the mountain side.

10. With dour frown on brow and pouting mouth, the hound growled at the chow.

Confusion of Words like "Hot" and "Heart": This may be thought of as a kind of substitution since it results in different words sounding alike. It is an Eastern and Southern localism which never occurs among general American speakers.

Method 1: Practice reading aloud the following paired words while being especially careful to make them distinctly different in sound. Test yourself by asking one or more listeners to differentiate the paired words at some distance.

stock—stark	shopper—sharper	dot—dart
hock—hark	toddy—tardy	shop—sharp
lock—lark	top—tarp	totter—tarter
shock—shark	cot—cart	gobble—garble
dock—dark	yon—yearn	gods—guards
cotton—carton	cod—card	hod—hard
pot—part	hot—heart	gob—garb
Don—darn	bock—bark	bobber—barber
Lodge—large	Bonnie—barny	watt—wart
mock—mark	cop—carp	shock—shark
pod—pard	clock—clark	cot—cart

Method 2: Practice reading the following sentences aloud while being especially careful to make the similar-sounding words distinctive and recognizable.

1. In the barny shop, Bonnie was trying to be a sharper shopper.
2. She carried a large cotton bag and a paper carton into the lodge.
3. They put a "tarp" on top of the dock in the dark.
4. Part of our stock is in the pot and part is out in the park.
5. Bob removed the barb from the cod and stuck it in a card.
6. They had the cot on the cart.
7. He hit the dot with the dart.
8. Doc made a mark in the dark.
9. The "cop" caught a carp in the park.
10. It was a "potty" party—very hot but no heart.

Omissions

Omissions of sounds and syllables are rather common, and the problem has already been treated in a general way in previous drills aimed at the development of careful enunciation. However, a few specific types of omission need further emphasis here, because some omissions have become such firmly established habits that drills in careful and vigorous enunciation may not result in the avoidance of such omissions.

Omitting or weakening Medial Consonants: For example, the letters in parentheses indicate consonant sounds that are frequently omitted in the following words: gen(t)lemen, pi(c)ture, in(t)ellectual, reco(g)nize, su(g)gest, frien(d)ly, mo(d)ern, and insi(st)s. Review the exercises starting on page 191 to check this tendency.

Omitting Medial Syllabic Vowels: For example, the letters in parentheses indicate syllabic vowel sounds that are frequently omitted in the following words: (fam(i)ly, veg(e)table, temper(a)ture, fin(al)ly, re(al)ly, exper(i)ment, and parli(a)ment. Again review the exercises starting on page 191.

Omission of the "h" from the "hw" Combination: This fault may be thought of as either an omission or a substitution, depending upon whether one regards "hw" as a single sound or a combination of two sounds. It is a fairly widely distributed fault although there are several regional concentrations of this fault.

Method 1: Practice reading the following paired words, while working for the proper contrast in sound:

way—whey	wide—why'd	wise—why's
watt—what	wig—whig	woe—whoa
WAC—whack	wither—whither	world—whirled
wail—whale	weather—whether	wish—whish
wear—where	wite—white	wile—while
wax—whacks	wine—whine	word—whirred
weal—wheel	wire—why're	we eat—wheat
wen—when	were—whir	woo—whew
wet—whet	witch—which	wee—whee
wit—whit	wive—why've	why—"Y"

Method 2: Practice reading the following sentences, being especially careful not to omit the "h" sounds of the "hw" combinations:

1. We wonder whether the wheat, which the witch would eat, would wither without wet weather.
2. With a whistle, a whish, a whang, and a whack of the whip, they whizzed and whirled around the world.
3. Where whigs wear wigs, they care not a whit for whimsical wit.

4. Why should we wimper or whine for whiskey or wine?

5. This is the way to separate curds from whey.

6. When ready to remove the wen, he sharpened his knife on the wet whetstone.

7. When one uses the word "whirred" where "wear" should be used, he is talking nonsense.

8. Whistle while you work, whittle when you're irked, and whisper when you shirk.

9. The white whale whizzed past the wide wharf.

10. Why a mere whiff of smoke would make him wheeze and whistle like a sickly whelp.

Omitting the "ɪ" *of the* "aɪ" *Diphthong:* A Southern localism.

Method 1: Practice uttering the "a" and "ɪ" sounds separately; then quicken the sequence of uttering them alternately until you succeed in making a smooth glide from "a" to "ɪ." Repeat many times until you can enunciate a clear "aɪ" diphthong.

Method 2: Practice reading aloud the following word pairs, being very careful to make the sounds distinctly different by enunciating the full "aɪ" diphthong in one word of each pair:

my—ma	guide—god	side—sod
I—ah	height—hot	sight—sot
buy—bah	hide—hod	type—top
bind—bond	like—lock	tired—tarred
kite—cot	mile—moll	tire—tar
dine—Don	night—not	tight—tot
dike—Doc	pike—park	wide—wad
fire—far	ride—rod	buyer—bar
gibe—job	right—rot	pie—pa
dial—doll	mire—mar	blight—blot

Method 3: Practice reading aloud the following sentences, being especially careful to articulate the complete "aɪ" diphthong:

1. I'm too tired to dine with Don; so he'll probably have me tarred and feathered.

2. I got tar on my tire when driving far from the fire.

3. Never bar a buyer who rides the rods.

4. It's never hot at this height on the pike to the park.

5. A wise wife of the quiet type might buy white pine.

6. I must hide my eyes from the white light.

7. Such a live wire and likeable liar is likely to shine every night.

8. She had a fine time with a nice "guy" with kind eyes who smoked a vile pipe.
9. Don't let the mire mar such a wide wad of tar.
10. My ma did not serve pie to pa at night.

Confusion in the Use of the "u" *and* "ju" *Sounds:* Confusion is caused by the fact that speakers using the Eastern standard of American speech commonly use the "ju" sound in words for which general American and Southern speakers use only the "u" sound. Some dictionaries add to this confusion by showing a preference for the "ju" sounds, thus disregarding differences in standards.

Method 1: Contrast the vowel sounds used in the following word pairs:

booty—beauty	fool—fuel	moot—mute
boot—butte	who—hue	moor—Muir
cootie—cutie	Lou—lieu	pooh—pew
coo—cue	moo—mew	ooz—use
food—feud	mood—mewed	oo—you

Method 2: Determine carefully whether, according to the preferred standard of American speech used in your region, you should use "u" or "ju" in each of the following words. If necessary, practice the use of these words until you can use the preferred sounds easily and without any hesitation.

absolute	dew	fluke	flute	news
allude	dubious	illuminate	jewel	Nubian
allusive	dude	gubernatorial	hue	nude
annuity	due	institution	July	sewer
assume	duel	institute	June	student
astute	Duke	lubricate	Knute	stupid
attitude	dune	lugubrious	lewd	suit
attune	dupe	numerous	Lucy	toupee
blue	duty	numeral	Luke	tube
chew	enthusiasm	platitude	lute	tulip
choose	fluent	luminous	neural	tumult
deuce	fluid	neutral	neuter	tune

Additions

Additions of extraneous sounds are relatively rare. Some errors—such as those indicated by the sound symbols enclosed in parentheses in the words ath(ə)letic, griev(ɪ)ous, and fil(ə)m—have become conventionalized to some extent and are hence more a matter of pronunciation than enunciation. Most additions of extraneous sounds, however, seem to result from foreign-language influence or from a lack of precision in articulation.

Adding Extraneous "g" *or* "k" *Sounds after* "ŋ": Some speakers (usually because of a foreign-language influence) tend to add a "g" or a "k" sound after every "ŋ" sound. For example, such words as "singing" and "going" might be pronounced "sɪŋgɪŋg" and "goʊɪŋk."

Method 1: Practice enunciating the "ŋ" sound and each of the vowel sounds, alternating in repeated-and-rapid sequence and without uttering a "g" or "k" sound between. For example, when alternating "ŋ" and "i" be very careful that it does not become "ŋ-gi, ŋ-gi," etc.

Method 2: Practice reading the following word pairs. In one of each pair the "g" sound or the "k" sound is properly enunciated while in the other it is not. Be sure to make this distinction in your practice.

longing—longer	flinging—single	hanged—bungle
hanger—hunger	belonging—spangle	hanging—sprinkle
springer—linger	tongue—jangle	seemingly—gangle
singer—finger	singing—jingle	singsong—strangle
stringer—sinker	thronging—anger	songster—angular
kingly—English	longing—language	ringlet—fungus
banging—jungle	clinging—tingle	stringy—anchor
wringer—wrinkle	ringing—rankle	youngster—banker
bringing—congress	flinging—tangle	unwittingly—mangle
stringer—anguish	hang on—dangle	sing up—struggle

Method 3: Practice reading aloud the following sentences, being particularly careful to add no extraneous "g" or "k" sounds improperly.

1. After singing a single song, the English singer did not linger longer.

2. The king of the tangled jungle—singed and strangled with lungs full of smoke—lunged into a dangling vine and hanged himself.

3. Cringeing behind a door that was hanging on one hinge, the angry stranger suffered pangs of hunger.

4. When the angular bungler caught her finger in the wringer,

she used stronger language than did the gangling shingler who was stung by a bee when clinging to the top rung of his ladder.

5. The "g" sound is uttered properly in only four of the following words: ping, pong, bingo, winging, wrangling, stronger, tingling, bringing, banging, ringing, and stringing.

6. In such phrases as "strung up," "wrong about," "hang on," "sing out," "hung over," and "among us," the tendency to insert extraneous "g" sounds is strong.

7. The word groups "sin—sing—sink," "ban—bang—bank," "sinner—singer—sinker," "tan—tang—tank," and "kin—king—kink" should be easy to distinguish in terms of sound.

8. After a long harangue by the singular young gangster, the angry throng was ready to string up their own ring leader.

9. Bring along a long, strong string or thong in order to hang up the gong.

10. A struck gong will ring, a plucked string will twang or sing, and a tight valve will ping.

A Strong Glottal Click: On initial vowels of emphatic words a strong glottal attack (a kind of coughing sound) is sometimes very noticeable and unpleasant, especially when the voice is amplified electronically.

Method 1: Practice reading aloud and emphatically the following sentences while attempting to soften the initial attack upon the beginning vowel sounds. If possible, record and study the results.

1. You ask me to acknowledge that arrogant ape? Why, that's absolutely assinine!

2. All right! I'll alter my attitude! But it is an apathetic and ignorant audience nevertheless!

3. An author, did you say? He's nothing but a back-alley agitator and an insolent anarchist.

4. Oh, oh, oh, ouch! Get out, you ignorant oaf!

5. The empty-headed imbecile ate up all the evidence.

6. An arrogant amateur actor is always apt to alter it.

7. With an angry oath the other officer ousted the obstinant agent.

8. You can't learn to operate any other instrument in eight easy lessons.

9. The infamous idiot often offered his evil influence but obviously envied even his enemies.

10. There was an odd odious oil oozing out over the ice.

Eliminating other Faults in Enunciation

There are many other errors in enunciation that may be classified as dialectal difficulties, localisms, or problems of individual speakers. Any attempt to mention them all, and to devise drills aimed at the elimination of each, would be both tedious and unnecessary.

A pattern of effective drill material is set by the exercises included herewith, and each student should be able to devise further drills (perhaps with the aid of his instructor) for his own use whenever he becomes conscious of any particular fault of enunciation that he needs to eliminate.

8.

American Standards of Pronunciation

As indicated previously, pronunciation is the auditory form of a single word; and a good or acceptable pronunciation of a word is established as a conventional pattern by usage among cultured speakers. Any conventional or familiar combination of speech sounds making up a recognizable word pattern involves the following elements:

1. The use of exact phonetic units or accurate speech sounds.
2. A customary sequence of speech sounds within each syllable.
3. The conventional division of the word into syllables, if it has more than one syllable.
4. The conventional degrees of accent and subordination of the various syllables, involving both the relative loudness and durations of the syllables.
5. A conventional melody or inflectional pattern.

Each of these elements suggests a way in which a word may be varied or mispronounced.

Standards of Pronunciation

A speech standard, like any other standard, may be defined as that which has been established as a model or pattern to be followed or imitated. Any standard may be established either by the direction of a recognized authority or by the gradual development of convention resulting in general consent or acceptance. In the case of English speech, there seems to be a wide-spread assumption that a single standard exists so that there can be only one correct way of uttering each spoken word in the language, just as there is only one way of spelling each written word. Such an assumption may be either the cause or the effect of the common use of such terms as the "King's English" and "correct English pronunciation." Because of this assumption, there is a general tendency for each English-speaking individual to accept unquestioningly as correct the pronunciations of all common words to which he has become accustomed. In the case of new or uncommon words, he is likely to imitate with confidence the first speakers who pronounce these words in his presence with an air of self-assurance. In rare or exceptional cases, the average individual —being motivated by curiosity or doubt as to the "correct pronunciation" of a word—may resort to a dictionary which he considers the ultimate authority in the matter of pronunciation. Once a person has created a personal standard of all his pronunciations in the manner just described, he tends to be smug about it, to the extent that he regards all obvious deviations from it by other speakers to be a result of ignorance, affectation, or crudity.

Several centuries ago the English-speaking world was small enough so that the English King and his court society might have comprised the center and source of all English culture. The King might then have been an authority capable of establishing cultural standards for the entire English-speaking world by his own manner of behavior; and the "King's English" might have meant a specific standard of correct pronunciation used by the King. But times have changed. The English-speaking world now surrounds the earth, and English culture is so widely distributed that it cannot possibly have any generally recognized center and source of all that is correct and proper. There are today many recognized centers of English culture; and in different parts of the English-speaking world the spoken language has developed into divergent dialects that differ one from another not only in the pronunciation of individual words but also in the rhythmic and inflectional patterns of rapidly flowing speech.

Throughout the past years there have always been champions of the "King's English" or some ideal single standard of correct English pronunciation; but the combined efforts of these champions failed to arrest the growth of diversification in the pronunciation of the spoken language. There are still champions of a single standard of correct English speech, but they cannot all agree upon what standard should be established universally nor can they devise an effective means of establishing any single standard that might be agreed upon.

Nearly all authorities who specialize in the field of the spoken language now agree that the one criterion of good pronunciation is cultured usage. Any standard of English pronunciation is said to be correct if it is used by a sufficiently large number of cultured or well-educated people. Standards may vary in different regions; and the best pronunciation in any region is the pronunciation used by the majority of cultured people living within that region. A different pronunciation used by a minority of cultured people in a region (although not preferred) may be quite acceptable and should never be considered as incorrect.

The exact characteristics of a standard of good speech that has been established by cultured usage within any region may be rather elusive because it is impossible for every individual to confer with all the cultured people within his region and to observe how the majority of them pronounce all the words that he might wish to use. Moreover, the cultural standing of those observed must be a matter of personal judgment.

Fortunately, the pronunciations of the great majority of

English words are consistent enough in common usage at all cultural levels within any region to permit a person to determine, without difficulty or confusion, the pronunciations that are established and acceptable in this region. It is only the relatively few words that are commonly pronounced differently by different speakers in the same regions that cause difficulty. Sometimes such differences in pronunciation seem to result from differences in cultural backgrounds; as, for example, when the word "deaf" is pronounced "dif," it suggests a low-level or antiquated cultural background. Such a "mispronunciation" causes little confusion because it is usually rare and an obvious deviation from modern usage even among the majority of speakers of less than average education. When, on the other hand, the word "bade" is pronounced "beɪd,' its deviation from cultured usage is not so obvious. Many well-educated speakers adopt this pronunciation suggested by the spelling and never seem to notice how it differs from that used by the majority of cultured speakers. But a good dictionary can help to clear up any confusion in such cases.

It should be understood, however, that a dictionary is not an authority that establishes the correct way of pronouncing words. An American dictionary, for example, is a compilation of words with pronunciations indicated. These pronunciations seem to the editors of the dictionary to be used by the majority of cultured people throughout the country. The editors, of course, are expert observers in the matter of pronunciation; consequently, when a clear-cut decision can be made as to which of two or more possible pronunciations of the same word is used by the majority of cultured people throughout the country, the editors of a dictionary can be trusted to indicate that decision accurately.

Unfortunately, there are some really troublesome English words for which different pronunciations are used with about the same frequency by speakers who seem equally well educated or highly cultured. Even the editors of our best dictionaries seem to add to, rather than to clear up, the confusion in many of such cases. One dictionary lists two or more alternative pronunciations of a troublesome word that are in common use by cultured speakers. These alternatives are listed in the order of preference, this order being based upon the editors' estimate of the comparative frequency with which the different pronunciations of the word are used by cultured speakers throughout the country. Another dictionary might list the same or even a slightly different group of alternative pronunciations for the same word and have them listed in a different order of preference. In such cases, an individual can only choose the pronunciations that seem to be used most frequently by careful speakers in his own community.

Pronunciation Standards in the United States

Although there are a great many slight variations of speech in common use in different areas of the United States, there are only three distinct types of speech that are used by sufficiently large numbers of cultured people over areas of sufficient size to be recognized as standards of American speech. These three standards are known as (1) the Eastern standard, used in the New England states; (2) the Southern standard, used in the Southeastern states; and (3) the general American standard, used in the rest of the country. There are, of course, no sharply defined boundaries separating the areas in which these standards are most commonly used, and there are many local and cultural differences from the prevailing standard in each region. But, in terms of popular usage, about two-thirds of the population of the United States use the general American standard of speech, about two-ninths use the Southern standard of the old and deep South, and only about one-ninth use the Eastern standard. It is, therefore, obvious that, on the basis of usage by the majority of cultured Americans in the country as a whole, the general American standard has a great preferential advantage; but, on the basis of tradition, the Eastern standard has what might be called a classical advantage.

The Eastern standard of American speech is more similar to the cultivated South-British speech of Oxford and cultured London (which still possesses a high degree of traditional prestige) than is any other American standard. Also, American stage diction, that has been taught for over a hundred years by schools of oratory and elocution as well as by many modern dramatic schools and teachers of interpretation, is substantially the same as the Eastern standard of speech, with varying degrees of South-British influence. It is not surprising, therefore, that the users of the Eastern standard or of a carefully cultivated stage diction should assume a superiority for their pronunciation of the English language.

The desirability of a cultivated stage diction is still assumed widely by professional interpreters—both actors and platform readers—although it has been abandoned generally by public speakers. Also the traditional belief in the aesthetic value of a stage or platform diction seems to be steadily losing ground.

A hundred years ago, when professional actors were hired to play a series of different roles in a permanent stock company, the possession of a highly cultivated stage diction was an essential qualification for employment in the best companies and for public approval. But today, an actor is hired to play only one role in a single play on a run-of-the-show basis, and his need for a cultivated diction of any kind will usually depend upon the cultural level of the role that he plays. Some actors might actually find a cultivated diction used subconsciously to be a handicap when applying for uncultured types of roles. At any rate, an uncultured Eastern standard of speech is of no more value professionally than is an uncultured general American standard.

In the motion-picture industry, the demand for the traditional stage diction is even less frequent than it is in the legitimate theater. Motion-picture actors, like their colleagues of the theater, are usually hired to play only roles of particular types which may or may not need cultivated diction. When a cultivated diction is required for a motion picture, either a South-British or a good general American diction might satisfy the demand as well as a cultivated stage diction. Hollywood usually demands good or highly cultivated speech, but it does not consistently demand speech of only one particular standard. Except that the Southern standard is usually reserved for Southern characters, motion-picture speech has a fairly wide representation of standards—both British and American.

In its early days the radio industry was extremely speech conscious because the radio executives were evidently convinced that, through radio, America could be taught to prefer a single standard of good speech. People having cultivated stage diction or an Eastern standard of speech were preferred for broadcasting positions; and once a year, for several years, an award was made to the radio announcer of America judged to have the best voice and diction. The judges obviously preferred the best examples of the Eastern standard, or a British diction. In other ways, also, a strong influence was exerted upon broadcasters to develop a single standard of radio speech similar to Eastern or stage diction. However, such efforts failed to eliminate Southern and general American standards from the airways, and gradually radio executives gave up the attempt to establish a single standard of good speech in America. Good radio speech today is the best speech of the region from which any particular program is initiated. *The NBC Handbook of Pronunciation,* compiled by James F. Bender under the supervision of the National Broadcasting Company and published in 1944, follows the general American standard of pronunciation. In a preliminary statement, Mr. Bender explains this adherence in the following words:

> From a realistic point of view, that pronunciation is best that is most readily understood, and that pronunciation is most readily understood that is used by most people. Thus a standard of pronunciation for the American broadcaster is reasonably based upon the speech heard and used by the radio audience that the broadcaster reaches. This means that the broadcaster should use the pronunciation that is spoken by the educated people of the area served by the station. . . . When a broadcaster speaks over a powerful station or a nation-wide hook-up, he desires to use a pronunciation that is readily understood by the majority of his listeners. In such an event, the broadcaster would be well advised to use a pronunciation widely known among phoneticians as "General American," the standard presented in this book.

So far the television industry has taken no consistent stand upon the matter of speech standards; but since television is drawing its talent from radio and motion pictures as well as from the legitimate theater, it seems probable that no definite nation-wide preference for a particular standard of speech will ever be adopted.

Although today many platform readers and actors may prefer and find definite advantage in a cultivated stage diction that is similar to the Eastern standard of American speech, the demand for such a diction in all professional fields in which speech plays an important part is no longer unanimous. Good speech, however, that is both distinct and cultured (whatever its standard may be) is still very valuable to anyone, especially to any trained speaker or interpreter who wishes to speak effectively from stage, screen, studio, platform, or pulpit to cultured audiences.

Speech Standards and Their Relative Beauty

Early in the twentieth century an important objective in speech training was the development of beauty in the spoken language; and at that time a cultivated stage and platform diction was taught to students of oratory and elocution for the sake of enhancing the beauty of their speech. In later years, teachers of speech abandoned or at least de-emphasized this objective because it tended to encourage affectation and artificiality in speaking. Today the functional qualities of speech are much more highly esteemed than are any aesthetic qualities. Unobtrusive clarity of speech and the effectiveness of communication are considered to be much more desirable than any beauty of speech, especially if that beauty would in any degree distract the attention of a listener from the message communicated.

It must be admitted that unobtrusive or natural beauty in the sounds of one's speech is highly desirable. And, if it could be proved that one standard of English pronunciation is basically more beautiful than any other, then the development of that standard should be worthwhile, especially for an actor or reader who may need to communicate forms of highly polished literature in which the aesthetic qualities conveyed by the sounds of the spoken language are particularly important.

The relative beauty of different standards of English speech is often argued; and so long as it is possible to compare a highly cultivated speech of one standard with average or uncultured speech of another, some people will undoubtedly be convinced that some one standard is more beautiful than any other. However, the beauty of the spoken language depends primarily upon the vocal tones of the speaker and precision and smoothness of his enunciation, rather than upon his standard of pronunciation. It is possible, of course, that users of one standard might acquire, through imitation, a greater tendency towards harsh or unpleasant vocal tones than users of another standard. It is often alleged, for example, that the vowel tone in the word "bird" is more harsh and unpleasant as the word is pronounced by the average native of Chicago than the vowel tone used for the same word by the average native of Boston. There may be a tendency for many users of the general American standard to vocalize relatively tense and harsh tones when uttering the "ɝ" sound, but it would be impossible to prove that a cultivated speaker using the general American standard could not utter an "ɝ" sound that is just as relaxed and beautiful (at least to the ears of general American speakers) as the "ɜ" sound substituted for it by a cultured speaker who uses the Eastern or Southern standard of American speech. It is pointed out also that general American speakers use the "æ" sound in a number of words (about a hundred words perhaps) for which the Eastern American speaker uses either "a" or "ɑ" sounds. It happens that there is a much greater tendency to nasalize an "æ" sound than an "a" or "ɑ" sound, especially when it is preceded or followed by one of the nasal consonants—"m," "n," "ŋ." It is inferred, therefore, that general American speakers have a greater tendency towards nasality than do Eastern speakers. Any possible effect of the slightly greater frequency of the "æ" in the general American standard could be only negligible; and, furthermore, if the first vowel sound in the word "mammy" is less pleasant than the first vowel sound in the word "mamma," then the fault is one of vocalization and not one of pronunciation. One vowel can be vocalized just as pleasantly as the other; so there should be no reason for a trained speaker to substitute one sound for the other in an effort to improve the beauty of his speech.

Beauty of speech, depending upon pleasant vocal tones and clear, easy, flowing enunciation of well-chosen words, may be developed while using any standard of English speech. If a particular standard such as a stage diction is to be preferred over any other, the preference should be based upon traditional or professional associations or prestige rather than upon an assumption of superiority in terms of beauty.

Improvement of Pronunciation

The first step towards improving pronunciation is the development of an open mind and unbiased attitude towards such improvement. As previously indicated, everyone tends to be smug about the pronunciations to which he is accustomed; and nearly everyone is afraid that any changes in his speech will make him a laughingstock among his acquaintances because he believes that such changes will make him seem different or brazenly affected. Such resistance to change is an old problem, for it has impeded many kinds of improvement and progress. No one can improve his speech unless he really wants to badly enough to run the risk of being laughed at, and unless he is willing to fight against the kind of social inertia that resists all changes of old and familiar habits.

Once a person really wants to improve his pronunciation, he needs to find out what changes should be made, and he must decide whether he wants merely to improve his pronunciation according to the local standard or if he wants to develop a new and different standard for professional expediency.

If a person wishes to change his standard of pronunciation —as by the development of a highly polished stage diction, for example—he should realize that such a change involves long and careful training and practice for the sake of forming both auditory memory images and muscular memory images of new pronunciations to be used easily and subconsciously. He should realize also that such training and practice should be undertaken only on an all-or-none basis. In other words, only a little training and practice would be worse than none at all because only a partial change of standard would result in a ludicrous mixture of old and new standards and a self-conscious manner of speaking that would make a speaker sound ridiculous and seemingly affected. An actor or reader might learn to change his standard of pronunciation for a single role or program just as he might learn any kind of dialect. But to change effectively one's standard of pronunciation for unrehearsed speaking would necessitate intensive ear training and long practice periods equivalent to at least a two-semester college course or a long series of private lessons. The direction of such a process is beyond the scope of this book.

If a person wishes to improve his pronunciation according to his own standard, he must develop a word consciousness so that he notices slight variations in pronunciation which he normally has ignored. And he must develop a curiosity as to which of various pronunciations of the same words are used most frequently by cultured speakers who use the same standard of speech. A good dictionary will provide the easiest means of satisfying this curiosity; so any person interested in improving his speech should develop a habit of using a dictionary frequently. A person should not only learn the preferred pronunciations of words that are pronounced in various ways, but he should also practice both speaking and hearing them until he can use the preferred pronunciations spontaneously, without stumbling, and without hesitation, and also without giving the newly learned sounds any undue emphasis.

Short of changing one's speech standard, the most difficult adjustments that a person might need to make are those necessary for the elimination of localisms or foreign dialects. Localisms, which are commonly (although not very accurately) called accents, are speech sound variations from the prevailing standard that are common in relatively small areas. In the Southwest, for example, the general American standard is generally used, but a few Southern characteristics of speech are quite common as localisms. These variations from the conventional and cultured standard may take the form of adding, changing, or omitting conventional phonetic units; they may be in the nature of unusual syllable divisions or accents; or they may merely be a matter of slightly abnormal inflectional patterns. The first step in the process of eliminating a deviation is that of developing a vivid awareness of it. This may be very difficult not only because the deviation may be very slight or subtle but also because after hearing a deviation for many years, the person who uses it would consider it entirely normal and exactly like the conventional standard. The exercises at the end of Chapter 7 include drills to aid those needing help in the elimination of a number of common localisms.

Summary

The most understandable speech is the most familiar speech. Good or preferred pronunciations of words are established as a result of consistent use by a majority of cultured speakers. The pronunciation of any word having more than one syllable may involve: (1) the use of specific phonetic units, or the accuracy of speech sounds, (2) uttering phonetic units in the proper order, (3) making conventional divisions of words into syllables, (4) using the customary degree of accent or subordination of each syllable, and (5) using a normal inflectional pattern.

Divergent standards of English pronunciation, established by usage, have been developed throughout the English-speaking world. Three recognized standards of pronunciation—each having many minor variations—are used in the United States. About two-thirds of our population use the general American standard, about two-ninths use the Southern standard, and about one-ninth use the Eastern standard. The Eastern standard, used by cultured New Englanders, is the most similar to cultured South-British speech and to American stage diction. For this reason it is favored by many professionals employed in motion pictures, radio, and television, although it is seldom favored at all by public speakers living outside of the New England area.

Improvement in pronunciation requires the development of an unbiased attitude towards pronunciation changes. Then any person attempting to improve his pronunciation must practice listening to, and articulating, the changes until he has formed both new auditory images and new muscular images for the new pronunciations so that he may use them spontaneously and smoothly without self-consciousness or undue emphasis.

Any attempt to change one's standard of speech—as for the development of a cultured stage diction—should not be entered into lightly or for too short a time, because a partial change of one's standard is worse than none at all since it would result in a ridiculous mixture or inconsistency of speech standards.

Questions

1. What is meant by a phonetic unit?
2. Have you ever been taught to sound out words according to spelling? Do you believe such teaching to be of value?
3. Differentiate pronunciation from enunciation.
4. In what five ways may pronunciations vary? Give examples.
5. When may poor enunciation become a matter of pronunciation?
6. Upon what kind of memory image does one's pronunciation depend?
7. What do one's muscular memory images determine?
8. Is a pronunciation ever literally correct or incorrect? Explain.
9. What is the one criterion of good pronunciation?
10. Is a dictionary an authority in the matter of pronunciation?
11. What three pronunciation standards are used in the United States?
12. What standard do you use?
13. Are you aware of any localisms in your speech?
14. What standards are commonly preferred in various professional fields?
15. What are the chief obstacles to be met when attempting to improve one's pronunciation?

16. Why should one attempt to change one's standard of speech only on an all-or-none basis?

EXERCISES

Purpose: To gain practice in using preferred pronunciations in rapid reading.

Method 1: Look up the pronunciations of the italicized words in the following paragraphs in a good American dictionary and memorize both the preferred pronunciations (listed first by the dictionary) and the meanings. Practice reading the paragraphs until you can read them rapidly and smoothly without hesitation or stumbling over the preferred pronunciations.

1. Some French words like *bouillon, foyer, guillotine,* and *denouement* may either retain their French pronunciations or be almost completely Anglicized, but other French words such as *façade, fatigue, faux pas, hors d'oeuvre,* and *rendezvous* would sound ridiculous if Anglicized.
2. The *autumnal* design painted by a skillful *artisan* with *aniline* dyes upon the window *valance* gave no suggestions of the *valence* of chemical elements nor of a *process* associated with the *quarantine* or the new *vaccine.*
3. In the cavity of a small *niche gouged* out of the *conduit* leading from the *slough* into the *reservoir* was an *irate Gila* monster that dared anyone to *trespass.*
4. In attempting to understand the *diverse* but *equable program* of the *executor,* you should take *cognizance* of his *Aryan egotism* and his experience with *demagogy, bureaucracy, et cetera.*
5. Because of his *garrulousness,* his *bovine* mentality, and his *Buddhist ideology,* they issued an *indictment* against him which was without *precedent.*
6. Like a *regatta,* the *armada* moved out past the *buoy.* The last *fortnight* had proven their position *untenable.* The *premier's egotism* and *braggadocio* were no longer *discernible* when the *allied pro rata* cost of the campaign was revealed.
7. The *irascible* captain, an *absolute misanthrope,* held a huge *conch* in one hand and *maritime almanac* in the other as he stared through the *interstice* at the broken *hawser* over the *bowsprit.* He knew that it would be impossible to *placate* his captors.

8. Miss Laurette Burton, daughter of a well-known *chiropodist,* entertained last evening in honor of her *fiancé,* who recently returned from *Copenhagen.* The *hospitable library* of the Burton *domicile* was *exquisitely decorated* with *bouquets* of *gladiolas.* The wedding is *scheduled* for July after Miss Burton completes her studies at *Bryn Mawr.*

9. The university *comptroller* has just announced that the Department of *Economics,* during the summer *recess,* published *data* resulting from extensive *research* in post-war *finance* and the *hostile* influence of inflation. *Inquiries* concerning this research may be mailed to the Department of Economics. No other *address* is needed.

10. She was a *naïve* but *vivacious ingénue* in *mauve* skirt and yellow *blouse.* He was an *athletic* young man in *khaki* uniform. They were sitting in the *Bijou* Theatre watching Dr. *Jekyll* and the *bestial* Mr. Hyde.

11. With *admirable* speed two *juveniles* were apprehended and arrested by the local *constable.* They were then *indicted* for the *despicable* trick of launching a fake relief drive for their own benefit. The boys admitted their guilt but made *futile* efforts to pass off their *pretense* as *infantile mischievousness.* Local authorities *guarantee* immediate *chastisement.*

12. The *harassed* judge, after reading the *illustrated advertisement,* removed his *pince-nez* and glared at the *disputants.* A *pianist* of considerable *prestige* and *temperament* was suing the owner of the local *aviation* school because the planes disturbed him *during* his hours of practice. Should music take *precedence* over pilot training?

13. It was an *isolated* spot in the *Italian* mountains. The private surveyed the wrecked jeep with a *dolorous* expression. The damage was *irreparable.* Even the *chassis* had been twisted and broken. A hasty inventory revealed that he had one can of *K-ration,* a *chocolate* bar, and few *caramels,* while his canteen contained only a little *cognac* instead of water. His little accident gradually assumed *catastrophic* proportions.

14. It was *table d'hote* dinner—and what *victuals!* The *hors d'oeuvres* consisted of *anchovies, canapés* with *Roquefort* cheese, salmon *sauté,* and sliced *pomegranate* covered with syrup.

15. Then we had *consommé* and tomato *purée.* The main course consisted of *fricassee* of chicken and steak with *Worcestershire* sauce. There were hot rolls with *gooseberry* jam and finally *almonds* and *pecans.* Being so overloaded with *proteins,* it's a wonder we lived to remember the *menu.*

16. From *Buenos Aires* came a *rotund* little man who was *agile* in spite of his *obesity*. His *gallant* speech, *chivalric* manners, and *poignant repartee* seemed quite *incongruous* with his physical *grossness* and *Herculean* strength.

17. He was a *senile academician* with eye-shade on *forehead, disheveled* hair, stained *waistcoat,* and baggy *breeches* of some *worsted* material. He looked like a *burlesque caricature* of a *doughty* old *pedagogue.*

18. However, he was an *astute* professor of *zoology* with a *facile* mind. His *acumen* and *assiduity* in his own field were *indisputable.* He was greatly respected by all his *confreres.* He was slightly *deaf* and afflicted with *diabetes,* which accounted for his *cadaverous* appearance and his way of *ogling* everyone who spoke to him.

19. It was *positively* and *indisputably* a case of *plagiarism.* But she faced the charges with *calm docility* and *subtle* display of *naïveté.* The *consummate* skill of her acting was so *poignant* that it completely *deluded* the jurors.

20. The *experimental process* was interrupted by a tremendous explosion. The *apparatus* was wrecked and the *statistical data* of the research were *lamentably* jumbled. The chemist uttered some *puerile cliché* about *condolences* being *superfluous* and immediately started the *menial* task of clearing away the *debris.*

21. To *promulgate* such a *panegyric* at this time would hardly be *decorous. Alumni* disapproval of the *Chancellor*'s *patronizing* manner has often been expressed. No *alumnus* or *alumna* would accept gracefully any attempt at *aggrandizement* through such a *brochure.*

22. Leaving the *Manor,* the Duke strolled down the *boulevard towards* the *promenade.* He looked *neither* to the right nor to the left or *vice versa.* He had committed a *faux pas* but with an *equanimity* that *forebade censure.*

23. A stage *aspirant,* who dreams only of fancy *costumes* and *amour,* is *comparable* to any *ebullient dilettant* who flits about the art *museums. Either* might better spend her *leisure* time dreaming up a *trousseau.*

24. An *affluent* young *architect* of *Los Angeles* wanted to build an *amphitheater* for his *Alma Mater.* After carefully considering every *detail,* he drew up plans, submitted them to a *contractor* and *bade* him estimate the *cost.* This contractor being an alumnus of the same school, made the grand *gesture* of giving his services *gratis.*

25. From the *Appalachian* Mountains and the *bayous* near *New Orleans* to the *mesa* country of the Northwest, political *contumely*

and *chicanery* are *prevalent*. Political *combatants* indulge in *derisive* and *devastating* oratory.

26. The *Elizabethan dramatists* were more interested in the sounds and *connotative* values of words than in dictionary definitions. To Shakespeare, a star or a *column* might be "*chaste*." In writing, he had in mind a *boisterous clientele* rather than an *esoteric critique* by some critic. The *divers* elements of Shakespeare's audiences never suffered *ennui*.

27. The *envelope* must be either in the *garage* or the *granary*. The *inanity* and *impious obscenity* of that letter must never be discovered. The *fragile Jacques* threw off his *lethargic* pose and began a feverish search.

28. The *maestro* was writing his *memoirs*. He pictured himself as a combination of *Epicurean, cosmopolite,* and *impresario*. But his *genealogy* bothered him. It was *indisputably incongruent* with his *indecorous behavior*.

29. The *homogeneity* and *esprit de corps* of this *juvenile* gang in its own *habitat* made it a *formidable* and *inhospitable* group. With a ferocious *grimace* the leader hammered on the box with his *gavel*. He knew that *obeisance* was *obligatory* and that the law of the gang was *implacable*.

30. The *mercantile* establishment next to the *Lyceum Theatre* and fronting the *Esplanade* near the *quay* was a *potpouri* of *architectural* types. The building had a *decorative façade* of *ceramic* tile from the local *kiln*. It was topped with a *globular* construction on the *roof* that looked like *papier mâché*.

31. It was an *interminable soporific* lecture on the *hygienic* effects of a *saline* solution sprayed into the *pharyngeal* cavity and other *respiratory* passages. He presented one *irrefutable* argument after another with a *suavity* and an air of *omniscience* that was *positively nauseating*.

32. The *saturnine Junker* general of the *Nazi* party used his personal *stationery* decorated with a *vignette* of *sword* and *swastika* in issuing his *succinct ultimatum*. The prisoners must be released or the *Viscount* would be shot.

33. The manager's *protegé*, in a *beige ensemble*, stood like a *prima donna* next to the *proscenium* arch gazing through her *lorgnette* with *feline hauteur* at the *entrepreneur* as she informed him that she was to play the *titular* role.

34. He was a *wizened* little man who, up to the time that his wife gave birth to *quintuplets*, had spent a *tedious* existence in the *squalor*

of a *Chicago* tenement. Now as he gazed at the *stupendous scenic panorama* of *Yosemite* Park, his face *softened.* He could only utter *sacrilegious blasphemy* intended to express admiration.

35. The *vivacity* and *spontaneity* of her response, when she saw the *tiara,* were very unlike the *sanguine urbanity* that he had expected. It gave him a *piquant soupçon* of what he could expect after the *nuptial* ceremony. He no longer regarded their coming marriage as merely an open *sesame* to the upper *stratum* of society.

36. He was a *tenacious* young man, and he knew that he would be *penalized* if he failed to finish the job. Like a *pugnacious reptile* he crawled under the *tarpaulin* with a blow-torch in his hand and *soot* on his nose. He had to apply the blow-torch to the *apparatus* in order to raise the *temperature* enough to *soften* the *solder,* then *simultaneously* bend the wires and hold them in place.

37. She was *debonair* and *chic*—having been schooled in the American brand of *coquetry*—but English society gave her a feeling of *impotence.* The *blatant cacophony* of London and the talk of *halfpenny, twopenny,* and *twopence* confused her. So she continued her trip through *Gloucester* and *Edinburgh.*

38. The *demesne* of a Duke was a center of culture. The *patronage* of the nobles during this *regime* resulted in both moral *decadence* and the *maintenance* of a high cultural level. The *details* of *progress* were not apparent until the last *decade* of this *era.*

39. The *exigency* of the moment demanded action. The *vagrant, Danish equilibrist*—sick of his *banal* existence—handed back the *coupon,* unbuttoned his coat, removed his *jabot,* and walked down the street. He knew a man who owned a *mobile calliope,* that worked like a player-piano—one only had to pull a *lever* and it operated automatically. He wanted to *inveigle* that man into selling it.

40. *Abdominal* pain, *nausea,* and a *febrile* condition *suggested* acute *appendicitis* or *ptomaine* poisoning but the doctor diagnosed the trouble as *diphtheria* and gave him a mixture of *herbs*—principally *digitalis.*

41. A courteous but *peremptory gendarme* confiscated the *automobile* of an *attaché* from *Marseilles* and accused him and the *garrulous aviatrix* of *espionage.*

42. The *milieu* of the *drama* was a *patio* surrounded by *adobe* walls of the principal building of a huge *hacienda.* The *dramatis personae* consisted of a *dour Don Juan,* an *irascible Goucho,* and an *anemic señorita.*

43. The *blackguard* confided *sotto voce* that any *secretive* or *cir-*

cuitous attempt to *impugn* the *veracity* of the *humble liaison* officer would be *preferable* to any *inflammatory protestation.*

44. It was a *restaurant* with unusual *cuisine.* The *chef* was evidently an eccentric *culinary* genius. We had *lyonnaised scallops* with *mayonnaise* loaded with *endives* and *truffles.* The desert consisted of a *pistachio* sundae with sliced *apricot.*

45. He had been known as an *abstemious diabetic.* His *ambrosia* had consisted of one cup *per diem* of *pekoe* tea with a dash of *saccharine.* But now he had obviously been *drowning,* or at least *diluting,* his sorrows with *wassail.*

46. The *aurora borealis* appeared to *hover* close over the *forecastle* as a *nascent seismic tremor* shook the deck of the whaleboat as a barely *discernible* sound of a *glacial avalanche* reached their ears.

47. Before becoming *acclimated,* they all suffered from *respiratory* and *pulmonary* disorders resulting in *inflammation* of the *pharynx,* the *larynx,* and the *trachea*—also *flaccid expiratory* muscles, *rheumy* eyes, and *bizarre* fantasies.

48. Like an *automaton* but with an air of *nonchalance,* the aristocrat mounted the *guillotine.* He would not *grovel* or attempt to *placate* his *proletarian* captors even to avoid his *quietus.* A courteous smile for his *valet* was his final *beau geste.*

49. A *docile* little *dachshund* named *Cleopatra* was a *staunch ally* of every *mongrel interloper haunting* the neighborhood until an outbreak of *rabies* forced *curtailment* of all *canine promiscuity.*

50. The *Nevada* Music Association presented a musical *fantasia,* including his *concerto* for *pianoforte* and *cello* with *orchestral* background and a *choral* rendition of a *cantata* based on one of the *psalms.*

Method 2: Look up the pronunciations of the following words in a good American dictionary. If you are familiar with the word, compare your habitual pronunciation of it with the preferred pronunciation listed in the dictionary. Make a list of all words for which you have not used the preferred pronunciation, and practice these unfamiliar pronunciations by putting them in original sentences and reading them many times aloud. Continue such practice until you can pronounce each word smoothly without hesitation whenever you wish to use it or whenever you find it in print.

Words Having Confused Vowel Sounds

abdomen
absorb
acetic
Adonis
again
agile
albino
amenable
aquiline
area
asked
aunt
aye
been
betroth
bosom
bowline
bravo
brooch
broom
buoyant
cabal
cadaver
candelabra
Caucasian
clique
concavity
courtesan
creek
crystalline
Danish
deluxe
derisive
desperado
dilute
ebullient
ego
elephantine
elite
erred
esplanade
facile
feline
Florentine
fraternize
Gael
gala fete
garrulous
genuine
globule
gondola
gums
harem
hearth
heinous
hog
hoof
hovel
ignoramus
inflammable
jocund
jodhpurs
kimono
libertine
lingerie
Mary
negligee
obesity
oblique
pajamas
pathos
patron
pedagogue
pell-mell
penal
Pharaoh
Philistine
phonic
plebeian
precocious
profile
projectile
quinine
radiator
recuperate
requiem
robot
room
root
route
respite
seance
serpentine
servile
stanch
status
tapestry
tenacity
verbatim
wound
wrath

Words Having Confused Consonant Sounds

Archangel
archives
asphyxiate
association
auxiliary
berserk
brochure
Burmese
cache
catsup
censure
chagrin
chaldron
chameleon
chamois
chandelier
chaperone
charade
charlatan
chartreuse
chasm
chateau
chautauqua
chimpanzee
Chinese
choreography
communiqué
crescendo
czar
desist
dinghy
diphtheria

escape
executor
exemplary
exit
exotic
exude
exultation
garnishee
gesticulate
gibbet
gibberish
grease
greaser
hiccough
Japanese
larynx
licorice
liege
luxury
machinations
Maltese
Marchioness
mirage
morose
Moslem
moths
naphtha
nauseating
nauseous
orgy
pamphlet
persist
piquant
presentiment
ruse
schism
schizophrenia
schottische
scintillating
scion
ski
sociable
suggestion
sumac
talisman
tissue
transient
vase

Words Having Confused Accents

absolute
acclimatization
adult
advertisement
Agatha
alias
allied
amateur
ambiguity
amicable
applicable
cerebral
clandestine
comparable
connotative
communal
contumely
deviation
demoniacal
devastating
dictator
dirigible
divan
eczema
formidable
illustrative
inapplicable
incognito
incomparable
inebriety
inexplicable
infamous
inhospitable
insurance
irrelevant
irreparable
irrevocable
kilometer
laboratory
lamentable
maniacal
mustache
non-combatant
obligatory
oasis
occult
perfume
preferable
prevalent
recalcitrant
refutable
renaissance
reputable
revocable
ribald
ribaldry
robust
romance
satiety
umbrella

Words with Sounds Added or Omitted

In some cases omissions may result from poor enunciation rather than from confusion as to the proper pronunciation; but when an omission resulting from poor enunciation becomes common enough, it can result in a change of conventional pronunciation. For example, omitting the "ð" sound from the word "clothes" is considered poor enunciation although such an omission is virtually universal, but omitting the first "n" sound in the word "government" has recently been recognized by editors of more than one dictionary as common enough among cultured speakers to become a characteristic of the preferred pronunciation.

alveolar
apostles
apropos
Arctic
argot
artists
balm
boatswain
bowline
caffeine
calf
calm
casual
chasten
christen
clangor
clapboard
clothes
corduroy
depths
diamond
discs
epistle
escape
every
exhalation
exhaust
exhort
exhilarate
experimental
extraordinary
family
fasten
February
fifths
flaccid
generally
gentleman
government
gristle
hangar
handkerchief
hasten
heir
herb
humble
hygiene
hygienic
impugn
indict
indictment
kiln
leeward
leghorn
lineament
listen
literally
literature
maintenance
medieval
miniature
mistletoe
modern
often
oleomargarine
palm
picture
poem
police
porcelain
presumptuous
privilege
probably
proteins
psalm
pseudonym
pumpkin
qualm
quandary
raspberry
really
recognize
risks
salve
sophomore
sophomoric
sovereign
subtle
suggestion
sword
temperature
towards
vegetable
veterinarian
wrestle
waistband

Words of Foreign Origin That Are Anglicized in Varying Degrees or Not at All

aqua vitae
ballet
buffet
bas-relief
bivouac
blasé
bona fide
boudoir
cabaret
carillon
castanet
chaise longue
chauffeur
coiffeur
communiqué
connoisseur
corpus delicti
crepe de Chine
cretonne
critique
reveille
ricochet
roué
ruse
sabotage
debut
debutante
depot
detour
dilettante
distingué
eau de cologne
encore
entr'acte
en route
epitome

espionage	Giuseppe	naïveté	première
exeunt omnes	gourmet	Navajo	prestige
Fahrenheit	hara kiri	surveillance	prima facie
faux pas	in absentia	tableau	prodigy
fiancée	intrigue	Terpsichore	quadrille
finale	lieu	Terpsichorean	quasi
finis	limousine	tête-à-tête	recherché
forte	lingerie	niche	reconnaissance
foyer	madame	Notre Dame	regime
sachet	mademoiselle	nuance	rendezvous
scenario	mezzanine	omelet	repertoire
souvenir	mirage	omniscience	toreador
subpoena	modiste	Parisian	trousseau
suite	moire	parquet	vaudeville
gauche	monsieur	persiflage	via
geisha	morale	premier	vice versa

Geographic Names

Albuquerque	Chatham	Houston	Sahara
Alleghany	Chelsea	Iowa	Santa Fe
Amiens	Cheyenne	Joliet	Sault Ste. Marie
Appalachian	Chihuahua	Lancaster	Schenectady
Arkansas	Colorado	Le Havre	Schuylkill
Banff	Connecticut	Marlborough	Seine
Baton Rouge	Danzig	Miami	Sioux City
Belfast	Des Moines	Moscow	Spokane
Bucharest	Detroit	Mojave	St. Helena
Buena Vista	Dieppe	Newfoundland	Syracuse
Butte	Dubuque	Oberammergau	Terre Haute
Cairo	Duquesne	Portsmouth	Thames
Calais	Greenwich	Poughkeepsie	Tucson
Cayenne	Helena	Prague	Wilkes-Barre
Cayuga	Himalaya	Rio Grande	

Words to Which Extraneous Sounds Are Often Added

across	attacked	column	crowned
athlete	barbarous	dilate	elm
athletics	boisterous	diminutive	film

grievous	momentous	portentous	stupendous
height	one-legged	Roquefort	tarpaulin
idea	pomegranate	statistical	tremendous

Miscellaneous Words Pronounced in Various Ways

abyss	actual	altercation	anthropoid
accelerate	adept	ameliorate	archaic
accent	adversary	amenities	archeology
accepts	aerial	anesthesia	aria
accidentally	agape	anesthetists	armada
acoustics	alkaline	anomaly	asbestos
acme	agate	anesthetize	artisan
acts	Alpine	anonymous	auspices
auxiliary	deficit	guile	marshmallow
aversion	defile	harbinger	matricide
azure	demolition	heigh-ho	meerschaum
ay	demonstrable	hosiery	melancholy
baton	dentine	humor	mimetic
beatific	denunciation	hundred	minute (adj.)
bedizen	deposition	hundredth	monetary
bequeath	depths	hydrangea	morpheus
bravado	desiccate	hypochondria	municipal
breadth	desists	idealization	nape
brevity	desultory	ideology	narrator
bromide	detonate	idol	neuralgia
brusque	dictionary	idyl	nomad
buccal	didactic	ignominy	obdurate
bucolic	digress	environs	oboe
Buddha	dilemma	envoy	octopus
Buddhism	discretion	epoch	opus
bureau	dismal	equine	orangutan
bureaucracy	docility	esoteric	overture
burro	dubious	euphony	pageant
cadaverous	duodenum	glazier	patriot
calcimine	dynasty	global	patronage
caliph	eerie	immutable	paunch
calumny	egotism	improvisation	pedagogy
candidate	egret	inalienable	pedantic
cantaloupe	elucidate	indigent	penchant
caricature	enervate	indolence	peony

carton
cavalry
celibacy
cello
chaos
choir
choleric
cogent
cognizance
comfortable
compatriot
consists
coronet
corollary
correlate
corrugate
corsage
costume
courteous
cupola
cyclic
dahlia
dias
datum
daunt
debacle
debauched
recuperate
relevancy
renunciation
requiem
resource
retroactive
righteous
risks
rotogravure
routine
rudiment
saga
sagacity
salient
enigmatic
enunciation
envelope
Eustachian
evangelical
excerpt
exemplary
falcon
familiarize
figure
flaunt
forthwith
fortnight
franchise
fraternize
fulsome
furniture
gallows
gamut
gape
gaunt
get
geyser
ghoul
grandios
guffaw
gubernatorial
slavic
sleazy
sloth
slough
sobriety
sophomoric
sough
specious
stationery
stereotype
strenuous
strew
strychnine
suave
inertia
inspiratory
integral
interminable
interpellate
inundate
iodine
irreconcilable
Islam
itinerary
jaguar
jaundice
jaunt
joust
just
laconic
laryngeal
lithe
longevity
ludicrous
lugubrious
magnanimity
maladroit
malefactor
malevolent
malinger
maritime
tenable
tenacious
textile
threepence
thresh
tincture
tirade
tortoise
tournament
tranquil
transact
transient
transition
traverse
percolate
peremptory
perspiration
photogravure
pitcher
placate
plebiscite
pleurisy
portraiture
postscript
predecessor
prelude
premature
pretense
profligate
project
prologue
promulgation
protestation
provocative
pulmonary
quadruple
quarantine
querulous
raillery
recipe
recluse
twentieths
ubiquitous
undulatory
unfrequented
unison
usurp
usury
various
viaduct
viking
violoncello
virile
virtue
visor

sanguine
saunter
scrupulous
scurrilous
sentient
sheik
short-lived
simile
swarthy
swath
sycophant
syllabic
tabernacle
taciturn
taunt
temerity
tremor
trespass
trough
truculent
tumult
turbine
tureen
twelfths
visual
vituperative
waft
warrior
werewolf
whorl
wonder
yearling

PART II

Tonal Communication

9.

The Speech Intonation Pattern and Meaning

THE preceding chapters of Part I are chiefly concerned with the mechanics of voice improvement and the development of clarity and conventional accuracy in the articulation of words spoken in rapid sequence. The approach is an objective one since the attention of the learner is directed to the physical processes which may lead to the desired improvement.

In Part II the approach becomes subjective as the attention of the learner is directed away from the physical mechanics of vocalizing and articulating speech and towards the psychological motivations that bring about the vocal variations that make up the intonation patterns of speech. Part II is concerned with the development of vocal and timing flexibilities which can and should be used only in the spontaneous composition of expressive sound patterns.

Part II deals with: (1) the nature and importance of speech intonation patterns as a means of communication, (2) the factors involved in the spontaneous composition of intonation patterns, and (3) the development of the types of vocal and timing flexibilities that are needed for effective tonal communication.

The Nature of Speech Intonation Patterns

A speech intonation pattern is often called a speech melody because, like a melody in music, it consists of variations in pitch, time, force, and quality of sound. Although there is this basic similarity between speech intonation and music, there are also two very important dissimilarities that should be noted.

First, a melody in music is an end in itself, while a speech intonation pattern is only a means to an end. When listening to music, a person's attention is directed to the melody pattern as a thing of beauty to be admired for its own aesthetic qualities; but when a person listens to speech, his attention is directed to the ideas and feelings expressed by the speaker, and the speech intonation pattern is merely the means of making these ideas and feelings apparent. Whenever a speech intonation pattern obtrudes itself into the listener's consciousness, it ceases to be an effective means of communication.

The second dissimilarity between the melody patterns of music and speech is revealed by the fact that the melody in music may be written down in readable symbols so that it can be reproduced, but there are no symbols that can accurately record all the changes of a speech intonation pattern. In music the changes in pitch, time, and force are uniform, regular, and easily perceptible; but in speech the changes are not uniform or regular and they are often too rapid and too subtle for accurate perception or analysis.

A story often told, which illustrates the communicative effectiveness of a speech intonation pattern, relates that Madame Modjeska, the great Polish actress, was asked by a group of American ladies to recite for them something in her native language. Rather reluctantly she complied with the request. Her audience was moved to tears by the sound pattern of what they supposed was a selection of great dignity and pathos. Madame Modjeska's husband, however, was much amused by his wife's recital and its effect upon the audience because she was merely reciting in a dramatic fashion the Polish multiplication tables. Ridiculous as this performance may have seemed to Madame Modjeska's husband, its effect was real, and it illustrates the power to influence a listener's response by means of one's speech intonation pattern alone.

Factors Determining Speech Variety

A speech intonation pattern consists of variations in the force, pitch, and quality of the voice and in the timing of articulated words and syllables while speaking. These variations occur automatically as spontaneous expressions. The number and degree of such changes are determined by a number of factors which may be outlined as follows:

1. *Tonal expression* of thoughts and feelings expressed verbally. The tonal pattern reinforces, modifies, and supplements that which is uttered verbally.

2. *The speech personality,* which is dependent upon fixed personality traits, appearance, and speech habits of the speaker as well as upon a type of role-playing resulting from his adaptation to the specific speech situation.

3. *Basic skills of the speaker,* which include: (a) his ability in auditory guidance of expressive speech sounds—depending upon his ear training through listening experience; (b) his degree of flexibility and spontaneous control of changes in vocal force, pitch, and quality; and his spontaneous control of variations in the timing of words and of pauses.

The tonal expression of thoughts and feelings is discussed in the present chapter; the other determining factors (except for ear training—see Chapter 6) are discussed in following chapters.

Vocal Variations and Meaning

The most widely recognized function of the speech intonation pattern is that of reinforcing and supplementing the verbal language. Vocal changes are made spontaneously as a result of the speaker's attempt to communicate certain thoughts and feelings to others. The number and degree of the various kinds of vocal changes depends largely upon the number and variety of thoughts and feelings expressed, the relative vividness and significance of those thoughts and feelings in the speaker's consciousness, the keenness of the speaker's desire to communicate them to his listeners, and the speaker's skill in oral communication.

A study of expressive intonation patterns reveals that different speakers use individualistic patterns that are never exactly alike. Even when two people express seemingly identical thoughts and feelings under the same circumstances, their melody patterns of speech are distinctly different. This is partly because of their difference in backgrounds and speech habits, and partly because of different speech personalities; but even that part of the speech intonation pattern that is expressive of logical meanings is also different because of differences in the viewpoints of the speakers which result in variations in the relative significance they attach to the words. Nevertheless, the tonal expression of meanings is conventionalized sufficiently to permit the average listener to understand perfectly the intended meanings as they are clearly expressed by different speakers and in different manners.

Some vocal variations accomplish the same functions in speech that punctuation marks accomplish in the written language. A pause, for example, might take the place of a comma; an upward inflection of pitch might have the same significance as a question mark; and a downward inflection might have the same meaning as a period. Many other vocal variations indicate changes in the thought process and various relationships between different parts of the same sentences. Transitions or changes in thought, contrasts, climaxes, echoes, and parenthetical relationships, for example, may be expressed clearly by vocal changes. Other vocal changes are used to make apparent many types of subtle suggestions, insinuations, and nuances that the speaker cannot or does not wish to express verbally.

Emphasis and Subordination: Perhaps the most common function of vocal variations is that of gaining the effect of emphasis and subordination. Emphasis is a means of giving greater prominence to important or significant words, while subordination is a means of giving less prominence to relatively unimportant words. When a person talks, he senses the fact that some of his words carry much greater loads of meaning or emotional significance than do other words; so he emphasizes proportionally the more important words and subordinates the less important ones. The many different levels of emphasis and subordination account for a large part of the vocal variations that make up the intonation patterns of speech.

Kinds of Emphasis and Subordination: The effects of emphasis and subordination in speech are always gained through variation or contrast of force, pitch, timing, and quality. Whether the contrast be chiefly in force, pitch, timing, or quality determines the kind of emphasis, while the degree of contrast and the suddenness of change usually determines the strength of emphasis.

In order to illustrate the use of different kinds of emphasis, suppose that the simple sentence, "I will not," be vigorously emphasized. Literally this sentence expresses a refusal to perform some act, and that is all. It does not indicate the nature of the act, the attitude of either the speaker or the listener, or the kind of situation that motivates the refusal. Obviously, a person speaking that line must have some idea of the motivating situation before he would know the meaning to be communicated and hence the degree and kind of emphasis that would be appropriate. Even if the words were "flipped off" with a casual unconcern, the attitude of the speaker would motivate some degree of variation in emphasis and subordination, and hence an expressive intonation pattern.

Suppose that "I will not" were uttered spontaneously by an aggressive person who has been asked to perform a very unpleasant task by a presumptuous individual who has no right to ask it. As such a speaker utters the sentence, either "will" or "not" receives a primary emphasis which is chiefly force emphasis. The word receiving the force emphasis is uttered with a louder voice than other words which are subordinated by holding down their volume. If the emphasized word is much louder than the subordinate words, and if it is uttered with a sudden burst of loudness, then it is said to have strong force emphasis.

It should be noted, however, that force emphases, like pitch, time, or quality emphases, are never used with complete independence of each other. When a force emphasis results in the utterance of a word or syllable in a louder voice, the pitch of the voice usually rises also, and the word or syllable is also prolonged in duration, and the quality of the voice may change to reflect the speaker's mood or attitude. In other words, any word or syllable that is emphasized by force, contrasts with other words and syllables not only in force, but also to somewhat lesser degrees in pitch, time, and quality as well. The term force emphasis means merely that the greatest degree of contrast is in force. Likewise, pitch emphasis results from greater contrast in pitch than in force, time, or quality; and time emphasis has the greatest contrast in time.

Now suppose that the sentence, "I will not," is uttered by an irritable person who is in a petulant mood because he has been asked by a member of his own family to perform an unpleasant or menial task. In his utterance, the word "not" is apt to receive the primary emphasis which is apt to be a strong pitch emphasis. The higher and more suddenly the pitch rises on the word "not" the stronger will be the emphasis.

Once again, suppose "I will not" is uttered by a determined speaker with well-controlled emotions, who is replying to a persistent associate who has repeatedly asked him to do something that he has consistently refused to do in the past. This time either "will" or "not" may receive the primary emphasis which is likely to be of the time variety—the emphatic word being prolonged in utterance with perhaps also a prolonged pause before or after the emphatic word.

Finally, suppose that the speaker is a squeamish person who has been asked to perform a very disgusting task. This time the world "not" is apt to receive the primary emphasis by way of a change in the quality or tone of voice—the tone used on the word "not" expressing repugnance or extreme disgust. This is called quality emphasis and it will vary in strength as the quality used on the emphatic word communicates a stronger or milder attitude of disgust.

Since the four kinds of emphasis are not used independently but are usually mixed, an infinite variety of emphasis and subordination is possible. Very slight variations in the degree and proportions of force, pitch, time, and quality used for emphasis and subordination are expressive of very subtle variations in thoughts and feelings. Listeners are usually very quick to sense the meanings expressed by even the subtlest variations of force, pitch, timing, and quality used in speech.

Variations in Speech Content

As indicated in Chapter 1, one of the factors that determines a speaker's effectiveness in communication is having something to say—thoughts and feelings to be communicated. The essential nature of this factor seems self-evident, but exactly what is meant by having something to say is not so evident. There are so many different kinds and levels of meaning and so many different degrees of significance that having something to say needs further examination.

A person may talk a great deal, for example, without saying anything of significance that the listener does not already know. Consequently, his speech may be said to be empty because its effect upon the listener is negligible. At the other extreme, a single inspired line composed by a great poet, scholar, or orator may be so packed full of intellectual and emotional significance that it would tax the perceptive power of even the most intelligent reader or listener who attempts to understand it fully.

If a speaker has something to say, he presumably has a specific purpose which may be stated in terms of the response that he wishes to stimulate within his listeners. A speaker may wish to influence or change in some way the attitudes or feelings of his listener or listeners; he may want to influence or modify the listeners' convictions, opinions, or even their behavior in some specific way; he may wish to instruct or inform his listeners by means of definition, description, or explanation; or he may wish merely to give those who listen some degree of satisfaction or pleasure by sharing with them an interesting or amusing narrative or experience. In other words, when a speaker has something to say, he expects the saying of it to stimulate a specific and desired response; and the content of his speech may be measured in terms of the amount of new or significant materials that may be communicated to the listener for the purpose of gaining the desired response.

A speech may lack content in terms of its verbal composition alone—being made up of only vague and rambling generalities—because the speaker lacks knowledge, experience, and interest in the field discussed or perhaps because he lacks the skill to organize and present his thoughts verbally. However, he may be able to express adequately by means of tonal expressions all the thoughts and feelings that he succeeds in expressing verbally. On the other hand, a speech might lack content in terms of its intonation pattern alone. Such a lack may result either from the speaker's failure to realize the full significance of the words that he utters or from an overly reserved manner of speaking plus perhaps a lack of skill in tonal expression. If for example an interpreter attempts to deliver a meaningful speech without understanding completely its intellectual and emotional significance, his intonation pattern would surely fail to communicate that part of the verbal content that he does not perceive. On the other hand, a speaker may perceive and express verbally many meanings to which he cannot give adequate tonal expression because of either an overly reserved habit of speaking or a lack of vocal flexibility and control, or both.

The amount and variety of meanings contained in speech materials prepared by accomplished speakers or writers are revealed or suggested partly by the literal meaning of the language, partly by the connotative suggestions of words and general style of composition, partly by the implications inherent in the context, and partly by the rhetorical devices employed. The total content of any material composed by a competent speaker or writer is not something that can be grasped by a reader or interpreter in the process of reading through that material only once or even a half-dozen times. Assuming that the interpreter has sufficient background and imagination to understand and appreciate the material fully, he must study it very carefully, weighing every word and every phrase and pondering over the implications of the whole. In some cases, he may need to study word definitions in order to discover the exact sense intended. He must gain a degree of familiarity with the material that permits a full realization of the exact relationship of each part with every other part and with the whole. And he must practice reading the material aloud while carefully listening, in order to become fully aware of the sound and rhythmic values of the material that might reinforce its meaning. Without such study, an expressive intonation pattern cannot be fully motivated.

The Inevitability of Intonation Patterns

It is impossible for a parson to speak aloud without initiating some kind of intonation pattern. Whether that pattern be effective or ineffective in terms of oral communication, it is inevitable.

As an illustration of an ineffective intonation pattern, suppose that a first-grade pupil is demonstrating his mastery of a lesson in reading by naming the words that make up the printed sentence, "See the dog run." If this pupil merely calls out the words without any realization of their combined meaning, he is likely to utter each word with approximately the same degree of loudness, the same level of pitch, the same duration, and the same vocal quality—hence he neither emphasizes nor subordinates any word more than the others. One might conclude that this pupil's reading lacks any intonation pattern at all, but this is not true. His intonation pattern is ineffective because it fails to reinforce the meaning of the words uttered, but it does reveal clearly the real situation. It reveals, for example, the fact that the child is naming words rather than expressing ideas: it reveals his state of mind, his mental effort in recalling the names of the words, and perhaps his self-satisfaction over his success. It might also reveal something of his family background.

Suppose that this same pupil, after naming the words of the sentence, suddenly realizes their meaning and he repeats the words with their literal meaning rather vaguely in mind. In his utterance of these words, he now composes an intonation pattern that is more varied than before, with the individual words being emphasized or subordinated to some degree. The meaning of the sentence is still not very vividly expressed because, after all, a first-grade pupil is not an expert interpreter; but his intonation pattern does reinforce to some extent the verbal expression besides showing the child's attitudes and background.

Once again, suppose that the same child utters the same words spontaneously in describing the action of a new puppy which he has just received as a gift and over which he is very much excited. Although the literal meaning of the words is unchanged, the vividness and emotional significance of the action of the dog are greatly increased, and the vocal contrasts, giving the effects of emphasis and subordination, are also greatly increased. One or more of the words is probably uttered as a little scream or shrill squeal of delight. Which word or words receive the strongest emphasis and which type of emphasis predominates depends upon what thoughts and feelings are dominant at the moment of utterance. This depends upon the background of the child and upon his exact attitudes towards his listener, towards the dog, towards the dog's action, and towards himself as owner of the dog. Different children uttering the same words under seemingly identical circumstances would use different intonation patterns because of different speech habits, different backgrounds, and different reaction tendencies.

Under all circumstances, however, whether a speaker expresses thoughts and feelings or merely utters meaningless words, his speech will always have an intonation pattern. If this intonation pattern does not help the speaker in gaining a desired response from his audience, it will undoubtedly gain an undesirable response. In other words, when an intonation pattern is not right it is wrong, because it cannot remain neutral by signifying nothing.

Summary

A speech intonation pattern, like a melody in music, consists of variations in pitch, force, timing, and quality. But it is unlike a musical melody in two important respects. First, it is only a means to an end while music is an end in itself. And second, its changes are not regular and uniform enough to permit it to be written down, like music, in readable symbols.

A speech intonation pattern must be composed spontaneously, its form being determined by the following factors:

1. The tonal expression of thoughts and feelings.
2. The speech personality—including the speaker's habits of speech.
3. The auditory and vocal skills of the speaker.

The most widely recognized function of vocal variations is that of indicating or reinforcing the exact meanings intended by the speaker. Although different speakers would use somewhat different intonation patterns in expressing substantially the same meanings, the vocal changes used by virtually all speakers are conventionalized sufficiently to permit the average listener to understand their meanings.

Some vocal changes accomplish the same functions as punctuation marks accomplish in written language. Other changes indicate contrasts, climaxes, parenthetical relationships. But the most common function of vocal changes is that of giving the effect of varying degrees of emphasis and subordination. The effects of emphasis are gained by variations in force, pitch, time, and quality. Such variations are not used independently but are usually mixed in varying proportions and degrees to express subtle differences in meaning.

Meanings conveyed by speech may be translated in terms of the specific listener response that the speaker desires. A speech may lack content verbally, if the words can communicate very little that is new or significant to a listener. On the other hand, a speech may lack content because of its intonation pattern, if the speaker fails to communicate meanings because he either fails to understand or because he lacks the vocal skill to give them effective expression.

The meanings contained in speech materials are revealed by a literal interpretation of the language, by the connotative suggestions of the words, by the style of composition, by the context of the whole speech, and by the rhetorical devices used. The discovery and assimilation of such meanings by an interpreter requires careful and extended study, including oral rehearsal for the sake of becoming aware of sound values.

It is impossible to speak aloud wthout initiating an intonation pattern. If that intonation pattern does not aid communication, it is almost sure to damage it because tonal expression can never remain meaningless.

QUESTIONS

1. Why does the development of effective intonation patterns demand a subjective approach?
2. In what ways is a speech intonation pattern like a melody in music?
3. In what two important respects is an intonation pattern unlike a musical melody?
4. What attributes of the voice are varied to make up a speech intonation pattern?
5. What are the three factors that determine the form of the speech intonation pattern?
6. If a person reads words without any comprehension of their meaning, will his reading have a speech intonation pattern?
7. Why does the expression of thoughts and feelings result in vocal variations?
8. Define emphasis and subordination.
9. When speaking a sentence, does a change in the type of emphasis used change the literal meaning of the sentence?
10. If two different people speak the same words under identical circumstances, will they use identical intonation patterns of speech?
11. Should all the syllables of an emphatic word be emphasized equally?

12. Is it possible to emphasize all the words in a single sentence?
13. Is it possible to subordinate all the words in a single sentence?
14. What usually determines the strength of emphasis?
15. If a person speaks a sentence with no emphasis or subordination, would his speech have no intonation pattern?
16. What is meant by speech content?
17. Differentiate the lack of content when due to verbal expression and when due to tonal expression.
18. What might account for a lack of content in the intonation pattern of a speech having good verbal content?
19. In what ways is verbal content of speech material revealed?
20. Explain the inevitability of the speech intonation pattern.

Exercises

I—*Purpose:* To observe the changes in meaning or inference brought about by changing the words emphasized and the types of emphasis used in interpreting the same sentence.

Method: Repeat the following sentence, emphasizing the italicized word or words first by increasing the force or loudness of the voice on the emphatic word or words, then by raising the pitch, then by prolonging the time duration. Also pause before and after the italicized word or words and notice the emphatic effect. Then repeat the sentence several times while adopting a different attitude or mood each time. For example, repeat it gaily as though suppressing laughter, then sadly as though suppressing tears, then angrily, then disgustedly, etc. Emphasize the italicized word or words in whatever manner seems most fitting and notice the resulting vocal qualities on the emphatic words. Also experiment with strong and weak emphasis to become entirely aware of the means of increasing the strength of emphasis.

1. *I* won't do it. 3. I won't *do* it. 5. *I* won't *do* it. 7. I *won't do* it.
2. I *won't* do it. 4. I won't do *it*. 6. *I* won't do it. 8. I *won't* do *it*.

II—*Purpose:* To develop a critical consciousness of the different intonation patterns used when varying the interpretations of the same sentences.

Method: Practice interpreting the following sentences in the various manners indicated under each, and observe carefully the differences in the resulting intonation patterns. Use a recording device if possible as a means of improving your opportunity to observe your pattern. Also observe other speakers attempting the same interpretations and compare their intonation patterns with yours. Read to others varying the order of the various interpretations and see if they can recognize your intended interpretation each time.

1. Your performance was marvelous.

a. *Enthusiastically*—as though addressed to an intimate friend
b. *With forced politeness*—polite but very unenthusiastic
c. *Sympathetically*—as though comforting someone who is weeping because of a caustic criticism
d. *Insistently*—meaning, "I said it before and I insist that it's true."
e. *Surprised and pleased*—as though addressed to a child who did amazingly well
f. *With insolent indifference*—in a haughty and condescending manner
g. *Sarcastically*—in a nasty and insulting manner
h. *Incredulously*—meaning, "I said your performance was marvelous? Why, that's ridiculous!"
i. *Enviously and self-pityingly*—meaning, "I wish my performance had been half as good."
j. *Tauntingly*—showing amused and jeering ridicule
k. *Thoughtful agreement*—meaning, "As I think it over, I realize that that is probably true."

2. I know I shouldn't have done it.

a. *Irritatedly*—meaning, "I have admitted it, so don't keep on pestering me about it."
b. *Ashamedly*—meaning, "I can't forgive myself for being such a fool."
c. *Indifferently*—meaning, "All right, I did it—so what?"
d. *Ingratiatingly*—meaning, "I'm sorry. Please forgive me."
e. *Fearfully*—meaning, "I'm terribly frightened of the consequences."
f. *Saucily*—meaning, "I know it wasn't proper, but it was lots of fun."
g. *Egotistically*—meaning, "Although it is common practice, it should have been beneath my dignity."
h. *Thoughtfully*—meaning, "But what else could I have done?"
i. *Decisively*—meaning, "So let's not discuss it any further."
j. *Tragically*—as though suffering from tragic consequences.

k. *Angrily*—meaning, "I admit it, but you are making entirely too much of it."

3. I'd love to.

a. *Enthusiastically*—meaning, "I can't think of anything I'd rather do."
b. *Doubtfully*—meaning, "I think I would, but I'm not sure."
c. *Suspiciously*—meaning, "I wonder what kind of joke you are trying to play on me."
d. *Adoringly*—meaning, "I'd go anywhere with you."
e. *Maliciously*—meaning, "If I do, it will serve you right."
f. *Teasingly*—meaning, "You wouldn't like it, but I might just do it anyway."
g. *Graciously*—meaning, "It would be no trouble at all."
h. *Longingly*—meaning, "I'd give anything to be able to."
i. *Denying an unwillingness*—meaning, "On the contrary, I'd really like to."
j. *Scoffingly*—meaning, "Why, such an idea is ridiculous."
k. *Questioningly*—meaning, "You think so, do you?"

4. Why don't you go?

a. *Angrily*—meaning, "Go away and let me alone!"
b. *Curiously*—meaning, "I can't understand why you don't."
c. *Coaxingly*—meaning, "Please, won't you go along?"
d. *Disgustedly*—meaning, "Your reason for not going is silly."
e. *Reprovingly*—meaning, "Everybody is decent enough to go except you."
f. *Sorrowfully*—meaning, "Your not going is a terrible disappointment."
g. *Flippantly*—meaning, "What difference would it make?"
h. *Sternly*—meaning, "It's your duty to go and you know it."
i. *Urgently*—meaning, "We shall really need you there."
j. *Amusedly*—meaning, "It would be a big joke, if you went."
k. *Pleadingly*—meaning, "I won't be able to stand it without you there."

5. It looks easy.

a. *Surprisedly*—meaning, "And I thought it would be so hard."
b. *Doubtfully*—meaning, "But looks may be deceiving."
c. *Negatively*—meaning, "But it is probably very difficult."
d. *Happily*—meaning, "And it should be delightful."

e. *Incredulously*—meaning, "Why, that's ridiculous."
f. *Scoffingly*—meaning, "It's silly to say you can't do it."
g. *Insistently*—meaning, "It does too look easy."
h. *Exasperatedly*—meaning, "And yet I'm so clumsy I can't do it."
i. *Sarcastically*—meaning, "And you were fool enough to think it would be easy."
j. *Questioningly*—meaning, "Do you really think it looks easy?"
k. *Egotistically*—meaning, "It'll be no problem at all for me."

III—*Purpose:* To practice and observe various interpretations of a single word.

Method: Act out the following scenes as completely as you would if they were parts of a play.

Scene 1—Situation—Your best boy or girl friend, who has been out of town, has promised to call you on the telephone as soon as he or she returns. The call is now long overdue and you are worried. Then the telephone rings.

You (answering eagerly): Yes?
Telephone (A strange voice asks if it is you speaking.)
You (disappointed but curious): Yes.
Telephone (The speaker identifies self as an old friend whom you have not seen for over a year.)
You (surprised and cordial): Yes!
Telephone (He says that he is calling from the local hospital.)
You (a little anxiously): Yes?
Telephone (He says that he has brought your friend to the hospital.)
You (shocked and very worried): Yes?
Telephone (He says that they have had a slight accident.)
You (fearing the worst): Yes!
Telephone (He asks if you can come to the hospital immediately.)
You (convinced of a real tragedy but trying to be brave): Yes!
Telephone (Your friend's voice breaks in telling you to hurry.)
You (very much relieved): Yes.
Telephone (Sound of two people laughing.)
You (realizing that you are the victim of a so-called joke): Yes!
Telephone (Your friend asks if you are mad about it.)
You (furious): Yes! (And you hang up.)

Scene 2—Situation—You are a college student and are in your room studying for your last final examination when the telephone rings.

You (answering but irritated at the interruption): Hello.

Telephone (The long-distance operator tells you that there is a call for you from your home town.)

You (after a long pause, you wonder if there is anyone on the line): Hello?

Telephone (No answer.)

You (another pause—then afraid that you have been cut off): Hello?

Telephone (Nothing but several meaningless clicks.)

You (exasperated and a little angry): Hello!

Telephone (Suddenly your father's voice says): Hello.

You (surprised and delighted): Hello.

Telephone (He asks if you have finished your examinations yet.)

You (feeling sorry for yourself): No.

Telephone (He says that he is driving through and could pick you up at noon tomorrow if you are free by then.)

You (wailing because your last examination is at 1 P.M.): No!

Telephone (He asks if you have enough money for bus fare home.)

You (apologizing because you should have): No.

Telephone (He asks if you received the letter telling you that your best friend will visit you at home.)

You (delighted over the prospect): No.

Telephone (He asks teasingly if it isn't a love affair rather than an examination that is delaying your trip home.)

You (scoffing at the idea): No.

Telephone: Goodbye. Don't fail your examination.

You (a little worried at your prospect of passing it): No. (Hang up).

IV—*Purpose:* To gain practice in giving clear tonal expression to meaningful and relatively complicated materials.

Method: Practice reading the following selections aloud until you can deliver them with spontaneity and ease, giving full tonal expression to all meanings:

1. I tell you earnestly and authoritatively (I know I am right in this) you must get into the habit of looking intensely at words, and assuring yourself of their meaning, syllable by syllable—nay, letter by letter. . . . You might read all the books in the British Museum (if you could live long enough) and remain an utterly "illiterate," uneducated person; but if you read ten pages of a good book, letter by letter,—that is to say, with real accuracy,—you are forevermore in some measure an educated person. The entire difference between

education and noneducation (as regards the merely intellectual part of it), consists in this accuracy.

A well-educated gentlemen may not know many languages,—may not be able to speak any but his own,—may have read very few books. . . . But whatever language he knows, he knows precisely; whatever word he pronounces, he pronounces rightly; above all, he is learned in the peerage of words; knows the words of true descent and ancient blood, at a glance, from words of modern canaille; remembers all their ancestry, their intermarriages, distant relationships, and the extent to which they were admitted, and the offices they held, among the national noblesse of words at any time, and in any country.

But an uneducated person may know, by memory, many languages, and talk them all, and yet truly know not a word of any;—not a word even of his own. An ordinarily clever and sensible seaman will be able to make his way ashore at most ports; yet he has only to speak a sentence of any language to be known for an illiterate person: so also the accent, or turn of expression of a single sentence, will at once mark a scholar. And this is so strongly felt, so conclusively admitted, by educated persons, that a false accent or a mistaken syllable is enough, in the parliament of any civilized nation, to assign to a man a certain degree of inferior standing for ever.

John Ruskin

2. To-morrow, and to-morrow, and to-morrow,
Creeps in this petty pace from day to day
To the last syllable of recorded time;
And all our yesterdays have lighted fools
The way to dusty death. Out, out, brief candle!
Life's but a walking shadow, a poor player
That struts and frets his hour upon the stage
And then is heard no more; it is a tale
Told by an idiot, full of sound and fury,
Signifying nothing.

from *Macbeth*
by William Shakespeare

3. The earth is the Lord's and the fulness thereof, the world and they that dwell therein;

For he hath founded it upon the seas, and established it upon the floods.

Who shall ascend into the hill of the Lord? or who shall stand in his holy place?

He that hath clean hands, and a pure heart; who hath not lifted up his soul unto vanity, nor sworn deceitfully.

He shall receive the blessing for the Lord, and righteousness from the God of his salvation.

This is the generation of them that seek Him, that seek thy face, O Jacob.

Lift up your heads, O ye gates; and be ye lifted up, ye everlasting doors; and the King of glory shall come in.

Who is this King of glory? The Lord strong and mighty, the Lord mighty in battle.

Lift up your heads, O ye gates; even lift them up, ye everlasting doors; and the King of glory shall come in.

Who is this King of glory? The Lord of hosts, He is the King of glory.

Psalm XXIV

4. I will lift up mine eyes unto the hills, from whence cometh my help.

My help cometh from the Lord, which made heaven and earth.
He will not suffer thy foot to be moved:
He that keepeth thee will not slumber.
Behold, He that keepeth Israel shall neither slumber nor sleep.
The Lord is thy keeper;
The Lord is thy shade upon thy right hand,
The sun shall not smite thee by day, nor the moon by night.
The Lord shall preserve thee from all evil;
He shall preserve thy soul.
The Lord shall preserve thy going out and thy coming in,
From this time forth, and even for evermore.

Psalm CXXI

5. The quality of mercy is not strain'd.
It droppeth as a gentle rain from heaven
Upon the place beneath. It is twice blest:
It blesseth him that gives and him that takes.
'Tis mightiest in the mightiest; it becomes
The throned monarch better than his crown.
His scepter shows the force of temporal power,
The attribute to awe and majesty,
Wherein doth sit the dread and fear of kings;
But mercy is above the sceptered sway;
It is enthroned in the hearts of kings;

It is an attribute to God himself;
And earthly power doth then show likest God's
When mercy seasons justice. Therefore, Jew,
Though justice be thy plea, consider this,
That in the course of justice, none of us
Should see salvation. We do pray for mercy,
And that same prayer doth teach us all to render
The deeds of mercy. I have spoke thus much
To mitigate the justice of thy plea,
Which if thou follow, this strict court of Venice
Must needs give sentence 'gainst the Merchant there.

from *The Merchant of Venice*
by William Shakespeare

6. Esau Wood sawed wood. Esau Wood would saw wood. All the wood Esau Wood saw Esau Wood would saw. In other words, all the wood Esau saw to saw Esau sought to saw. Oh, the wood Wood would saw! And oh! the wood-saw with which Wood would saw wood. But one day Wood's wood-saw would saw no wood, and thus the wood Wood sawed was not the wood Wood would saw if Wood's wood-saw would saw wood. Now Wood would saw wood with a wood-saw that would saw wood, so Esau sought a saw that would saw wood. One day Esau saw a saw saw wood as no other wood-saw Wood saw would saw wood. In fact, of all the wood-saws Wood ever saw saw wood Wood never saw a wood-saw that would saw wood as the wood-saw Wood saw saw wood would saw wood, and I never saw a wood-saw that would saw as the wood-saw Wood saw would saw until I saw Esau Wood saw wood with the wood-saw Wood saw saw wood. Now Wood saws wood with the wood-saw Wood saw saw wood.

Anonymous

10.

The Speech Personality

IN Chapter 1 personality is defined as, "the total of all the attitudes that an individual habitually assumes towards himself, towards those with whom he comes in contact, towards mankind in general, and towards the conventional opinions and ideals of his social world." It seems obvious that an attitude, whether it be temporary or permanently fixed by habit, affects one's manner of speaking. A person with a querulous attitude, for example, might be expected to use a plaintive or whining speech pattern, and either the speech pattern or the attitude motivating it might became habitual. A kindly, gracious attitude, on the other hand, might be expected to motivate a pattern of speech suggesting friendliness, sympathic understanding, and intimacy.

A speech personality may be defined as the total personal impression that a speaker gives of himself while speaking to one or more listeners. In casual, daily discourse a person's speech personality is likely to be identical with his everyday personality; but when a person is faced with a speech situation in which he feels the need to make a particular kind of impression upon one or more listeners who do not know him intimately, he normally tries to alter his casual, everyday attitudes and manner of speaking in hopes that he may make a more favorable impression upon his listeners in order that he may increase his influence over them. Such an assumed attitude and manner of speaking—being motivated like "company manners" by a desire to make a favorable impression—might be only a temporary result of adapting oneself to a particular kind of speech situation; but when such an adaptation is made again and again as a speaker repeatedly adapts himself to the same kind of speech situation, it might become fixed as a speech-personality trait that may be assumed more or less automatically whenever the speaker meets a similar speech situation.

It is quite possible for a person who speaks frequently in distinctly different speech situations in which he attempts to make distinctly different impressions upon his listeners, to develop two or more distinctly different speech personalities. A minister, for example, might develop one speech personality for his weekly sermons, another personality for small and relatively intimate meetings with church workers such as a ladies' auxiliary group, another personality for large political or service club groups, and still another personality for his visits to ailing or bedridden parishioners. Such variation of speech personality does not mean that the minister speaks unnaturally or insincerely in any of the different speech situations. It means merely that he attempts to make the best impression upon his listeners in contrasting situations so as to increase the effectiveness of his communication or influence in each.

A speech personality should always be evaluated not in terms of how truly or to what degree it reveals the nature of the speaker, but rather in terms of its effect upon the listener or listeners. When a speech personality is effective, the personal impression given by the speaker is a favorable one which serves to reinforce both the communicative and persuasive powers of his speech; but, when the speech personality is ineffective, it serves only to decrease or cancel out the speaker's potential influence upon his audience.

The nature of the personal impression that a speaker gives

depends upon both the particular speech situation and the effectiveness of the speaker's adaptation to that situation.

The Speech Situation

The nature of a speech situation is determined by all the conditions, circumstances, and human relationships in the speaker's and listeners' present environment which might serve to determine the attitudes of the speaker and listeners towards each other and the listeners' predisposition to react in a particular manner to the speaker's influence. The attitudes or predisposition of the listeners is determined by a number of factors such as the following:

1. The number and kinds of listeners present—their age, sex, experience, and cultural background.
2. The physical environment and the emotional atmosphere accompanying it.
3. The occasion for speaking and any established conventions or customs governing listener behavior upon such an occasion.
4. Any previous knowledge that the listeners have of the subject to be discussed by the speaker, and any fixed attitude or bias that the listeners hold towards the speech objective.
5. Any previous knowledge that the listeners have of the speaker—his reputation, rank, position, accomplishments or the lack of any of these.

Obviously, speech situations—being dependent upon many variable factors—are subject to great variation. And it follows that a speaker's ability to adapt his speech personality so as to be effective in a particular speech situation depends partly upon his ability to sense or evaluate accurately that speech situation.

An Effective Speech Personality

The speaker's means of revealing, or of involuntarily suggesting, his speech personality includes his physical appearance, his general grooming and style of dressing, his posture, his manner of walking and moving, his voice, his way of pronouncing and articulating his words, his manner and facility in expressing his thoughts and feelings verbally, and many of the vocal changes constituting the intonation pattern of his speech. In other words, the speech personality is revealed by the general appearance of the speaker and in the various aspects of his speech behavior.

The general appearance of the speaker is dependent upon his physical appearance and his general grooming, including his manner and style of dressing.

The physical appearance of the speaker is dependent upon such uncontrollable factors as size and proportions or build of body, as well as facial features, complexion, and natural coloring of hair. Occasionally, listeners may be very much impressed, either favorably or unfavorably, by a speaker's physical appearance; and such an impression might serve to increase or decrease the listeners' susceptibility to the speaker's influence. However, a speaker's physical appearance, unless it be reinforced by other personality factors, seldom exerts as much influence upon the listeners' attitudes as it might exert upon the attitudes of the speaker himself. For example, a speaker who is unusually small or frail of body and who possesses homely features with perhaps a pimply complexion, might fail to gain any audience favor by virtue of his physical appearance; but he would probably not lose much in terms of listener susceptibility if he were able to maintain a positive, self-assured, and friendly approach to his listeners. Unfortunately, however, such a speaker is often prone to exaggerate, in his own mind, the effects of his physical appearance; and he either feels sorry for himself with the result that he becomes very self-conscious and apologetic in his approach to his listeners, or he overcompensates for an imagined handicap by becoming defiant, self-assertive, and seemingly egotistical in his manner of speaking. In either case, it is the speaker's attitude reinforced by his appearance, rather than his physical appearance alone, that tends to weaken greatly the listeners' responsiveness.

To be reasonably good-looking is usually an advantage to a speaker, but there may be some danger in a speaker's consciousness of his own good appearance because listeners usually resent any indication that a speaker is conscious of, or is inclined to take advantage of, his or her beauty—resentment being commonest, of course, among listeners of the same sex.

The grooming of a speaker is controllable and consequently it is usually more effective than his physical appearance in determining the listeners' responsiveness to his influence. Except in rare instances when a speaker may be very poorly dressed for economic reasons, the speaker's attitude is little affected by the quality of his clothes or grooming.

The cleanliness and neatness of a speaker's appearance, the taste shown by the cut and grooming of hair, the colors, style, and condition of clothing, and occasionally the amount and application of make-up are commonly held to be significant indicators of personality. Certainly anything very slovenly, bizarre, or even unconventional about the speaker's clothing or grooming could predispose the average listener to be somewhat resistant to his influence.

There are probably rather wide sex differences, age differences, and social-class differences in the responses of listeners to the grooming of male and female speakers. In general, however, the speech personality of the average speaker may be aided most by neatness and cleanliness of grooming and relative conservativeness of styles and colors of clothing.

The various aspects of speech behavior that reveal speech personality are of two types—those fixed by habit and those that result spontaneously from thoughts and feelings to which the speaker is currently responding.

Any speech habits that are so deep-seated that the speaker

is completely unconscious of them while speaking will be uncontrollable as long as the speaker allows them to operate automatically. As a matter of fact, the whole process of speaking is so tremendously complex that a speaker could not possibly control all aspects of it consciously when speaking extemporaneously; hence the speech process is inevitably governed largely by habit. The actor or interpreter may eliminate old speech habits to some extent by forming and substituting new ones during the rehearsal period—so his speech also is largely governed by habits that are both new and old. Even many of the ideas, beliefs, and attitudes that motivate one's speech may come to him automatically because they have been repeatedly associated with similar situations in the past. Such ideas, beliefs, and attitudes are commonly called stereotypes because of their frequent recurrence in the mind of the speaker and because of his unquestioning acceptance of them.

It is impossible ever to determine exactly how much of a person's speech behavior is part of a habitual pattern and how much is being guided, with some degree of conscious purpose, by thoughts, attitudes, and impulses that are relatively new and spontaneous. However, it seems obvious that any speaker must depend to some extent upon speech habits while speaking; and those parts of one's speech and speech behavior that are fixed by habit are usually recognized quite easily as being characteristic of the speaker, as well as of his family, his region, and his nation. They reveal the speaker's cultural background and usually some of his most basic personality traits that are not changed as a result of his adaptation to the speech situation.

Those parts of the speech pattern and speech behavior which are motivated by the thoughts and feelings to which the speaker is currently responding are controllable parts that are affected most by the speaker's adaptation to a particular speech situation. They are the principal bases of any distinctive speech personality. The most important controllable factors that determine the speech personality are the basic attitudes which the speaker adopts particularly for the speech situation. These may be identified as the attitudes of the speaker directed towards himself, towards the subject under discussion, and towards his listeners. These basic attitudes of the speaker arouse and stimulate listener attitudes towards the speaker and towards his speech objective; and it is these listener attitudes that determine the degree to which the listener resists or is amenable to the speaker's influence.

As an example of the effects upon an audience of a vocal quality which is determined by the speaker's basic attitudes, suppose that a handsome, tastefully dressed speaker, who is unknown to his audience, gives a seemingly very competent speech upon a very significant subject. However, he gives the impression that he is smug and conceited in his attitude towards himself, that he is indifferent and carelessly flippant in his attitude towards his speech materials, and that he is insolently condescending in his attitude towards his listeners. Is it not obvious that such a speech would be rendered ineffective by the speech personality? The basic attitudes of the speaker would inevitably arouse and stimulate listener attitudes that would render his audience resentful and highly resistant to his influence. As the speech situation varies, the basic attitudes of the speaker should vary. However, the basic attitudes that should be most effective in reinforcing the speaker's influence over his listeners in the average or most normal speech situations are fairly obvious, at least in general outline.

1. *Attitude Towards Self:* A speaker must seem to be self-confident and self-respecting if he wishes to inspire the confidence and respect of his audience. A weak, apologetic, tentative, or indecisive manner of speaking would make a lack of self-confidence obvious to an audience; and any careless, slovenly, or blatantly unconventional speech behavior

would seem to suggest the speaker's lack of normal pride, self-respect, or concern for the good opinion of others. In either case, the evident attitude of the speaker towards himself would tend to rob his speech of most of its personal reinforcement and persuasive power.

It is not easy for an inexperienced speaker who suffers from stage fright and self-consciousness, or especially for a speaker with a well-established inferiority complex, to play the role of a well-poised and self-confident speaker. However, even though learning to play such a role may be very difficult, it is never impossible; and it is of primary importance to anyone who wishes to become an effective speaker. When a speaker makes the effort to assume self-confidence and poised self-respect as attitudes that are rather new in his experience, he may tend to overplay the role to such an extent that he seems conceited, smug, and pompous. The effective playing of such a role requires a rather delicate adjustment. The exact degree to which a speaker should seem to be self-confident and self-respecting in order to gain a maximum reinforcement of his influence depends upon the exact speech situation. Any speaker therefore needs experience and practice in analyzing and adjusting to various speech situations in order that he may develop skill in making such adjustments.

2. *Attitudes Towards Speech Materials:* The speaker must show a lively interest in his speech materials and a firm conviction in the principles and beliefs that he supports while speaking, and he must show an active and simultaneous desire to communicate fully every detail to his listeners if he is to arouse any real audience interest and a willingness to respond favorably.

Although a speaker should always maintain a lively interest in his speech materials and he should always keep up a constant effort to communicate these materials to his listeners, his attitude towards the ideas and feelings that he expresses must be adjusted to the specific speech situation. The speech situation may vary as the listeners are predisposed to be interested or uninterested in the speech subject, and friendly or antagonistic towards the speech objective. The speaker's attitude towards the materials, therefore, should fall somewhere between the two extremes of indifference or careless flippancy on the one hand and didactic bigotry or fanaticism on the other.

Some subjects should inspire a different kind and degree of animation and interest than should others. To be too much animated and enthusiastic in discussing certain subjects might suggest insincerity of attitude and a gushing affectation in the manner of speaking. Such an impression, if given, might be just as damaging to the speaker's influence as indifference or flippancy of attitude and a dull, monotonous manner of speaking. The speaker must seek a middle ground that is well adjusted to his subject and to himself.

3. *Attitudes Towards the Listeners:* Above all, a speaker should always show a full awareness of his listeners as human beings, and he should be as friendly, sympathetic, and intimate in his attitude towards them as the specific speech situation permits. Speech situations may vary widely in terms of speaker-listener relationships; but in the great majority of public-speaking situations, the speaker should assume leadership or an attitude based upon an assumption that the listeners will react exactly as he wants them to react. This taking for granted that the listeners will respond favorably to his influence is perhaps the most basic element of leadership, for it shows the listeners that the speaker has assumed the role of the leader and conventional courtesy will usually cause them to acknowledge his leadership at least initially without challenge.

The assumption of leadership by a speaker does not mean that he needs to be dictatorial or overbearing in his manner of speaking. In fact, the persuasive power of a leader is much greater if leadership is accomplished by a quiet and relatively reserved manner of speaking because such a manner suggests maturity and a type of strength that goes with self-control. Nearly everyone recognizes a blustering manner of speech as indicative of weakness on the part of the speaker.

The greatest deterrent to an effective attitude towards one's listeners is stage fright or self-consciousness, which results typically in a negative attitude or a withdrawal from the audience. The speaker may seem to be in a state of shock and only vaguely aware of the existence of his audience. As a result he treats them with a cold, impersonal detachment. Unfortunately, this negative attitude often becomes habitual and might become fixed as a part of one's speech personality long after he has ceased to be bothered by stage fright and self-consciousness.

Speech Personality Not Based on Pretense

Adapting the speech personality to the specific speech situation in order to gain maximum control of audience responses is primarily a matter of properly adjusting basic attitudes. However, in the last analysis, the potential effectiveness of the speech personality is dependent upon the personal capacities and experience of the speaker himself. An attitude of self-confidence and self-respect, for example, can bolster the speaker's ego and make its full dimensions apparent, but it cannot be used to enlarge that ego and make it seem more impressive than it really is. A vital or lively interest in the speech material cannot be assumed as a matter of pure pretense. The speaker must possess enough experience or background and both intellectual and emotional perception to permit full understanding, and he must have enough imagination to supply some individuality or originality of viewpoint, and he must have enough vitality or emotional energy to support a vital or animated interest. A speaker may assume a positive or direct attitude towards an audience, but he must possess warmth and sympathy or fellow-feeling to make his direct manner of speaking really effective in terms of audience response.

No matter how great the personal qualities of the speaker, they may be easily hidden or disguised by poor adaptation of the speech personality to the speech situation. But no matter how skillfully a speaker may adapt his personality to the speech situation, he cannot assume convincingly a greatness or an impressiveness of personality that he does not possess.

An Ineffective Speech Personality

A speech personality may be said to be ineffective when it fails to reinforce the speaker's message to, or his influence upon, his audience, as described above. But also, ineffectiveness of speech might result from an obviously stereotyped intonation pattern. Such an intonation pattern results from a speech-personality stereotype which develops partly as a result of meeting almost identical speech situations with monotonous frequency so that the speaker gradually loses his spontaneity partly through boredom and partly through the imitation of other speakers who meet the same type of speech situation. Preachers, politicians, teachers, trial lawyers, auctioneers, sideshow barkers, student debaters, and students of elocution often develop characteristic intonation patterns that plainly suggest their respective professions or training. Such speech patterns and the speech personalities that are revealed by them are ineffective because of the lack of spontaneity and the resulting artificial and monotonous intonation patterns.

Occasionally, a kind of stereotyped pattern may develop that is unkind to both audience and speaker. This is a type of tense or screaming delivery resulting from a kind of fanatic fervor that the speaker evidently confuses with great sincerity in its early stages of development. Preachers and politicians are both subject to this type of emotional stereotype which usually results in vocal damage—chronic hoarseness or harshness of voice—and frequently in the loss of the voice entirely for short periods of time. Such speakers may seek vocal treatment or voice training, but the only remedy for such a difficulty is a complete change of speech personality—learning to temper sincerity with self-control and general relaxation.

It is perhaps true that listeners who frequently hear the same speaker in identical speech situations—as, for example, a church congregation or a class in school—may learn to respond to a stereotyped speech pattern in a stereotyped manner. Such a response might even be favorable. Nevertheless, any obviously stereotyped manner of speaking would have little immediate influence upon a new and independent listener.

Acting and Speech Personality

The kind of role-playing done by an actor is somewhat different from that done by a public speaker. The actor represents a stage character; consequently, he does not attempt to adapt his speech personality to a speech situation in order to reinforce his influence upon an audience. To the actor, speech situations are permanently fixed by the play and he speaks directly to other actors who are playing other stage characters in carefully rehearsed scenes. The actor's speech personality is carefully developed during a rehearsal period—even to the extent of eliminating many old speech habits and forming new ones—and it may be intended to make an unpleasant impression upon the audience rather than always a favorable one.

The actor learns to interpret his stage character's attitudes towards himself, towards the thoughts and feelings expressed, and towards other characters in the play. And although he seldom has any occasion to speak directly to his audience, the actor must never forget that his ultimate objective is to stimulate a specific type of response in that audience—the desired response being one that will lead to full understanding and maximum appreciation of the play.

Summary

A speech personality results when a speaker alters his basic attitudes and manner of speaking in order to give a more favorable impression of himself to his listeners and thus increase his influence over them.

A person's speech personality results from his adaptation to a specific speech situation, which is determined by the number and kinds of listeners present, the environment, the occasion, and any existing attitudes of the listeners towards the speaker and his subject. When a speaker adapts his speech personality frequently to very similar speech situations, a speech personality develops that becomes a familiar role that is easy for him to play. When a speaker frequently meets distinctly different speech situations, it is quite possible that he may develop two or more distinctly different speech personalities or roles.

Speech personalities may be effective or ineffective depending upon the speaker's ability to evaluate and adjust himself to various speech situations. The speech personality is revealed by the speaker's appearance and all aspects of his speech behavior. The most adaptable attributes of speech personality include general grooming and basic attitudes that the speaker assumes towards himself, towards his speech materials, and towards his listeners.

An effective speech personality in an average speech situation might result from clean, neat, and conservative grooming, and the following basic attitudes: self-confidence and self-respect, animated interest in speech materials and an active desire to communicate them to others, complete awareness of the audience and as much friendliness and intimacy towards that audience as the situation may justify.

An ineffective speech personality might result from poor adaptation to a particular speech situation resulting from a poor analysis of the situation or from an underplaying or overplaying of the proper role. Sometimes speakers develop ineffective stereotyped speech personalities and speech intonation patterns as a result of meeting identical speech situations with monotonous frequency. Such stereotypes result partly from stereotyped attitudes and partly from the imitation of other speakers who already have a stereotyped speech pattern.

The type of role playing done by an actor differs from that done by a public speaker because the actor speaks directly to other actors in a fixed play situation. The actor's speech personality is identical to that of his stage character which is developed during an extended rehearsal period. The actor's influence upon the audience is not a personal and direct influence. It is aimed towards a complete understanding of and a full appreciation of the play as a whole.

Questions

1. Why is one's speech personality usually different from his general or everyday personality? When is it alike?
2. If a speech personality results from a kind of role playing, is it necessarily somehat artificial? Explain.
3. Why is an effective speech personality closely associated with leadership ability?
4. To what extent do you consider the speaker's physical appearance important in determining the speech personality?
5. Is the speaker's general grooming as important as his physical appearance in determining his speech personality?
6. In analyzing a speech situation what factors need consideration?
7. What aspects of speech behavior are most adjustable when adapting oneself to a speech situation?
8. What basic attitudes towards oneself are usually the most effective?

9. What basic attitudes towards the speech materials are usually most effective?

10. What basic attitudes towards the listeners are usually most effective?

11. Give examples of speech situations in which any of the basic attitudes need to be different from those usually recommended.

12. Can the speech personality be based upon pure pretense?

13. Does a speaker inevitably give an impression of his speech personality whenever he speaks?

14. What might account for a stereotyped pattern of speech?

15. How does the speech-personality problem of an actor differ from that of the public speaker?

EXERCISES

I—*Purpose:* To gain practice in making a variety of adjustments of one's speech personality.

Method: Practice delivering the following selections while attempting to give different impressions of your speech personality. Make out for each trial a personality check sheet (an example of which is given following the selections below) to indicate the exact impression you are attempting to give. Have a number of listeners fill out the same kind of check sheet after hearing you deliver a selection. Then compare your check sheet with those of your listeners to see how well you succeeded in giving the intended impression.

1. * But don't you see that the whole trouble lies here. In words, words. Each one of us has within him a whole world of things, each man of us his own special world. Then how can we ever come to an understanding if I put in the words I utter the sense and value of things as I see them: while you who listen to me must inevitably translate them according to the conception of things each one of you has within himself. We think we understand each other, but we never really do.

from *Six Characters in Search of an Author**
by Luigi Pirandello

2. Christ chose an image which was familiar when He said to His disciples, "Ye are the salt of the earth." This was His conception of their mission, their influence. They were to cleanse and sweeten the

* From SIX CHARACTERS IN SEARCH OF AN AUTHOR by Luigi Pirandello: Used by permission of E. P. Dutton and Company, Inc., and Dutton Everyman Paperbacks.

world in which they lived, to keep it from decay, to give a new and more wholesome flavor to human existence. Their function was not to be passive but active. The sphere of their action was to be this present life. There is no use in saving salt for heaven. It will not be needed there. Its mission is to permeate, season, and purify things on earth.

from "Salt"
by Henry Van Dyke

3. * A library may be very large; but if it is in disorder, it is not so useful as one that is small but well arranged. In the same way, a man may have a great mass of knowledge, but if he has not worked it up by thinking it over for himself, it has less value than a far smaller amount which he has thoroughly pondered. For it is only when a man looks at his knowledge from all sides, and combines the things he knows by comparing truth with truth, that he obtains a complete hold over it and gets it into his power. A man cannot turn over anything in his mind unless he knows it; he should, therefore, learn something; but it is only when he has turned it over that he can be said to know it.

from *The Art of Literature*
by Arthur Schopenhauer*

4. Liberty is not a social question. Civil liberty is not social equality. We are equal only in rights. No two persons are of equal weight or height. There are no two leaves in all the forests of the earth alike—no two blades of grass—no two grains of sand—no two hairs. No two anythings in the physical world are precisely alike. Neither mental nor physical equality can be created by law, but recognizes the fact that all men have been clothed with equal rights by Nature, the mother of us all.

by Robert Ingersoll

5. If to do were as easy as to know what were good to do, chapels had been churches and poor men's cottages princes' palaces. It is a good divine that follows his own instructions; I can easier teach twenty what were good to be done, than be one of the twenty to follow mine own teaching. The brain may devise laws for the blood, but a hot temper leaps o'er a cold decree; such a hare is madness the youth, to skip o'er the meshes of good counsel the cripple. But this reasoning is not in the fashion to choose me a husband. O me, the word choose! I may neither choose who I would nor refuse who I

dislike; so is the will of a living daughter curbed by the will of a dead father. Is it not hard, Nerissa, that I cannot choose one nor refuse none?

from *The Merchant of Venice*
by William Shakespeare

6. Arise, shine; for thy light is come, and the glory of the Lord is risen upon thee.

For, behold, the darkness shall cover the earth, and gross darkness the people: but the Lord shall arise upon thee, and His glory shall be seen upon thee.

And the Gentiles shall come to thy light, and kings to the brightness of thy rising.

Lift up thine eyes round about, and see: all they gather themselves together, they come to thee; thy sons shall come from far, and thy daughters shall be nursed at thy side.

Then thou shalt see, and flow together, and thine heart shall fear, and be enlarged; because the abundance of the sea shall be converted unto thee, the forces of the Gentiles shall come unto thee.

Isaiah LX

Speech Personality Check Sheet

A check mark placed anywhere along the line between opposite attitudes indicates the degree of attitude shown—the central point being neutral.

I—*Attitudes Towards Self:*

Self-confidence ______ . . . . . Indecisiveness
Pride ______ . . . . . Humbleness

II—*Attitudes Towards Speech Materials:*

Enthusiastic Interest ______ . . . . . Indifference
Eagerness to Communicate ______ . . . . . Flippancy or Carelessness

III—*Attitudes Towards the Listeners:*

Direct and Personal ______ . . . . . Indirect and Aloof
Friendly and Intimate ______ . . . . . Unfriendly and cold
Dominant over ______ . . . . . Submissive to
Approving ______ . . . . . Disgusted with or Critical of

Suggested Basic Attitudes for Practice (many of which are usually undesirable):

1. Timid and lacking self-confidence, and withdrawn from listeners —aloof
2. Overbearing and aggressive while showing no respect for listeners
3. Humble and apologetic, also highly respectful, towards the listeners
4. Enthusiastic and eager to communicate, also direct and friendly towards the listeners
5. Flippant and indifferent towards speech material and condescending towards the listeners
6. Ingratiating, as though addressed to an antagonistic audience which you respect
7. Firm and authoritative but not unfriendly towards the listeners
8. Egotistical and disgusted with the listeners, who are treated as fools
9. Self-confident but friendly towards audience and highly respectful towards speech material
10. At least five attitudes of your own choice.

11.

Developing Vocal Flexibilities

As indicated in Chapter 8, a speech intonation pattern results from tonal communication and consists of variations in the force, pitch, and quality of voice and in the timing of articulated speech. An effective speech intonation pattern is infinitely complex and can never be consciously or completely analyzed or controlled. Any speaker's intonation patterns must be composed spontaneously as the mind is occupied with the thoughts and feelings to be communicated. The exact form of the intonation pattern is determined by such factors as:

1. The speaker's established speech habits resulting from early imitation.
2. His speech personality resulting from adaptation to the speech situation.
3. The completeness and vividness of his perception of the thoughts and feelings to be communicated.
4. His ability to respond freely to his speech materials without being inhibited by fear or social anxiety.
5. His vocal flexibilities or the degree to which his voice is capable of expressing fully, by means of many and rapid variations, all the communicative impulses motivated by the speech material and speech situation.

In the present chapter, we are chiefly concerned with the development of vocal flexibilities. However, such flexibilities can be developed only as a result of practice or experience in the effective communication of a great variety of speech materials. To be of value as practice, the process of communicating such materials must be accompanied by vividness of perception and by free or uninhibited responses.

Force Variations and Control

The force or loudness of speech sounds or syllables is varied continually in any normal speech. The chief purpose of force variations is that of gaining the effect of accent and emphasis or subordination. Although force is only one of four types of emphasis, it is the most obvious type and the only type that is generally recognized as emphasis by the layman. In fact, the words "emphasis," "stress," "beat," and "accent" are commonly used interchangeably as though there were no real difference in their meanings.

As indicated previously, force emphasis results from contrast in loudness. Emphatic words and syllables (because only the accented syllables are emphasized in polysyllabic words) are uttered with increased loudness, force, or vigor of articulation, thus making them contrast with the weaker sounds of subordinate words and unaccented syllables. The speed of change is perhaps as important as the degree of contrast in determining the strength of force emphasis. The rapid changes of staccato or explosive speech gain a much stronger effect of emphasis than do the slower changes of an even slightly drawling speech. Therefore, we may say that the strength of force emphasis is determined both by the degree of contrast in loudness and by the speed of change.

Force emphasis or accent may be applied to syllables, words, phrases, or whole sentences, or even to paragraphs. In a polysyllabic word like "dictionary," for example, three degrees of stress are represented by the syllable receiving the primary accent, that receiving the secondary accent, and the two subordinate syllables that receive no accent. In any sentence the various words may receive any number of different degrees of force emphasis or subordination depending upon their various levels of significance or importance; or perhaps differences in levels of loudness might indicate relationships such as those of "echoes" or of contrasts. A whole phrase might be emphasized or subordinated by means of force or the lack of it, as, for example, when a speaker wishes to call attention to an important slogan, or when he wishes to indicate a parenthetical relationship. It is also quite common for a public speaker or interpreter to build up in loudness and emotional intensity a particularly important sentence or a whole section of a speech in order to gain the effect of a climax.

Motivation and Types of Force Emphasis

A person might say that force emphasis is the most dynamic type of emphasis because it indicates personal forcefulness or self-assurance on the part of the speaker. Anyone who uses force emphasis is motivated by some degree of self-assertiveness or by any of such associated traits or attitudes as anger, pride, arrogance, conceit, self-confidence, maturity, certainty, authority, or positiveness. The number of words emphasized by force and the strength of the force emphases used are usually directly proportional to the speaker's degree of aggressiveness and self-assurance. On the other hand, a speaker who avoids the use of force emphasis in his speech gives the impression of being meek, timid, immature, apathetic, unconcerned, uncertain, irresolute, or submissive because he seems to speak without positive self-assurance or he seems to lack an active interest in what he is saying.

Force emphasis may vary in type, depending upon the kind of speech sounds that receive the greatest degree of stress. Almost all syllables that may be emphasized are made up of two kinds of speech sounds—vowels and consonants. Force emphases may result from the vowel sounds of emphatic words or syllables being uttered with a relatively loud voice. This is the most common form of force emphasis. When used only moderately in terms of the number of words emphasized, and in strength of emphasis, this type gives the impression that the speaker is self-confident and somewhat authoritative. But if this type of emphasis is greatly increased both in amount and degree of strength, it suggests a domineering speaker who has given way to an overmastering emotion such as anger or scorn. In other words, the effect of much strong force emphasis on vowel sounds is that of bombastic speech resulting from unsuppressed, self-assertive emotions.

Another type of force emphasis results from increasing the vigor and precision of consonant utterance while holding down the loudness of vowel sounds. This type of force emphasis gives the impression of suppressed or pent-up emotions. The attitudes or emotions expressed are the same as those expressed by the vowel type of force emphasis, the difference being in the degree to which these attitudes or emotions seem to be suppressed or controlled. The strength of a pent-up aggressive emotion seems to be increased as the apparent effort that is required to suppress it is increased. Great strength of this type of emphasis is attained by holding down the loudness of the vowel tones on emphatic words and syllables to scarcely more than a tense whisper while the consonants are articulated with explosive violence. This type of emphasis, when used only in a weak or moderate degree, gives the impression of vitality and a crisp, decisive, and self-assured manner of speaking. In very strong degrees, however, it suggests violent but carefully controlled emotions of rage, hate, disgust, maliciousness, or repugnance.

The techniques of forceful delivery can best be developed by practice in the interpretation of materials requiring all kinds and degrees of various self-assertive emotions both suppressed and unsuppressed. A considerable amount of practice in vigorous articulation while under strong emotional stress may be necessary because many speakers tend to become relatively "tongue-tied" when they attempt to give vent to strong emotional feelings. Such practice in forceful speaking also involves good breath support and other factors governing the strength and basic quality of voice (discussed in Chapter 4) as well as clear articulation. Both the physical and emotional strength and vitality necessary for forceful speaking may be developed gradually as a result of regular and systematic exercises in forceful speaking.

Pitch Variety in Speech

In all normal speech the pitch of the voice is constantly changing. It changes in two ways. One way may be called a step change and the other a glide change or inflection. Any change in vocal pitch is dependent upon a change in vocal-cord adjustment. When the vocal-cord adjustment is changed during the "break" between syllables, the resulting pitch change is called a step because one syllable ends on one pitch and the following syllable begins on another, with a split second of silence or near silence separating the two. The glide or inflectional change, on the other hand, results from a change in vocal-cord adjustment made during the utterance of a syllable. Consequently, the voice is heard in the process of changing pitch so that a listener hears not just two pitches but every gradation of pitch as the vocal tone glides upward or downward.

The inflectional changes in pitch are the most subtle, the most complex, and the most frequently used in speech; and hence they are the most characteristic of conversational patterns of speech. Not a syllable is uttered, by way of normal conversation, that is not inflected in some way and some degree. The glide may be upward, or downward, or both in turn; but the change may be so rapid or so slight that the ear, although sensing some variation, cannot determine its exact nature. To eliminate these glide changes from one's speech by sustaining the same pitch on each syllable would instantly change the effect from that of speaking to that of chanting or singing.

Although any specific inflection in a speech pattern may contribute to the communication of a clearly understandable meaning or inference, that inflection by itself may be meaningless. It is the general pattern rather than individual inflections that is meaningful. However, one important generalization may be made concerning individual downward and upward inflections. Downward inflections tend to be strong and decisive while upward inflections seem weak and suggestive of incompleteness. A downward inflection or pitch glide always suggests completeness, finality, or certainty. Downward inflections, when used with strong force emphases, will contribute to the effect of positiveness, dominance, and aggressiveness, and hence they are often called strong inflections. Upward inflections, on the other hand, may be called weak because they suggest a lack of completeness, a questioning, or an uncertainty. When upward inflections are used in conjunction with a lack of force emphases, the suggestion is given of timidity, uncertainty, or of weak submissiveness.

Pitch emphasis, like force emphasis, results from contrast. Emphatic words, or syllables are uttered with high pitches that contrast with the lower pitches of subordinate words and syllables. The strength of a pitch emphasis is determined by the degree of pitch change and, to some extent, by the speed of change. Very strong pitch emphasis often causes the voice to "crack" or break into a falsetto quality.

Both step and glide changes of pitch and all types of inflections may be used for emphasis, although all pitch changes are not necessarily emphatic in nature. High pitches are made effective as emphasis only by contrast with low pitches; consequently, emphatic speech is usually highly varied in pitch, particularly if it is relaxed rather than tense.

Pitch Range, Key, and Optimum Pitch

The pitch range of a person's voice is a measure of the difference between the highest and the lowest pitches which he is capable of vocalizing. Such a difference may be measured in terms of the musical unit called an octave, which consists of eight full steps in pitch on the musical scale. Voices of different people may vary from a poor range of only about one octave to an excellent range of two and one-half octaves or higher. Ordinarily, a speaker who has an excellent pitch range will use only a fraction of it when speaking.

The key pitch of a person's voice is that pitch to which his voice returns most often when speaking. It is the basic pitch level from which the voice varies both upward and downward but to which it consistently returns. The key pitch is usually somewhat lower than the middle of the pitch range used in speaking because the vocal pitch varies upward from the key more often and to a greater degree than it varies downward.

The optimum pitch of a person's voice is that pitch at which his voice flows with maximum ease and resonance. If a person should start at the very bottom of his vocal pitch range and should sing the musical scales upward, he would find one pitch (usually somewhat below the middle of his range) at which his voice seems stronger and fuller in quality, although less effort seems to be required to vocalize that particular pitch than others. This is the optimum pitch at which an individual's voice operates at maximum efficiency.

Obviously, a person should usually key his speech at his optimum pitch level, in order that he might use his voice most efficiently and effectively. However, many people pitch their voices considerably above their optimum pitch levels while speaking. This tendency is especially common among women who speak with relatively thin basic qualities of voice. A high pitch key and thinness of quality usually go together, and are discussed as a vocal fault in Chapter 4. Nervousness, uncontrolled excitement, or any very tense emotional state plus a lack of self-control usually results in a relatively high key pitch of the voice; and any speaker, having a relatively weak voice, who attempts to speak loudly in a large hall or auditorium, almost invariably raises his key pitch to a high level. Although an interpreter will occasionally need to use a high key pitch for the purpose of characterization, a high key pitch is generally undesirable for two reasons. First, it suggests a kind of character weakness that is typified by a lack of self-control; and second, it results in a kind of high-pitch monotony since the key pitch is so close to the top of the vocal range that the voice cannot vary upward enough to give sufficient pitch variety.

Development of Pitch Variety and Control

Training for the most effective use of pitch variation in speaking may or may not involve the process of widening one's vocal pitch range. There is no fixed requirement in speech arts for a pitch range of any particular width. However, anyone having a vocal pitch range of less than one and one-half octaves should regard it as a serious limitation of his communicative potential for any kind of effective speaking before the public. An actor or oral interpreter might need a somewhat wider vocal pitch range than that which might seem adequate to a speaker who must express only his own thoughts and feelings in a manner governed by his own speech personality. An actor or interpreter should probably aim to build up his controllable pitch range to at least two to two and one-half octaves.

Exercises used for widening the pitch range of the singing voice should be equally as effective in widening the range of the speaking voice because, after all, it is the same voice. A student of vocal music sings up and down the width of his voice range during daily practice sessions, while striving for the same ease and resonance of vocalization at the extremities of his range as in the middle. When the muscular strain of forcing the voice to the upper and lower extremes of its range has been decreased by practice, the student can usually extend his range by adding a step lower or higher; then the new extended range is practiced in a never-ending attempt to decrease the strain of vocalization at the extremities of the range and to push out its limits.

One may learn to use and control subtle and meaningful pitch variations of wide range by practice and many varied experiences in communicating significant and imaginative materials that are relatively rich in implied meanings. The study of such materials should be aimed at:

1. Building up a vivid perception of every detail of all thoughts and feelings to be communicated, particularly those that are implied or suggested rather than only those that are clearly expressed verbally.
2. Stimulating within oneself a vital interest in all thoughts and feelings to be communicated and an eagerness to communicate them fully in every detail.
3. Freeing oneself from all inhibiting influences in order to respond easily to thoughts and feelings expressed without embarrassment or fear of seeming too demonstrative.
4. Adapting one's manner of speaking to the audience's capacity to understand.

The degree of the speaker's eagerness to communicate depends upon the degree of importance or significance of the speech materials and how difficult it might seem to get the listeners to understand fully all intended meanings. As the importance or significance of speech material increases, the speaker's motivation or enthusiasm increases and the vitality and animation in his manner of speaking increases; hence the pitch variation also increases. As speech material becomes more difficult to understand, or as the listener's apparent capacity for understanding decreases, the speaker (sensing an increased difficulty of communication) increases his effort to communicate and his variation of pitch automatically increases. When, for example, a speaker talks to very young children, he almost invariably uses a wider pitch range than he normally uses when speaking to adults.

The flexibility and control of pitch needed for expressive speech can be developed only through practice in the vocalization of expressive speech rather than by any calisthenic type of exercises. The degree of a person's expressiveness in speaking will grow gradually as a result of speaking experience which stresses the motivational factors mentioned above.

The Variety and Control of Voice Qualities

There are many words used to designate various voice qualities. A person may speak of thin, full, deep, shallow, orotund, pectoral, sepulchral, guttural, and aspirate qualities of voice. He may also use terms that are suggestive of the manner of producing various qualities as when he speaks of chest, throat, mouth, head, and nasal resonances. A few terms handed down to us by some of the more florid teachers of the old schools of elocution and oratory, and used now principally with satiric intent, liken voice qualities to shapes and colors, as, for example, a "round" or "pear-shaped tone" and a "greenish" or "lavender quality." Then there are hundreds of descriptive terms that are usually suggestive of the effect of voice qualities upon a listener. Examples of such terms include "gravel voice," "honeyed" or "dulcet tones," "harsh and rasping qualities."

All terms designating voice qualities, however, are vague and are used principally to refer to the general basic qualities that are characteristic of various speakers rather than to describe the numerous variations in the quality of voice used by one individual while speaking. As previously indicated, the basic or characteristic qualities of a person's voice are determined by both the physical structure of his vocal mechanism and his muscular habits of vocalization. These muscular habits of vocalization involve principally the routine adjustments of the resonating chambers and habitual muscular adjustments that affect vocal cord vibration. A person's basic quality of voice is not a fixed and unchanging quality; it is rather a basic similarity of various qualities that are all recognizable as characteristic of his voice.

The quality of any person's voice changes constantly while he is speaking because the muscles controlling the size and shape of his resonating chambers and the muscles around and in his vocal cords are alive and in constant movement. It would be impossible for a person to speak without changing his vocal quality. All vowel sounds, for example, differ in vocal quality. Each vowel is formed by a fairly definite modification of the mouth cavity by means of conventional adjustments made by the lips, jaw, and tongue muscles. These adjustments have been learned and are made automatically while speaking. Other adjustments, principally in the size of the throat cavity, are also made automatically for the purpose of matching each variation of pitch with a cavity change that will give each pitch an effective resonator. Changes of this kind result naturally in changes of voice quality, although such quality changes are merely incidental to pitch changes and have no communicative significance.

The one kind of quality change that is significant, and hence important to students of the speech arts, is the kind that is expressive of the emotional accompaniment of speech. Such changes help to communicate shifts in feeling or attitude on the part of the speaker. They add that characteristic of voice that is called a personal quality or warmth and color; and the speaker who lacks such variations of vocal quality gives the impression of being impersonal, cold, aloof, and unfeeling.

The Emotional Accompaniment of Speech

We often speak of intellectual and emotional behavior as though the two were different and independent functions of a human being. Actually, however, all human behavior that is consciously performed involves both intellectual activity and some kind and degree of emotion or feeling.

Speech is a kind of human behavior that is, for the most part, consciously motivated, and hence it involves both thought and feeling. Of course, a feeling of contentment or repose, or an attitude of casual indifference or boredom, may motivate a manner of speaking that seems unemotional in the sense that the speaker is neither upset nor excited. However, excitement is a relative term, and as long as a speaker is conscious he is subject to some degree of excitement. Being reposed is a feeling, and indifference is an attitude. Let us suppose, as an example, that a person, acting as a club treasurer, presents a routine report of a number of insignificant receipts and expenditures at a meeting of the club. Nothing in the nature of oral reading or speech could be less conducive to emotional communication; yet the person making such a report will inevitably assume certain attitudes that are determined by the situation and his speech personality, and these attitudes will be communicated by his manner of speaking or reading the report.

All that is needed to arouse a number of feelings and attitudes in any speaker is some degree of consciousness of a speech situation and of a speaker-listener relationship. And all such feelings and attitudes are expressed simultaneously by the manner of speaking—particularly by changes of voice quality. Of course, the emotional state of a speaker may be heightened in terms of increased awareness of situation, excitement, and physical tension; and when this happens, a greater number and degree of emotional feelings will be communicated by the vocal qualities.

Quality Emphasis

We usually think of speech emphasis as an oral device by means of which a single word in a phrase or sentence is given prominence. If a word or accented syllable is uttered with a sudden increase of force, a raised pitch, or a prolonged duration, the effect is always emphatic, and the degree of emphasis in each case depends, at least to some extent, upon the degree of change or contrast.

Emphasis by change of vocal quality, on the other hand, is different and relatively rare. All changes in voice quality do not accomplish an effect of emphasis. Only the vocal quality changes that reflect marked changes in emotional feeling result in emphatic effects; and it is the relative degree of change in emotional intensity rather than the degree of vocal change that determines the strength of quality emphasis. There is also a tendency for quality emphasis to be used not merely to give prominence to single words but also to strengthen any climax, consisting possibly of several sentences in a public speech, in an oral reading, or in the scene of a play. The building of a climax may be accomplished by a gradual mounting of emotional tension that is shown principally by change of voice quality.

To emphasize a single word by means of a change in voice quality will accomplish about the same function in speech that the ejaculation accomplishes in language. In fact, the reader may illustrate for himself the use of quality emphasis by speaking with appropriate feelings such ejaculatory words as "ouch," "bah," "alas," and "whoopee." The voice qualities that are expressive of the appropriate feelings will possess emphatic force because of the feelings expressed, not because of the vocal changes. Besides ejaculations, any words suggesting strong emotional feelings may be uttered with sudden changes of quality expressing those feelings and thus gaining the effect of emphasis. Even sounds that are not words at all, such as a derisive hoot, a dismayed cry, an agonized groan, a disgusted snort, or a choking sound of suppressed laughter may have strong emphatic values that are communicated principally by the voice qualities.

Because of our habitual social reserve, the intense feelings that would motivate strong quality emphases are usually inhibited. Our speech may reflect many mild attitudes, feelings, and impulses, as well as many well-controlled emotions, by means of vocal quality changes but with very little effect of emphasis because of the mildness of the feelings communicated. Any uninhibited manner of speaking with much quality emphasis usually seems overly theatrical, melodramatic, and insincere, except when such a manner of speaking is used for comic effect by means of burlesque or caricature.

Training for Quality Variations

All significant quality variations of the voice are expressive of some feelings, emotions, attitudes, impulses, or the like. No one can explain exactly how various voice qualities are made, nor could anyone produce a particular voice quality merely from a description of it, if he had such a description. A voice quality can only be produced as a part of a general response which is chiefly physical in nature and which is popularly known as an emotional response. Training for the development of flexibility and control of voice quality must, therefore, be the indirect and subjective process of learning to communicate various kinds and degrees of feelings and attitudes effectively. Practice must be guided by an imagination which should enable the learner to understand fully the stimulating situations, and by a physical or emotional responsiveness which will insure that a proper degree of excitement and tension is aroused by each situation. Any degree of emotion actually felt by an interpreter either while preparing or while communicating emotional material will depend upon his own degree of physical or emotional responsiveness. Some degree of physical or emotional responsiveness, however, is always essential to any control of vocal qualities.

Summary

An expressive intonation pattern is made up of variations in the force, pitch, and quality of voice, and in the timing of articulated speech. A speaker's ability to compose expressive intonation patterns depends upon his vocal flexibilities and upon his ability to motivate fully a great variety of speech materials that provide vocal experience of great variations in force, pitch, and quality.

Force variations are motivated principally by self-confident and self-assertive attitudes or feelings on the part of the speaker—the amount and strength of force emphases being directly proportional to the speaker's aggressiveness or dominance. Force emphasis varies also in type as either the vowels or consonants receive the greater degree of stress. The type of force emphasis used by a speaker depends upon his degree of self-control or repression—bombastic or unrepressed speech is characterized by loud vowel emphases, and strongly motivated but repressed speech is distinguished by explosive or vigorously articulated consonant sounds.

All normal speech is continually changing in pitch. Both step and glide changes serve to emphasize and subordinate words and syllables; and many other pitch variations are used by the speaker to reinforce and to modify, in a great variety of ways and degrees, his verbal expression.

The degree of pitch variation used in speaking is determined chiefly by the speaker's intellectual animation and degree of eagerness to communicate, and by the relative amount of meaning or content to be communicated and the apparent capacity of the listeners to understand.

The key pitch of a speaker's voice is the basic pitch which he uses most often in speaking; and his optimum pitch is that level at which his voice seems to flow most easily and most resonantly. His vocal pitch range is the measure of the difference between the highest and lowest pitches he can vocalize. A capable speaker usually keys his voice at his optimum pitch, and as occasion demands he should have within his control a vocal pitch range of approximately two octaves or more.

Vocal quality changes are chiefly expressive of emotions, attitudes or feelings, and they provide warmth, color, or a personal characteristic to one's speech. Although quality emphases that are applied to single words or sounds are relatively rare in daily speech because of our conventional social reserve in speaking, any type of public speech or interpretation usually calls for relatively more emotional expression by means of vocal quality variations.

Training for the development of flexibility and control of vocal quality variations is of an indirect nature involving chiefly practice in the communication of a great variety of kinds and degrees of emotional feelings and attitudes.

Questions

1. What are the two methods of applying force emphasis? Explain their variation in meaning.
2. When a polysyllabic word is strongly emphasized, how many syllables are usually given added stress?
3. Would you expect a parent to use more or less force emphasis than his son or daughter if they engage in an argument?
4. In a quarrel between a parent and child, who would be most likely usually to use force emphases applied to his vowels?
5. What factors determine the strength of force emphasis?
6. In what two ways does the pitch change in speech? Which is more common?
7. Would it be possible to record accurately a speech pitch pattern in musical symbols?
8. Contrast the general meanings conveyed by upward and downward inflection.

9. Define:
   a. Pitch range
   b. Key pitch
   c. Optimum pitch

10. How wide should a person's pitch range be for effective speech?

11. How might a person go about widening his pitch range?

12. How may a person go about developing a greater variety of pitch in speaking?

13. What determines the strength of a quality emphasis?

14. Is it possible to speak on a completely intellectual plane without communicating either emotion or attitude?

EXERCISES

I—*Purpose:* To practice the motivation and control of force emphases of both types and of various degrees of strength.

Method: Practice the following selections with varying degrees of force and repression. Try to determine the appropriate type of force emphasis and the degree of strength called for in each selection.

1. Avaunt! and quit my sight! Let the earth hide thee!
   Thy bones are marrowless, thy blood is cold!
   Thou hast no speculation in those eyes
   Which thou dost glare with!
   Hence, horrible shadow!
   Unreal mockery, hence!

from *Macbeth*
by William Shakespeare

2. The curse never fell upon our nation till now; I never felt it till now; two thousand ducats in that; and other precious, precious jewels. I would my daughter were dead at my foot, and the jewels in her ear! Would that she were hearsed at my foot, and the ducats in her coffin!

from *The Merchant of Venice*
by William Shakespeare

3. If I can catch him once upon the hip,
   I will feed fat the ancient grudge I bear him.
   He hates our sacred nation; and he rails,

Even there where merchants most do congregate,
On me, my bargains, and my well-won thrift,
Which he calls interest. Cursed be my tribe,
If I forgive him.

from *The Merchant of Venice*
by William Shakespeare

4. I'll tell thee: Life and death! I am ashamed
That thou hast power to shake my manhood thus;
That these hot tears, which break from me perforce,
Should make thee worth them. Blasts and fogs upon thee!
The untented woundings of a father's curse
Pierce every sense about thee!

from *King Lear*
by William Shakespeare

5. Villains, you did not so, when your vile daggers
Hack'd one another in the sides of Caesar.
You show'd your teeth like apes, and fawn'd like hounds,
And bow'd like bondmen, kissing Caesar's feet;
Whilst damned Casca like a cur, behind
Struck Caesar on the neck. O you flatterers!

from *Julius Caesar*
by William Shakespeare

6. Gentlemen may cry, "Peace, peace!" but there is no peace! The war is actually begun! The next gale that sweeps from the north will bring to our ears the clash of resounding arms! Our brethren are already in the field! Why stand we here idle? What is it that the gentlemen wish? What would they have? Is life so dear, or peace so sweet, as to be purchased at the price of chains and slavery? Forbid it, Almighty God! I know not what course others may take; but as for me, give me liberty, or give me death!

from *The War Inevitable*
by Patrick Henry

7. Out upon merry Christmas! What's Christmas time to you but a time for paying bills without money; a time for finding yourself a year older, and not an hour richer; a time for balancing your books, and having every item in 'em through a round dozen of months presented dead against you? If I had my will, every idiot who goes

about with "Merry Christmas" on his lips should be boiled with his own pudding, and buried with a stake of holly through his heart.

from *A Christmas Carol*
by Charles Dickens

8. In the name of the Commons of England, I charge all this villainy upon Warren Hastings, in this last moment of my application to you.

Therefore, it is with confidence that, ordered by the Commons of Great Britain, I impeach Warren Hastings of high crimes and misdemeanors.

I impeach him in the name of the Commons of Great Britain in Parliament assembled, whose parliamentary trust he has abused.

I impeach him in the name of the Commons of Great Britain whose national character he has dishonered.

I impeach him in the name of the people of India, whose laws, rights, and liberties he has subverted.

I impeach him in the name of the people of India, whose property he has destroyed, whose country he has laid waste and desolate.

I impeach him in the name of human nature itself, which he has cruelly outraged, injured, and oppressed, in both sexes. And I impeach him in the name and by the virtue of those eternal laws of justice, which ought equally to pervade every age, condition, rank, and situation, in the world.

from *Impeachment of Warren Hastings*
by Edmund Burke

9. Has the gentleman done? Has he completely done? He was unparliamentary from the beginning to the end of his speech. There was scarce a word he uttered that was not a violation of the privileges of the House. But I did not call him to order,—why? because the limited talents of some men render it impossible for them to be severe without being unparliamentary. But before I sit down, I shall show him how to be severe and parliamentary at the same time.

On any other occasion I should think myself justifiable in treating with silent contempt anything which might fall from that honorable member; but there are times when the insignificance of the accuser is lost in the magnitude of the accusation. I know the difficulty the honorable gentleman labored under when he attacked me, conscious that, on a comparative view of our characters, public and private, there is nothing he could say which would injure me. The public would not believe the charge. I despise the falsehood.

If such a charge were made by an honest man, I would answer it in the manner I shall do before I sit down. But I shall first reply to it when not made by an honest man.

The right honorable gentleman has called me "an unimpeached traitor." I ask why not "traitor," unqualified by any epithet? I will tell him: it was because he durst not. It was the act of a coward, who raises his arm to strike, but has not courage to give the blow. I will not call him villain, because it would be unparliamentary, and he is a privy counselor. I will not call him fool, because he happens to be chancellor of the exchequer. But I say, he is one who has abused the privilege of Parliament and the freedom of debate, by uttering language which, if spoken out of the House, I should answer only with a blow. I care not how high his situation, how low his character, how contemptible his speech; whether a privy counselor or a parasite, my answer would be a blow.

He has charged me with being connected with the rebels. The charge is utterly, totally, and meanly false. Does the honorable gentleman rely on the report of the House of Lords for the foundation of his assertion? If he does, I can prove to the committee there was a physical impossibility of that report being true. But I scorn to answer any man for my conduct, whether he be a political coxcomb, or whether he brought himself into power by a false glare of courage or not.

I have returned—not as the right honorable member has said, to raise another storm,—I have returned to discharge an honorable debt of gratitude to my country, that conferred a great reward for past services, which I am proud to say, was not greater than my desert. I have returned to protect that Constitution of which I was the parent and founder, from the assassination of such men as the right honorable gentleman and his unworthy associates. They are corrupt, they are seditious, and they, at this very moment, are in conspiracy against their country. I have returned to refute a libel, as false as it is malicious, given to the public under the appelation of a report of the committee of the Lords. Here I stand, ready for impeachment or trial. I dare accusation. I defy the honorable gentleman; I defy the government; I defy their whole phalanx; let them come forth. I tell the ministers, I will neither give quarter nor take it. I am here to lay the shattered remains of my constitution on the floor of this House, in defense of the liberties of my country.

from *Grattan's Reply to Mr. Cory*
by Henry Grattan

10. God's bread! it makes me mad. Day, night, late, early,
    At home, abroad, alone, in company,
    Waking or sleeping, still my care hath been
    To have her match'd; and having now provided
    A gentleman of princely parentage,
    Of fair demesnes, youthful, and nobly train'd,
    Stuff'd as they say, with honorable parts,
    Proportion'd as one's thought would wish a man—
    And then to have a wretched puling fool,
    A whining mammet, in her fortune's tender,
    To answer "I'll not wed, I cannot love;
    I am too young, I pray you pardon me!"
    But, an you will not wed, I'll pardon you.
    Graze where you will, you shall not house with me.
    Look to't, think on't; I do not use to jest.
    Thursday is near; lay hand on heart, advise:
    An you be mine, I'll give you to my friend;
    An you be not, hang, beg, starve, die in the streets,
    For, by my soul, I'll ne'er acknowledge thee,
    Nor what is mine shall never do thee good.
    Trust to't. Bethink you. I'll not be forsworn.

from *Romeo and Juliet*
by William Shakespeare

II—*Purpose:* To determine the pitch range of your voice and to find your optimum pitch.

Method: Starting at the lowest possible pitch, sing up the musical scale to your highest possible pitch. Also notice which pitch seems the easiest and most resonant.

III—*Purpose:* To develop a consciousness of the basic forms of inflections.

Method: Count from one to ten, uttering each number as indicated below:

1. With downward inflections—as though each number were definite, final, or certain.
2. With upward inflections—as though each number were a question or were tentative and uncertain.
3. With alternate downward and upward inflections.

4. With circumflex inflections—gliding up and then down.
5. With U-shaped inflections—gliding down and then up.
6. With alternate circumflex and U-shaped inflections.

IV—*Purpose:* To gain practice in speaking with maximum use of pitch variations

Method: Carefully prepare the following selections to be read in the manner indicated for each. In all cases work for an eagerness to communicate vividly every detail of literal and implied meaning.

1. Prepare the following four selections as though for an audience of small children. Work for enthusiasm and vividness, and do not worry about seeming too demonstrative or affected.

I have a little shadow that goes in and out with me,
And what can be the use of him is more than I can see.
He is very, very like me from the heels up to the head;
And I see him jump before me when I jump into my bed.

The funniest thing about him is the way he likes to grow—
Not at all like proper children, which is always very slow;
For he sometimes shoots up taller like an India-rubber ball,
And sometimes gets so little that there's none of him at all.

He hasn't got a notion of how children ought to play,
And can only make a fool of me in every sort of way.
He stays so close beside me, he's a coward you can see;
I'd think shame to stick to nursie as that shadow sticks to me!

One morning, very early, before the sun was up,
I rose and found the shining dew on every buttercup;
But my lazy little shadow, like an errant sleepyhead,
Had stayed at home behind me and was fast asleep in bed.

"My Shadow"
by Robert Louis Stevenson

2. He thought he saw a Buffalo
Upon the chimney piece;
He looked again, and found it was
His sister's Husband's Niece.
"Unless you leave this house," he said,
"I'll send for the Police!"

He thought he saw a Rattlesnake
That questioned him in Greek;
He looked again, and found it was
The Middle of Next Week.
"The one thing I regret," he said,
"Is that it cannot speak!"

He thought he saw a Banker's Clerk
Descending from the bus;
He looked again and found it was
A Hippopotamus.
"If this should stay to dine," he said,
"There won't be much for us!"

He thought he saw a Coach and Four
That stood beside his bed;
He looked again, and found it was
A Bear without a Head.
"Poor thing," he said, "poor silly thing!
It's waiting to be fed!"

He thought he saw an Albatross
That fluttered round the lamp;
He looked again, and found it was
A Penny Postage Stamp.
"You'd best be getting home," he said:
"The nights are very damp!"

He thought he saw a Garden Door
That opened with a key;
He looked again, and found it was
A Double Rule of Three.
"And all its mystery," He said,
"Is clear as day to me!"

"A Strange Wild Song"
by Lewis Carroll

3. In came a fiddler with a music-book, and went up to the lofty desk, and made an orchestra of it, tuned like fifty stomach-aches. In came Mrs. Fezziwig, one vast substantial smile. In came the three Miss Fezziwigs, beaming and lovable. In came the six young followers whose hearts they broke. In came all the young men and women employed in the business. In came the house maid, with her

cousin the baker. In came the cook, with her brother's particular friend the milkman. In they all came one after another; some shyly, some boldly, some gracefully, some awkwardly, some pushing, some pulling; in they all came, anyhow and everyhow. Away they all went, twenty couples at once; hands half round and back again the other way; down the middle and up again; round and round in various stages of affectionate grouping; old top couple always turning up in the wrong place; new top couple starting off again, as soon as they got there; all top couples at last, and not a bottom one to help them. When this result was brought about, old Fezziwig, clapping his hands to stop the dance, cried out, "Well done!" and the fiddler plunged his hot face into a pot of porter especially provided for that purpose.

from *A Christmas Carol*
by Charles Dickens

4. Read the following with alert and fanciful animation.

O, then I see Queen Mab hath been with you.
She is the fairies' midwife, and she comes
In shape no bigger than an agate stone
On the forefinger of an alderman,
Drawn with a team of little atomies
Athwart men's noses as they lie asleep;
Her wagon spokes made of long spinners' legs,
The cover, of the wings of grasshoppers;
Her traces, of the smallest spider's web;
Her collars, of the moonshine's wat'ry beams;
Her whip, of cricket's bone; the lash, of film;
Her wagoner, a small grey-coated gnat,
Not half so big as a round little worm
Prick'd from the lazy finger of a maid;
Her chariot is an empty hazelnut,
Made by the joiner squirrel or old grub,
Time out of mind the fairies' coachmakers.
And in this state she gallops night by night
Through lovers' brains, and then they dream of love;
O'er courtier's knees, that dream on curtsies straight;
O'er lawyers' fingers, who straight dream on fees; . . .
Sometimes she gallops o'er a courtier's nose,
And then dreams he of smelling out a suit; . . .
Sometimes she driveth o'er a soldier's neck,
And then dreams he of cutting foreign throats,

Of breaches, ambuscadoes, Spanish blades,
Of healths five fathom deep; and then anon
Drums in his ear, at which he starts and wakes,
And being thus frighted, swears a prayer or two
And sleeps again.

from *Romeo and Juliet*
by William Shakespeare

5. Read the following selection in a humble and ingratiating manner.

Most potent, grave, and reverend signiors,
My very noble and approv'd good masters,
That I have ta'en away this old man's daughter,
It is most true; true, I have married her:
The very head and front of my offending
Hath this extent, no more. Rude am I in my speech,
And little blest with the soft phrase of peace:
For since these arms of mine had seven years' pith,
Till now some nine moons wasted, they have us'd
Their dearest action in the tented field;
And little of this great world can I speak,
More than pertains to feats of broil and battle,
And therefore little shall I grace my cause
In speaking for myself. Yet, by your gracious patience,
I will a round unvarnish'd tale deliver
Of my whole course of love; what drugs, what charms,
What conjuration, and what mighty magic,—
For such proceedings I am charged withal,—
I won his daughter. . . .
Her father lov'd me, oft invited me,
Still question'd me the story of my life
From year to year,—the battles, sieges, fortunes,
That I have pass'd.
I ran it through, even from my boyish days
To the very moment that he bade me tell it;
Wherein I spake of most disastrous chances,
Of moving accidents by flood and field,
Of hair-breadth 'scapes i' the imminent deadly breach,
Of being taken by the insolent foe
And sold to slavery, of my redemption thence,
And portance in my travel's history;

Wherein of antres vast and deserts idle,
Rough quarries, rocks, and hills whose heads touch heaven,
It was my hint to speak,—such was the process:
And of the Cannibals that each other eat,
The Anthropophagi, and men whose heads
Do grow beneath their shoulders. This to hear
Would Desdemona seriously incline:
But still the house-affairs would draw her thence;
Which ever as she could with haste dispatch,
She'd come again, and with greedy ear
Devour up my discourse: which I observing,
Took once a pliant hour, and found good means
To draw from her a prayer of earnest heart
That I would all my pilgrimage dilate,
Whereof by parcels she had something heard,
But not intentively. I did consent,
And often did beguile her of her tears,
When I did speak of some distressful stroke
That my youth suffer'd. My story being done,
She gave me for my pains a world of sighs:
She swore, in faith, 'twas strange, 'twas passing strange;
'Twas pitiful, 'twas wondrous pitiful;
She wish'd she had not heard it, yet she wish'd
That heaven had made her such a man; she thank'd me,
And bade me, if I had a friend that loved her,
I should but teach him how to tell my story,
And that would woo her. Upon this hint I spake:
She lov'd me for the dangers I had pass'd,
And I loved her that she did pity them.
This only is the witchcraft I have used.
Here comes the lady; let her witness it.

from *Othello*
by William Shakespeare

6. Prepare to read the following selection with calculation, suspicion, and sarcasm.

You come to me, and you say,
"Shylock, we would have moneys:" you say so—
You, that did void your rheum upon my beard,
And foot me as you spurn a stranger cur
Over your threshold: moneys is your suit.

What should I say to you? Should I not say,
"Hath a dog money? Is it possible
A cur can lend three thousand ducats?" Or
Shall I bend low and in a bondman's key,
With bated breath and whispering humbleness,
Say this:
"Fair sir, you spat on me on Wednesday last;
You spurn'd me such a day; another time
You call'd me dog; and for these courtesies
I'll lend you thus much moneys?"

from *The Merchant of Venice*
by William Shakespeare

7. Prepare to read the following selection in a manner of relaxed intimacy but in a mood of pensive anxiety.

* I don't expect him to be like other people. I wouldn't want him to be. One of the things that makes him so much fun is that he's different. If he forgets an appointment it's because he's working and doesn't notice. Only I wish he had come tonight. I needed him so. Kaye, I'm frightened. For the first time, I'm frightened. It's three years now. The first year it didn't matter so much. I was so young. Nobody was ever so young as I was. I thought, they just don't know. But I'll get a good start and show them. I didn't mind anything in those days. Not having any money, or quite enough food; and a pair of silk stockings was always a major investment. I didn't mind because I felt so sure that that wonderful part was going to come along. But it hasn't. And suppose it doesn't come next year? Suppose it—never comes?

from *Stage Door**
by Edna Ferber and George S. Kaufman

8. Prepare to read the following selection—a speech of the famous Mrs. Malaprop—in an affected, gushing, or overly enthusiastic manner of the pretender of great social importance and culture.

Observe me, Sir Anthony—I would by no means wish a daughter of mine to be a progeny of learning; I don't think so much learning becomes a young woman—for instance—I would never let her meddle with Greek, or Hebrew, or Algebra, or Simony, or Fluxions

* From STAGE DOOR by Edna Ferber and George S. Kaufman, Copyright 1936, 1941, by Edna Ferber and George S. Kaufman. Used by permission of Edna Ferber and Dramatists Play Service.

or Paradoxes, or such inflammatory branches of learning; nor will it be necessary for her to handle any of your mathematical, astronomical, diabolical instruments; but, Sir Anthony, I would send her, at nine years old, to a boarding-school, in order to learn a little ingenuity and artifice. Then sir, she should have a supercilious knowledge in accounts; and, as she grew up, I would have her instructed in geometry, that she might know something of the contagious countries; above all, she should be taught orthodoxy. This, Sir Anthony, is what I would have a woman know; and I don't think there is a superstitious article in it.

from *The Rivals*
by Richard B. Sheridan

9. Prepare to read the following speech with great excitement and elation while being particularly careful to avoid keying the pitch so high that the result is a high-pitched monotony.

* Terry! Wake up! We're in the movies! Both of us! We're in the movies! They just heard from the Coast. . . . They liked the tests, and we're to go to the office tomorrow to sign our contracts. We leave for the Coast next week! Terry! Can you believe it! . . . Of course we'll only get little parts in the beginning. But there's that beautiful check every week, whether you work or not. And the swimming and the sunshine and those little ermine jackets up to here. No more running around to offices and having them spit in your eye. And a salary raise every six months if they like us. So at the end of three years it begins to get pretty good, and after five years it's wonderful, and at the end of seven years it's more money than you ever heard of.

from *Stage Door**
by Edna Ferber and George S. Kaufman

V—*Purpose:* To develop some consciousness and control of different basic vocal qualities.

Method: Prepare to read the following selections in the manners described:

a. As a pompous orator with a deep, booming, and sonorous quality.
b. As a "hick" character, with a high-keyed, nasal quality.
c. In a ghostly manner as though trying to scare your listeners.
d. As a sweet and very gentle old lady or gentleman.

e. As a sickly and complaining or whining person.
f. As a sour, vindictive person.
g. Attempting to disguise your voice so that no one can recognize it.
h. Attempting to imitate someone else who has a distinctive quality of voice.

1. Breathes there a man with soul so dead
Who never to himself hath said:
"This is my own, my native land"?
Whose heart hath ne'er within him burned
As home his footsteps he hath turned,
From wandering on a foreign strand?
If such there breathe, go mark him well;
For him no minstrel raptures swell;
High though his titles, proud his name,
Boundless his wealth as wish can claim,
Despite those titles, power and pelf,
The wretch concenter'd all in self,
Living shall forfeit fair renown,
And, doubly dying, shall go down
To the vile dust from whence he sprung,
Unwept, unhonored, and unsung.

from *The Lay of the Last Minstrel*
by Sir Walter Scott

2. Shakespeare exceeded all the sons of men in the splendor of his imagination. To him the whole world paid tribute, and Nature poured her treasures at his feet. In him all races lived again, and even those to be were pictured in his brain.

He was a man of imagination—that is to say, of genius, and having seen a leaf, and drop of water, he could construct the forests, the rivers and the seas. In his presence all the cataracts would fall and foam, the mists rise, the clouds form and float.

If Shakespeare knew one fact, he knew its kindred and its neighbors. Looking at a coat of mail, he instantly imagined the society, the conditions, that produced it and what it, in turn, produced. He saw the castle, the moat, the drawbridge, the lady in the tower, and the knightly lover spurring across the plain. He saw the bold baron and the rude retainer, the trampled serf, and all the glory and the grief of feudal life.

from *Shakespeare's Imagination*
by Robert G. Ingersoll

VI—*Purpose:* To gain experience in using a great variety of vocal qualities in expressing a variety of moods and feelings.

Method: Prepare to read the following selections seriously or in an exaggerated manner as the material seems to suggest.

1. The outlook wasn't brilliant for the Mudville nine that day;
The score stood two to four, with but an inning left to play.
So when Cooney died at second, and Burrows did the same,
A sickly silence fell upon the patrons of the game.

A straggling few got up to go, in deep despair the rest
Clung to the hope that springs eternal in the human breast,
For they thought, "If only Casey could but get a whack at that,
Ah, they'd put up even money now, with Casey at the bat."

But Flynn preceded Casey, as did also Jimmy Blake,
And the former was a no-good, and the latter was a fake,
So on that stricken multitude grim melancholy sat,
For there seemed but little chance of Casey's getting to the bat.

But Flynn let drive a "single," to the wonderment of all,
And the much despised Blakey "tore the cover off the ball."
And when the dust had lifted and they saw what had occurred,
There was Blakey safe at second, and Flynn a-hugging third.

Then from the gladdened multitude went up a joyous yell,
It rumbled in the valley, it rattled in the dell;
It struck upon the mountain tops, recoiled upon the flat;
For Casey, mighty Casey, was advancing to the bat.

There was ease in Casey's manner as he stepped into his place;
There was pride in Casey's bearing, and a smile on Casey's face.
And when responding to the cheers, he lightly doffed his hat,
No stranger in the crowd could doubt 'twas Casey at the bat.

And now the leather-covered sphere came hurtling through the air,
And Casey stood a-watching it in haughty grandeur there.
Close by the sturdy batsman the ball unheeded sped—
"That ain't my style," said Casey. "Strike one!" the umpire said.

Then from the benches, black with people, went up a muffled roar,
Like the beating of storm waves on a stern and distant shore;
"Kill him! Kill the umpire!" shouted someone on the stand.
And it's likely they'd have killed him had not Casey raised his hand.

With a smile of Christian charity great Casey's visage shone;
As he stilled the rising tumult and bade the game, "Go on;"
He signaled to the pitcher, once more the spheroid flew;
But Casey still ignored it, and the umpire said: "Strike two!"

"Fraud!" screamed the maddened thousands, an echo answered
"Fraud!"
But one scornful look from Casey, and the audience was awed;
They saw his face grow stern and cold, they saw his muscles strain,
And they knew that Casey wouldn't let that ball go by again.

The sneer is gone from Casey's lip, his teeth are clenched in hate,
He pounds with cruel violence his bat upon the plate;
And now the pitcher holds the ball, and now he lets it go,
And now the air is shattered by the force of Casey's blow.

Ah, somewhere in this favored land the sun is shining bright;
The band is playing somewhere, and somewhere hearts are light;
Somewhere men are laughing, and somewhere children shout,
But there is no joy in Mudville—mighty Casey has struck out.

"Casey at the Bat"
by Earnest L. Thayer

2. You might have said, dear me, there are a thousand things . . . varying the tone . . . For instance, . . . here you are: . . . Aggressive: "I monsieur, if I had such a nose, nothing would serve but I must cut it off!" Amicable: "It must be in your way while drinking; you ought to have a special beaker made!" Descriptive: "It is a crag! . . . a peak! . . . a promontory! A promontory, did I say? . . . It is a peninsula!" Inquisitive: "What may the office be of that oblong receptacle? Is it an inkhorn or a scissor-case?" Mincing: "Do you dote on birds, you have, fond as a father, been at pains to fit the little darlings with a roost?" Blunt: "Tell me, monsieur, you, when you smoke, is it possible you blow the vapor through your nose without a neighbor crying, 'The chimney is afire'?" Anxious: "Go with caution, I beseech, lest your head dragged over by that weight, should drag you over!" Tender: "Have a little sunshade made for it! It might get freckled!" Learned: "None but the beast, monsieur, mentioned by Aristophanes, the hipocamelelephantocamelos, can have borne beneath his forehead so much cartilage and bone!" Off-hand: "What, comrade, is that sort of peg in style? Capital to hang one's hat upon!" Emphatic: "No wind can hope, O lordly nose, to give the

whole of you a cold, but the Nor-Wester!" Dramatic: "It is the Red Sea when it bleeds!" Admiring: "What a sign for a perfumer's shop." Lyrical: "Art thou a Triton, and is that thy conch?" Simple: "A monument! When is admission free?" Deferent: "Suffer, monsieur, that I should pay you my respects: that is what I call possessing a house of your own!" Rustic: "Hi, boys! Call that a nose? Ye don't gull me! It's either a prize carrot or else a stunted gourd!" Military: "Level against the cavalry!" Practical: "Will you put it up for raffle? Indubitably, sir, it will be the feature of the game!" And finally in parody of weeping Pyramus: "Behold, behold the nose that traitorously destroyed the beauty of its master; and is blushing for the same!"—That, my dear sir, or something not unlike, is what you would have said to me, had you the smallest leaven of letters or of wit, but of wit, O most pitiable of objects made by God, you never had a rudiment, and of letters, you have just those that are needed to spell "Fool!"

from *Cyrano de Bergerac*
by Edmond Rostand

3. Grim and authoritative but also sympathetic

* Eddie, since the day you were hired here as a rookie, every pilot you've flown with has had to report on you. You've seen the forms we use. One line reads: "Reaction to emergencies." That line might just as well read "Nerve" or "Guts" or whatever you want to call it. Your reports are all excellent—except for that one line. There—on a lot of them—is a question mark. The boys weren't sure you had what it takes. When the time came for you to fly a mail run on your own, I knew we'd find out whether they were right or wrong. We did, last night. It cost us a twenty-five-thousand dollar airplane.—They've got your final check at the office.

from *Ceiling Zero**
by Frank Wead

4. With the pride and self-righteous rage of an opera star speaking to her father

You blame me for living out my life without asking you and the whole family for permission. And why should I not? Was I not without family? Did you not send me out into the world to earn my bread, and then disown me because the way I earned it was not to your taste? Whom did I harm? Against whom did I sin? Oh, if I had remained the daughter of the house, like Marie, who is nothing and does nothing without the sheltering roof of the home, who passes straight from the arms of her father into the arms of her husband; who receives from the family—life, thought, character, everything,—yes, then you would have been right. In such a one the slightest error would have ruined everything,—conscience, honor, self-respect. But I? Look at me. I was alone. I was as shelterless as a man knocked about in the the world, dependent upon the work of my own hands. If you give us the right to hunger—and I have hungered—why do you deny us the right to love, as we can find it, and to happiness, as we can understand it.

from *Magda*
by Hermann Sudermann

5. Planning with self-condemnation and disgust

Now I am alone.
O, what a rogue and peasant slave am I!
Is it not monstrous that this player here,
But in a fiction, in a dream of passion,
Could force his soul so to his own conceit
That from her working all his visage wan'd:
Tears in his eyes, distraction in 's aspect,
A broken voice, and the whole function suiting
With forms to his conceit? And all for nothing!
For Hecuba!
What's Hecuba to him or he to Hecuba,
That he should weep for her? What would he do,
Had he the motive and the cue for passion
That I have? He would drown the stage with tears
And cleave the general ear with horrid speech;
Make mad the guilty, and appall the free,
Confound the ignorant, and amaze, indeed,
The very faculties of eyes and ears.
Yet I,
A dull and muddy-mettled rascal, peak,
Like John-a-dreams, unpregnant of my cause,
And can say nothing; no, not for a king,
Upon whose property and most dear life
A damn'd defeat was made. Am I a coward?

Who calls me villain? Breaks my pate across?
Plucks off my beard and blows it in my face?
Tweaks me by the nose? gives me the lie i' the throat,
As deep as to the lungs? who does me this, ha?
'Swounds, I should take it: for it cannot be
But I am pigeon-liver'd, and lack gall
To make oppression bitter; or ere this
I should have fatted all the region kites
With this slave's offal: Bloody, bawdy villain!
O, Vengeance!
. . . . I have heard
That guilty creatures sitting at a play,
Have by the very cunning of the scene
Been struck as to the soul that presently
They have proclaim'd their malefactions;
For murder, though it have no tongue, will speak
With most miraculous organ. I'll have these players
Play something like the murder of my father
Before mine uncle: I'll observe his looks;
I'll tent him to the quick; if he but blench,
I know my course. The spirit that I have seen
May be the devil: and the devil hath power
To assume a pleasing shape; yea, and perhaps
Out of my weakness and my melancholy,—
As he is very potent with such spirits,—
Abuses me to damn me: I'll have grounds
More relative than this: the play's the thing
Wherein I'll catch the conscience of the king.

from *Hamlet*
by William Shakespeare

6. Showing reverence and the effusive love of a very young man

He jests at scars that never felt a wound.
But soft! what light through yonder window breaks?
It is the East, and Juliet is the sun!
Arise, fair sun, and kill the envious moon,
Who is already sick and pale with grief
That thou her maid art far more fair than she.
Be not her maid, since she is envious.
Her vestal livery is but sick and green

And none but fools do wear it. Cast it off.
It is my lady; O, it is my love!
O, that she knew she were!
She speaks, yet she says nothing: what of that?
Her eye discourses; I will answer it.
I am too bold; 'tis not to me she speaks.
Two of the fairest stars in all the heaven
Having some business, do entreat her eyes
To twinkle in their spheres till they return.
What if her eyes were there, they in her head?
The brightness of her cheek would shame those stars
As daylight doth a lamp; her eyes in heaven
Would through the airy region stream so bright
That birds would sing and think it were not night.
See, how she leans her cheek upon her hand!
O, that I were a glove upon that hand,
That I might touch that cheek!

from *Romeo and Juliet*
by William Shakespeare

7. A conflict of love and admiration with extreme jealous rage

It is the cause, it is the cause, my soul,—
Let me not name it to you, you chaste stars!—
It is the cause. Yet I'll not shed her blood,
Nor scar that whiter skin of hers than snow,
And smooth as monumental alabaster.
Yet she must die, else she'll betray more men.
Put out the light, and then—put out the light!
If I quench thee, thou flaming minister,
I can again thy former light restore,
Should I repent me; but once put out thy light!
Thou cunningest pattern of excelling nature,
I know not where is that Promethean heat
That can thy light relume. When I have pluck'd the rose,
I cannot give it vital growth again,
It must needs wither; I'll smell it on the tree.
Ah, balmy breath, that doth almost persuade
Justice to break her sword! One more, one more.
Be thus when thou art dead, and I will kill thee,
And love thee after. One more, and this the last;

So sweet was ne'er so fatal. I must weep,
But they are cruel tears: this sorrow's heavenly;
It strikes where it doth love. She wakes.

from *Othello*
by William Shakespeare

8. With reverence

The Lord is my shepherd; I shall not want.

He maketh me to lie down in green pastures; he leadeth me beside the still waters.

He restoreth my soul: he leadeth me in the paths of righteousness for his name's sake.

Yea, though I walk through the valley of the shadow of death,

I will fear no evil: for thou art with me; thy rod and thy staff they comfort me.

Thou preparest a table before me in the presence of mine enemies: thou anointest my head with oil; my cup runneth over.

Surely goodness and mercy shall follow me all the days of my life; and I will dwell in the house of the Lord for ever.

Psalm XXIII

9. With carefully controlled grief

The loved and the loving brother, husband, father, friend, died where manhood's morning almost touches noon and while the shadows still were falling toward the west.

He had not passed on life's highway the stone that marks the highest point, but being weary for a moment, lay down by the way-side, and using his burden for a pillow, fell into the dreamless sleep that kisses down his eyelids still, while yet in love with life and raptured with the world, he passed to silence and pathetic dust.

Yet after all, it may be best, just in the happiest, sunniest hour of all the voyage, while eager winds are kissing every sail, to dash against the unseen rock, and in an instant hear the billows roar above a sunken ship. For whether in mid-sea or 'mong the breakers of the farther shore, a wreck at last must mark the end of each and all. And every life, no matter if its every hour is rich with love and every moment jewelled with joy, will at its close become a tragedy as sad and deep and dark as can be woven of the warp and woof of mystery and death.

Life is a narrow vale between the cold and barren peaks of two eternities. We strive in vain to look beyond the heights. We cry aloud, and the only answer is the echo of our wailing cry. From the voiceless lips of the unreplying dead there comes no word; but in the night of death hope sees a star, and listening love can hear the rustle of a wing.

At His Brother's Grave
by Robert G. Ingersoll

12.

Time Variety, Tempo, and Rhythm

ALTHOUGH timing is always listed as one of the important speech variations, it is controlled by the articulators and does not depend upon any skill of vocalization. Consequently, skill in the timing of speech is not a matter of vocal flexibility.

As previously indicated, speech may be subdivided into speech sounds, syllables, words, phrases, and sentences; but when one considers the time pattern of speech, he is concerned primarily with the two elements that are called duration and pause. The length of time taken for the utterance of any one syllable is a duration, and the interruption between syllables (which may be also between words, phrases, or sentences) is a pause, even though it may be no more than a slight break in sound continuity rather than an actually discernible period of silence. Variations in the lengths of durations and pauses are referred to as variety of time in speech. As an example of such variety, notice the various lengths of syllable durations and the pauses that separate them when uttering rapidly the words "a re p-u-b li can" and "a d-e-m o c-r-a-t." Although it is very difficult to judge with any degree of accuracy the relative lengths of duration and pauses in rapid speech, the lines under each syllable and the spaces between these lines may illustrate at least a gross approximation of the relative lengths of durations and pauses respectively that a typical American speaker might use in speaking these words. The two accented syllables "pub" and "dem" and the final syllable "crat" have the longest durations. Accented syllables are always prolonged to some extent, but the syllable "crat" is prolonged merely as a matter of convention. Even in reversed order—"a democrat and a republican"—"crat" is still prolonged. Any slight differences in the lengths of other durations probably result from the speaker's natural rhythm of articulation or his state of mind at the moment of utterance and hence would have no apparent communicative value. The pause after the word "republican" tends to be lengthened because there is at least a potential phrase division at that point. There is also some sense of contrast between the meanings of "republican" and "democrat" that may be pointed up by such a prolonged pause. Any difference in the lengths of other pauses probably result from the speaker's natural rhythm of talking or his state of mind.

Any impulsive or spontaneous speaking will result in great variety of timing, which means greatly varied lengths of both durations and pauses. At times a speaker may speak very slowly because he is hampered by laborious thought or the careful choice of each word; at other times the words may seem to tumble over each other as the speaker's mind conceives whole phrases rapidly or as he utters only stereotyped thoughts and phrases very easily. The lengths of durations are varied chiefly for emphasis and subordination or as a matter of conventional habits of articulation. The lengths of pauses, on the other hand, are varied for the sake of dividing or showing contrast as well as for emphasizing.

Syllables are divided from each other by pauses or slight breaks in sound continuity that are usually of barely discernible length. Words are separated from each other by similar breaks in sound continuity that—unless lengthened for the sake of emphasis or sense contrast—are seldom any longer than the breaks between syllables. This running together of words without discernible pauses is what makes it so difficult for a language student to understand rapid speech in a foreign language even after he is able to read that language quite easily. Phrases are separated from each other by pauses that are distinctly longer than the breaks between syllables and words, and these pauses are often further prolonged to show sense contrasts or thought transitions. The pauses separating sentences are usually no longer than those between phrases, although prolonged pauses to show contrasts or thought transitions probably occur more often between sentences than between phrases.

Time Emphasis

Time emphasis depends upon contrasts in the lengths of durations and pauses. A word—or the accented syllable of a word—may be given prominence by prolonging its duration so that it contrasts with the shorter durations of subordinate words and syllables. A similar effect of emphasis may be obtained by lengthening the pause before or after, or both before and after, an important word or its phrase while other pauses are, by contrast, very short. The lengthened duration of a word or its accented syllable may serve only as emphasis; but a lengthened pause may serve to emphasize a word, a phrase, or an especially significant sentence, or it might indicate a transition, a contrast, or natural sense division.

The two types of time emphasis may be combined to strengthen the emphatic effect; and either or both may be combined with force, pitch, or quality emphasis for an addition of effect. To obtain the maximum strength of time emphasis upon a word, a speaker should increase the length of pause before the word (or before the phrase in which the word is located); then he should utter the word with a prolonged duration (or a prolonged accented syllable), and finally he should pause again after the word (or its phrase).

No one can say just how long a certain duration or pause should be in order to gain the maximum strength of emphasis. Within certain limits, the effect of emphasis is increased as the degree of time contrast is increased, but to prolong a duration or pause too much would accomplish nothing but to break the thought continuity and thus destroy the effect of emphasis. A speaker must depend upon a sort of intuitive feeling for rhythm that will enable him to use the proper degree of time contrast for the maximum effect of emphasis. This intuitive feeling is commonly called a sense of timing and is discussed later under the heading of "Speech Rhythm."

Speech Tempo

The tempo of speech means simply the speed of talking. Of course, the speed at which a person utters individual words varies greatly. Some subordinate words may be uttered as much as twenty times as fast as some emphatic words. But tempo does not refer to the speed of uttering single words; it denotes rather the over-all speed of uttering many words of varying lengths and of every degree of emphasis and subordination. Tempo is measured in terms of the number of words spoken per minute.

One individual may speak at different tempos when motivated by different moods or because of different degrees of familiarity with the subject under discussion. However, each person has what might be called his normal tempo of speaking or his most usual rate of talking. Different individuals have normal rates of talking that vary from an extremely slow tempo of about one hundred words per minute to a very rapid tempo of perhaps as many as three hundred words per minute.

There is no ideal tempo of speaking that is clearly superior to all others. However, a student of speech arts should attempt to avoid both extremely fast and the extremely slow tempos as his normal rate of talking. An extremely slow tempo may be well adapted to the speaker because of slow and cautious habits of thinking, but it is not well adapted to the average listener. The listener tends either to lose interest in speech of extremely slow tempo and stop listening, or he will listen and be annoyed because he continually anticipates what will be said before the speaker gets around to saying it. An extremely fast tempo, on the other hand, gives the impression of superficial and shallow chatter because it lacks the thought-inspired emphases of prolonged pauses and durations.

Speech Rhythm

Rhythm refers to a regularity of pattern. In all rhythm some element or fragment of pattern is repeated at fairly regular intervals— the intervals being in terms of either time or space. The beat of a tom-tom, for example, illustrates a simple and monotonous rhythm because the sound of a drum beat is repeated at regular intervals. The lines of print on this page also illustrate a simple rhythm because they are very similar in appearance, they are parallel, and they recur at equal space intervals.

Because of our familiarity with such simple and strong rhythms as those of marching bands, dance orchestras, and verse meters, we tend to think of all rhythms as the regular recurrence of some kind of beat or force accent. However, a rhythm may result from any kind of recognizable recurrence. Speech rhythm, for example, consists of the repetition at fairly regular intervals of any element or fragment of speech pattern which may be made up of force or accent, pitch or inflection, duration or pause, voice quality, or any patterned combination of any of these attributes.

Actually, speech rhythms are too subtle and too complicated for accurate perception and analysis. However, all speech is rhythmic, and all normal listeners are very sensitive to speech rhythms. They may sense speech rhythm as a quality of speech that seems characteristic of the speaker and expressive of his moods or attitudes. They do not actually recognize speech rhythms as such, for they are not consciously aware of all the recurring similarities in speech. They sense the rhythmic effect just as they might sense the meanings of words without noticing how each word is articulated.

Speech rhythms may be either pleasant or unpleasant to a listener. A smooth, easy rhythm, resulting not from any conscious control but from a well-integrated and spontaneous impulse to communicate certain vividly conceived thoughts and feelings that are expressed fluently and easily, will usually be very pleasant. On the other hand, a rough rhythm of unexpected and jarring irregularities caused by a poorly integrated or confused and disorganized state of mind, may be very unpleasant. The listener is in a position similar to that of the female member of a couple on a dance floor who is expected to follow the lead of her dancing partner. Both the listener and the dancer find a smooth and patterned lead is easier and pleasanter to follow than is a lead that is irregular, unpredictable, and labored.

Besides giving to the sound of speech a degree of pleasantness or unpleasantness, speech rhythm has a communicative function. The rhythm of speaking may be adjusted in terms of the time needed by the listener for clear perception and a maximum degree of comprehension. How well a speaker is able to make this rhythmic adjustment to his listeners depends upon the quality of his sense of timing. Such a sense is presumed by many people to be an innate capacity that a speaker or interpreter possesses in some degree as a gift of nature and which can be improved very little, if at all, by training or practice. Perhaps a sense of timing only seems to be innate because any conscious or objective effort to time one's speech effectively always results in poor timing and because no method of improving one's sense of timing by direct study or practice has ever been devised.

A sense of timing seems to depend upon the speaker's awareness of the degree of effort that is involved in the listeners' attempt to hear and understand the full significance of what he says. The speaker breaks up his speech into phrase units that seem easy enough but not too easy for the listeners to understand; he gives to each phrase, or its key word, just the right degree of time emphasis; and he pauses just long enough between phrases or sentences to permit the listener to grasp fully the significance of what has preceded or to show contrast or transitional relationship with that which follows. This regulation of the size of phrase units and timing exactly the lengths of durations and pauses to permit maximum ease of perception and understanding is not something that the speaker does consciously. It is not something that can be calculated or reasoned out logically. It must depend upon a feeling for the rhythmic thought process involved in comprehension.

Improvement of Timing, Tempo, and Rhythm

The effective use of time variety in speaking—being at least partly dependent upon the speaker's sense of timing—is the most difficult of all speech varieties to develop. Although the control of the timing of speech requires less by way of vocal flexibility or muscular skill than does the control of pitch, force, or quality, the effective timing of speech is more dependent than any other variety upon the degree of the speaker's spontaneity or upon a state of mind that will promote a free and impulsive flow of speech guided by a sense of the relative difficulty of communicating the full meaning of each word or phrase that is spoken.

To develop a high degree of spontaneity, and perhaps improve indirectly one's sense of timing, is a fundamental objective of any student of speech arts. Any spontaneous speaking, although it may have been carefully prepared and rehearsed, gives the impression of freshness or newness, as though the thoughts and feelings being communicated had just occurred to the speaker for the first time at the moment of utterance. The spontaneity of anyone's speech will depend upon the following essential conditions:

1. *A degree of mental concentration.* The mind should be occupied with the thoughts and feelings being expressed—not with the manner of expressing them or anything else. Any time that the mouth speaks one thing while the mind is thinking something else, the manner of speaking is likely to be mechanical and unexpressive, or expressive of something other than the ideas and feelings expressed verbally.

2. *A vivid awareness of the listener and the response desired from the listener.* An active desire to communicate specific ideas and feelings in order to stimulate specific responses in the listener is the strongest motivational factor leading towards the true spontaneity and effective timing of speech; yet this factor is perhaps the one most generally neglected by speakers and interpreters alike. They fail to follow through the entire process of communication because they concentrate too much of their attention upon the process of delivery, so that they are no more than only vaguely aware of their listeners' process of reception and reaction.

3. *Intellectual and emotional ease.* Any degree of mental labor accompanying speech will decrease the spontaneity of speaking. The intellectual effort involved in recalling thoughts and feelings and in translating them into well-organized and effective language tends to reduce the time variation in speaking and hence the spontaneity of speech. Even a speaker who speaks extempore must possess a high degree of glibness or verbal fluency in order to attain a high degree of spontaneity. The extemporaneous speaker, interpreter, or actor, on the other hand, must acquire a measure of intellectual ease through the study and thorough assimilation of the material to be communicated.

Emotional ease is closely associated with intellectual ease, but it is by no means identical. Emotional ease means freedom from any type of anxiety such as stage fright, self-consciousness, or a feeling of being poorly prepared or poorly qualified to speak before the particular audience. Such anxieties tend to make a speaker overly careful, with the result that he speaks in a measured or cautious manner with monotonous timing. Anxieties may be eliminated or greatly reduced by further preparation and practice.

4. *Freedom from any fixed habit of timing.* It is very easy to form unconsciously a fixed habit of timing speech delivery while studying the speech material. As a person starts to study any material for oral delivery (either ideas to be communicated extemporaneously or lines to be interpreted) his first oral expression will tend to be slow in tempo with a deliberate and monotonous timing that is characteristic of consciously self-critical oral composition or of careful sight reading. This first oral rendition and subsequent repetitions are entirely lacking in spontaneity or any sense of actually communicating ideas and feelings. One does not usually realize that the very act of repeating the materials over and over again in a deliberative and monotonous time pattern can result in his unconsciously learning that time pattern, so that by the time he has fully assimilated the speech materials he will have acquired a dull, unvaried rhythm as a habit which is very hard to eliminate.

As stated earlier, there is no ideal tempo which everybody should attempt to adopt as his natural tempo of speaking. Occasionally, a person may wish to speed up or slow down his natural tempo to avoid one extreme or the other. For any impromptu or extemporaneous speaker, such a process is extremely difficult because speech tempo is based upon deep-seated habits of thought. A speaker cannot speak faster than his mind will supply ideas and words to express them, and he might find it nearly as difficult to speak more slowly than his supply of ideas and words come to him. An interpreter or actor, however, may change his tempo of speaking prepared lines if he makes a definite and continued effort to do so during a rehearsal period. An extemporaneous speaker might benefit from similar drill periods, first by developing a desirable tempo while reading, or delivering memorized materials, then by attempting to develop the same tempo while practicing the delivery of extemporaneous materials. Such drills in tempo should be supplemented by vocabulary drills aimed at improving general fluency.

Rhythm of speech may be improved by any kind of practice that will improve ease, relaxation, and fluency. Any stumbling over unfamiliar pronunciations or difficult articulations, and any starting and abandoning of sentences because of failure to recall the words with which to finish them, will be very damaging to speech rhythm. Smooth, pleasant rhythms of speaking result from the perfect integration of the whole speaker—body, mind, and voice—operating easily and efficiently. A smooth rhythm of speaking is the trademark of a polished or skillful speaker.

Summary

The timing of speech is determined by the relative lengths of syllable durations and the lengths of pauses (or breaks in sound continuity) between syllables, words, and phrases. Variations in the length of syllable or word durations are used chiefly for the purpose of indicating relative emphasis or subordination, while the variations in lengths of pauses may be used for emphasis or to indicate thought divisions or transitions.

Effective timing of speech depends upon the degree of the speaker's spontaneity when speaking and upon his sense of timing, which seems to be an innate sense of rhythm which permits the speaker to time his speech in terms of the listeners' ability to comprehend the speech material presented.

Speech rhythm consists of the repetition at regular time intervals of similarities in force, pitch, timing, or quality or patterned combinations of any or several of these attributes. Speech rhythm is too subtle to be consciously controlled by a speaker or accurately analyzed by a listener. However, all speech is rhythmic, and the rhythm of speech is sensed by the listener as characteristic of the speaker and expressive of his moods and attitudes. A smooth and varied speech rhythm is pleasant and it contributes to the communicative power of speech.

Any attempt to improve the timing of speech must be aimed at the development of spontaneity and the urge to communicate. This may be accomplished by the development of a high degree of mental concentration upon the thoughts and feelings to be communicated, a vivid awareness of the desire to communicate, an intellectual ease and a freedom from anxiety, and a special effort to avoid the formation of habits of artificial timing in the process of studying material for oral delivery.

Questions

1. Define a syllable, a phrase, a pause, and a duration.
2. How may a word of more than one syllable be given a time emphasis?
3. What might be the purpose of prolonging a duration?
4. What might be the purpose of prolonging a pause?
5. What is meant by a speech tempo and how is it measured?
6. What is the approximate range of the natural tempos of different speakers?
7. Is it difficult or easy to change one's natural tempo of speaking extemporaneously?
8. Define rhythm and explain the nature of a speech rhythm.
9. Could you analyze in detail the speech rhythm of anyone's speech?
10. What makes a speech rhythm either pleasant or unpleasant?

11. What is meant by a speaker's sense of timing?

12. Is it possible to improve one's sense of timing through study or practice?

13. What conditions are essential to a high degree of spontaneity?

14. How may one improve his concentration and intellectual ease while communicating prepared materials?

15. How may a person avoid the formation of bad timing habits while studying materials to be communicated orally?

EXERCISES

I—*Purpose:* To develop an awareness of time patterns in normal speech.

Method: Attempt to analyze the time patterns of the following words, phrases, and lines, and illustrate the relative lengths of durations and pauses by means of lines and spaces.

1. information
2. imagination
3. intellectually
4. particularly
5. similarity
6. Pay no attention to them.
7. You can't take it with you.
8. which is not shown to be questionable
9. many centuries ago
10. with malice of forethought

11. The day is cold, and dark, and dreary;
It rains, and the wind is never weary;

12. Fourscore and seven years ago our fathers brought forth upon this continent a new nation, conceived in liberty, and dedicated to the proposition that all men are created equal.

II—*Purpose:* To develop conversational time patterns of completely spontaneous speech.

Method: Prepare the following selections for the greatest spontaneity possible.

1. Dora had a discreet friend, comparatively stricken in years, almost the ripe age of twenty, I should say, whose name was Miss Mills! Dora called her Julia. She was the bosom friend of Dora. Happy Miss Mills.

One day Miss Mills said: "Dora is coming to stay with me. She is coming the day after tomorrow. If you would like to call, I am sure papa would be happy to see you."

I passed three days in a luxury of wretchedness. At last arrayed for the purpose at a vast expense, I went to Miss Mills, fraught with a declaration. Mr. Mills was not at home. I didn't expect he would be. Nobody wanted him. Miss Mills was at home. Miss Mills would be.

I was shown into a room upstairs, where Miss Mills and Dora were. Dora's little dog Jip was there. Miss Mills was copying music, and Dora was painting flowers. What were my feelings when I recognized flowers I had given her!

Miss Mills was very glad to see me, and very sorry her papa was not at home, though I thought we all bore that with fortitude. Miss Mills was conversational for a few minutes, and then laying down her pen, got up and left the room.

I began to think I would put it off till tomorrow.

"I hope your poor horse was not tired when he got home at night from the picnic," said Dora, lifting up her beautiful eyes. "It was a long way for him."

I began to think I would do it today.

"It was a long way for him, for he had nothing to uphold him on his journey."

"Wasn't he fed, poor thing?" asked Dora.

I began to think I would put it off till tomorrow.

"Ye—yes, he was well taken care of. I mean he had not the unutterable happiness that I had in being so near to you."

I saw now that I was in for it, and it must be done on the spot.

"I don't know why you should care for being near me," said Dora, "or why you should call it a happiness. But, of course, you don't mean what you say. Jip, you naughty boy, come here!"

I don't know how I did it, but I did it in a moment.

I intercepted Jip. I had Dora in my arms. I was full of eloquence. I never stopped for a word.

from *David Copperfield*
by Charles Dickens

2. These were the honest days, in which every woman staid at home, read the Bible, and wore pockets—ay, and that too of a goodly size, fashioned with patchwork into many curious devices, and ostentatiously worn on the outside. These, in fact, were convenient receptacles, where all good housewives carefully stowed away such things as they wished to have at hand; by which means they often came to be incredibly crammed—and I remember there was a story current when I was a boy, that the lady of Wouter Van Twiller once had occasion to empty her right pocket in search of a wooden ladle, and the utensil was discovered lying among some rubbish in one

corner—but we must not give too much faith to all these stories; the anecdotes of these remote periods being very subject to exaggeration.

from *Knickerbocker's History of New York*
by Washington Irving

3. All the world's a stage,
And all the men and women merely players:
They have their exits and their entrances;
And one man in his time plays many parts,
His acts being seven ages. At first the infant,
Mewling and puking in the nurse's arms.
Then the whining school boy, with his satchel
And shining morning face, creeping like snail
Unwillingly to school. And then the lover,
Sighing like furnace, with a woeful ballad
Made to his mistress' eyebrow. Then a soldier,
Full of strange oaths, and bearded like the pard,
Jealous in honour, sudden and quick in quarrel,
Seeking the bubble reputation
Even in the canon's mouth. And then the justice,
In fair round belly with good capon lin'd,
With eyes severe and beard of formal cut,
Full of wise saws and modern instances;
And so he plays his part. The sixth age shifts
Into the lean and slipper'd pantaloon,
With spectacles on nose and pouch on side,
His youthful hose, well sav'd, a world too wide
For his shrunk shank; and this big manly voice,
Turning again toward childish treble, pipes
And whistles in his sound. Last scene of all,
That ends this strange eventful history,
Is second childishness and mere oblivion,
Sans teeth, sans eyes, sans taste, sans everything.

from *As You Like It*
by William Shakespeare

4. My friends: No one not in my situation can appreciate my feeling of sadness at this parting. To this place, and the kindness of these people, I owe everything. Here I have lived a quarter of a century, and have passed from a young to an old man. Here my children have been born, and one is buried. I now leave, not knowing

when or whether ever I may return, with a task before me greater than that which rested upon Washington. Without the assistance of that Divine Being who ever attended him, I cannot succeed. With that assistance, I cannot fail. Trusting in Him who can go with me, and remain with you, and be everywhere for good, let us confidently hope that all will yet be well. To His care commending you, as I hope in your prayers you will commend me, I bid you an affectionate farewell.

Farewell to Springfield
by Abraham Lincoln

5. I confess, standing here in this responsible situation, I do not understand this much-used and much-abused phrase—the "material age." I cannot comprehend—if anybody can I very much doubt—its logical signification. For instance, has electricity become more material in the mind of any sane or moderately insane man, woman, or child, because of the discovery that in the good providence of God it could be made available for the service and use of man to an immeasurably greater extent than for his destruction? Do I make a more material journey to the bedside of my dying parent or my dying child when I travel there at the rate of sixty miles an hour, than when I went thither at the rate of six? Rather in the swiftest case, does not my agonized heart become over-fraught with gratitude to that Supreme Beneficence from whom alone could have proceeded the wonderful means of shortening my suspense.

What is the materiality of the cable or the wire compared with the materiality of the spark? What is the materiality of certain chemical substances that we can weigh or measure, imprison or release, compared with the materiality of their appointed affinities and repulsion present in them from the instant of their creation to the day of judgment? When did this so-called material age begin? With the use of clothing; with the discovery of the compass; with the invention of the art of printing? Surely it has been a long time about. And which is the more material object—the farthing tallow candle that will not give me light, or the flame of gas which will?

No, ladies and gentlemen, do not let us be discouraged or deceived by any fine, vapid, empty words. The true material age is the stupid Chinese age, in which no new or grand revelations of nature are granted, because they are ignorantly and insolently repelled, instead of being diligently and humbly sought.

The Present Age
by Charles Dickens

6. And he said, A certain man had two sons; and the younger of them said to his father, Father, give me the portion of goods that falleth to me. And he divided unto them his living. And not many days after, the younger son gathered all together, and took his journey into a far country, and there wasted his substance with riotous living. And when he had spent all, there arose a mighty famine in that land; and he began to be in want.

And he went and joined himself to a citizen of that country; and he sent him into his field to feed swine. And he would fain have filled his belly with the husks that the swine did eat; and no man gave unto him. And when he came to himself, he said, How many hired servants of my father's have bread enough and to spare, and I perish with hunger! I will arise and go to my father, and will say unto him, Father, I have sinned against heaven, and before thee, and am no more worthy to be called thy son: make me as one of thy hired servants.

And he arose, and came to his father. But when he was yet a great way off, his father saw him, and had compassion, and ran, and fell on his neck, and kissed him. And the son said unto him, Father, I have sinned against heaven, and in thy sight, and am no more worthy to be called thy son. But the father said to his servants, Bring forth the best robe, and put it on him; and put a ring on his hand, and shoes on his feet; and bring hither the fatted calf and kill it; and let us eat and be merry: for this my son was dead, and is alive again; he was lost, and is found. And they began to be merry.

Now his elder son was in the field: and as he came and drew nigh to the house, he heard music and dancing. And he called one of the servants, and asked what these things meant. And he said unto him, Thy brother is come; and thy father hath killed the fatted calf, because he hath received him safe and sound. And he was angry, and would not go in: therefore came his father out, and entreated him.

And he, answering, said to his father, Lo, these many years do I serve thee, neither transgressed I at any time thy commandment; and yet thou never gavest me a kid, that I might make merry with my friends; but as soon as this thy son was come which hath devoured thy living with harlots, thou hast killed for him the fatted calf. And he said unto him, Son, thou art ever with me, and all that I have is thine. It was meet that we should make merry, and be glad: for this thy brother was dead, and is alive again; and was lost and is found.

St. Luke, XV

7. "The Babies—As they comfort us in our sorrows,
   let us not forget them in our festivities."

I like that. We have not all had the good fortune to be ladies. We have not all been generals, or poets or statesmen; but when the toast works down to the babies, we stand on common ground. It is a shame that for a thousand years the world's banquets have utterly ignored the baby, as if he didn't amount to anything. If you will stop and think a minute—if you will go back fifty or one hundred years to your early married life and recontemplate your first baby—you will remember that he amounted to a good deal, and even something over. You soldiers all know that when that little fellow arrived at family headquarters you had to hand in your resignation. He took entire command.

You become his lackey, his mere body-servant, and you had to stand around, too. He was not a commander who made allowance for time, distance, weather, or anything else. You had to execute his order whether it was possible or not. And there was only one form of marching in his manual of tactics, and that was the double quick. He treated you with every sort of insolence and disrespect, and the bravest of you didn't dare to say a word. You could face the death-storm at Donelson and Vicksburg, and give back blow for blow; but when he clawed your whiskers and pulled your hair, and twisted your nose, you had to take it. When the thunders of war were sounding in your ears you set your faces towards the batteries and advanced with steady tread; but when he turned on the terrors of his war whoop you advanced in the other direction, and mighty glad of the chance too. When he called for soothing-syrup, did you venture to throw out any side remarks about certain services being unbecoming an officer and a gentleman? No. You got up and got it. When he ordered his pap bottle and it was not warm, did you talk back? Not you. You went to work and warmed it. You even descended so far in your menial office as to take a suck at that warm, insipid stuff yourself to see if it was right—three parts water to one of milk, a touch of sugar to modify the colic, and a drop of peppermint to kill those immortal hiccoughs. I can taste that stuff yet.

from *The Babies*
by Samuel Clemens

13.

On Following Through

PERHAPS the most common weakness in courses for the improvement of voice and articulation is a failure to "follow through" after completing such a course, in order to insure the successful accomplishment of the course objective. This is due partly to the fact that the course objective is not limited to the course itself, and partly to a common lack of facilities for continued progress.

Course Objective

The course objective is to make as much progress as possible (which is very indefinite to say the least) towards establishing habits that might lead eventually to the fulfillment of an ultimate objective—the best possible voice and oral diction for effective communication that the individual is capable of developing. Like a study of vocal music, any serious attempt to improve one's manner of speaking for more effective communication is a continuing process that is not limited to any single course. In fact a student of voice and oral diction may make excellent progress without ever reaching a point at which he may regard his ultimate objective as fully accomplished.

Unfortunately, in a course dealing with speech in which the learner is attempting to break old habits and establish new ones, there is a very strong tendency for progress to stop as soon as the course ends. Furthermore, many students, when freed from the vocal discipline of such a course, soon revert back to old attitudes of complacency and to old speech habits, thus losing substantially all the benefits they may have acquired while taking the course.

It is extremely important, therefore, that the student of voice and articulation, when finishing such a course, should resolve to "follow through," either by means of continued and systematic practice of course exercises or by new and carefully controlled speech experiences. Such new experiences may be obtained in additional courses in speech, oral interpretation, or acting; or they may come from vocational or avocational activities involving speech.

Facilities for Continued Progress

The student of voice and articulation needs principally a place where he may practice speaking without disturbing the peace of his social community and without danger of embarrassment to himself. Such a place is needed while taking any kind of course requiring oral practice, but it is doubly important for any adequate process of "following through" the vocal development started in such a course. When a person is a student, he may have the courage to disturb the peace by making all sorts of unconventional noises because he has the excuse of being required to do so in order to maintain his academic standing in a course of study; but after the course is completed, he has no such excuse. Then any unusual vocal sounds become odd behavior that might seem to be unforgivable.

Everyone knows the difficulties that music students—both vocal and instrumental—often encounter in getting essential practice without too much disturbing the peace. Noises made by a would-be musician who is not even taking any course may be annoying to his neighbors, but such sounds are understandable annoyances which may or may not be accepted philosophically. But any kind of noise that may be recognized as speech sounds are quite a different matter, especially when they are made by someone who is not taking a course that requires making such noises. Moreover, any loud delivery of speech materials of an emotional nature or any garbled and discontented oral sounds may subject their maker to embarrassing misinterpretations or even to libelous rumors. But more probably, the fear of causing such misinterpretations or rumors will result in either no vocal practice at all, or the avoidance of the type of practice that might be expected to do the most good. Thus the lack of a place to practice vocal exercises without disturbing others may prevent any further progress towards the course objective.

Another badly needed facility is a listener, or a mechanical device—such as a tape recorder—that will permit the student to listen to his own speech sounds as others hear them. Otherwise faults may go undetected and be perpetuated by practice.

A sound-proof room and a tape recorder should provide the ideal facilities for "following through" the progress started in a course in voice and articulation.

Individual Objectives

Another essential to an effective process of "following through" after completing a course in voice and articulation is a careful analysis of the individual's needs for future development. Although any course aimed at the development of an effective manner of speaking may have an obvious objective in terms of the generalized student, it usually has very particularized objectives in terms of each individual student.

The objectives of each individual differ widely from those of others for two reasons:

1. Different students start out with different kinds and degrees of vocal or articulatory faults which require very different kinds and amounts of exercises and practice for correction.

2. Different students plan to prepare themselves for very different kinds of vocational and avocational activities which require various types of skill in oral communication that have very different degrees of difficulty in their development. One student, for example, who plans to become a clergyman might have a natural voice of excellent basic quality but be very weak in pronunciation and enunciation, and have a strong tendency towards monotonous and stumbling unevenness of delivery. On the other hand, another student (taking the same course in voice and articulation) who plans to become a stage actor might have excellent oral diction and vocal flexibility but a weak voice and poor basic vocal quality. Obviously, each student has very different course objectives; and both might make progress towards their respective objectives and still be in need of much improvement after completing the course. If each wishes to continue progress towards effective communication in their respective professions, they should have very specific ideas as to what a "follow through" process is supposed to accomplish.

Therefore, a final course objective should be that of defining specifically what each student needs most in terms of future improvement in his manner of speaking for his particular requirements in oral communication.

Summary

Any serious attempt to improve one's manner of speaking for effective communication is a continuing process that should not be limited to a single course of study. Consequently, the student should be prepared to "follow through" after completing a course in voice and articulation by continuing to practice. For such practice, a person needs a place where he can vocalize any kind of speech drill materials without being embarrassed because of the annoyance such drills might arouse in others. Furthermore, an effective process of "following through" should be based upon each student's knowledge of his particular needs for further development.

Questions

1. Why is there any need for a process of "following through" in the field of voice and articulation?
2. Describe the objective of a course in voice and articulation.
3. Why do the course objectives differ with each individual student?
4. How may a student "follow through" after completing a course in voice and oral diction?
5. What facilities does a person need for effective training in voice and articulation?

Exercises

Purpose: To gain a specific analysis of one's particular needs for future development.

Method: As you deliver one or more of the following selections, have a number of listeners indicate their analysis of your needs for future development by filling out a check sheet similar to the following:

Sample Check Sheet

Name of Speaker ______________________

The speaker aims to become (underline one): a platform speaker, a radio or T.V. speaker, a stage actor, a T.V. or movie actor, a platform reader, a social conversationalist, (Other) __________.

Speech Skills	*Excellent*	*Adequate*	*Poor*
Vocal Strength	___	___	___
Basic Voice Quality	___	___	___
Pronunciation	___	___	___
Clarity of Enunciation	___	___	___
Smoothness of Articulation	___	___	___
Speech personality (degree of adaptation)	___	___	___
Vocal Force Variety	___	___	___
Vocal Pitch Variety	___	___	___
Vocal Quality Variety	___	___	___
Timing of Speech	___	___	___

Any Noticeable Fault ______________________________________

____

____

Selections

1. Well, honour is the subject of my story.
I cannot tell what you and other men
Think of this life; but, for my single self,
I had as lief not be as live to be
In awe of such a thing as I myself.
I was born free as Caesar, so were you;
We both have fed as well, and we can both
Endure the winter's cold as well as he;
For once upon a raw and gusty day,
The troubled Tiber chaffing with her shores,
Caesar said to me, "Dar'st thou, Cassius, now
Leap in with me into this angry flood,
And swim to yonder point?" Upon the word,
Accoutred as I was, I plunged in
And bade him follow; so indeed he did.
The torrent roar'd, and we did buffet it
With lusty sinews, throwing it aside
And stemming it with hearts of controversy;
But ere we could arrive the point propos'd,
Caesar cried, "Help me, Cassius, or I sink!"
I, as Æneas, our great ancestor,
Did from the flames of Troy upon his shoulder
The old Anchises bear, so from the waves of Tiber
Did I the tired Caesar. And this man
Is now become a god, and Cassius is
A wretched creature, and must bend his body
If Caesar carelessly but nod on him. . . .
Why, man, he doth bestride the narrow world
Like a Colossus, and we petty men
Walk under his huge legs, and peep about
To find ourselves dishonourable graves.
Men at some time are masters of their fates;
The fault, dear Brutus, is not in our stars,
But in ourselves that we are underlings.
Brutus and Caesar: what should be in that "Caesar"?
Why should that name be sounded more than yours?
Write them together, yours is as fair a name;
Sound them, it doth become the mouth as well;

Weigh them, it is as heavy; conjure with 'em,
"Brutus" will start a spirit as soon as "Caesar."

from *Julius Caesar*
by William Shakespeare

2. And the Lord said unto Satan, Whence, cometh thou? Then Satan answered the Lord, and said, From going to and fro in the earth, and from walking up and down in it.

And the Lord said unto Satan, Hast thou considered my servant Job, that there is none like him in the earth, a perfect and an upright man, one that feareth God, and escheweth evil?

Then Satan answered the Lord, and said, Doth Job fear God for nought? Hast not thou made an hedge about him, and about his house, and about all that he hath on every side? Thou hast blessed the work of his hands, and his substance is increased in the land;

But put forth thine hand now, and touch all that he hath, and he will curse thee to thy face.

And the Lord said unto Satan, Behold, all that he hath is in thy power; only upon himself put not forth thine hand. So Satan went forth from the presence of the Lord.

And there was a day when his sons and his daughters were eating and drinking wine in their eldest brother's house:

And there came a messenger unto Job and said, The oxen were plowing, and the asses feeding beside them:

And the Sabeans fell upon them, and took them away: yea, they have slain the servants with the edge of the sword: and I only am escaped alone to tell thee.

While he was yet speaking, there came also another, and said, The fire of God is fallen from heaven, and hath burned up the sheep, and the servants, and consumed them; and I only am escaped alone to tell thee.

While he was yet speaking, there came also another, and said, the Chaldeans made out three bands, and fell upon the camels, and have carried them away, yea, and slain the servants with the edge of the sword; and I only am escaped alone to tell thee.

While he was yet speaking there came another and said, Thy sons and thy daughters were eating and drinking wine in their eldest brother's house: And, behold, there came a great wind from the wilderness, and smote the four corners of the house, and it fell upon the young men, and they are dead; and I only am escaped alone to tell thee.

Then Job arose, and rent his mantle, and shaved his head, and fell down upon the ground, and worshipped,

And said, Naked came I out of my mother's womb, and naked shall I return thither: the Lord gave, and the Lord hath taken away: blessed be the name of the Lord.

In all of this Job sinned not, nor charged God foolishly.

Job, I

3. You may talk o' gin and beer
When you're quartered safe out 'ere,
An' you're sent to penny-fights an' Aldershot it;
But when is comes to slaughter
You will do your work on water,
An' you'll lick the bloomin' boots of 'im that's got it,
Now in Injia's sunny clime,
Where I used to spend my time
A-servin' of 'Er Majesty the Queen
Of all them blackfaced crew
The finest man I knew
Was our regimental bhisti, Gunga Din.
He was "Din! Din! Din!
You limping lump 'o brick-dust, Gunga Din!
Hi'! slippery hitherao!
Water, get it! Panee lao!
You squidgy-nosed old idol, Gunga Din."

The uniform 'e wore
Was nothin' much before,
An' rather less than 'arf o' that be-ind,
For a piece o' twisty rag
An' a goatskin water-bag
Was all the field-equipment 'e could find.
When the sweatin' troop-train lay
In a sidin' through the day,
Where the 'eat would make your bloomin' eyebrows crawl,
We shouted "Harry By!"
Till our throats were bricky-dry,
Then we wopped 'im 'cause 'e couldn't serve us all.
It was "Din! Din! Din!
You 'eathen, where the mischief 'ave you been?
You put some juldee in it

Or I'll marrow you this minute
If you don't fill up my helmet, Gunga Din!"

" 'E would dot an' carry one
Till the longest day was done;
An' 'e didn't seem to know the use o' fear.
If we charged or broke or cut,
You could bet your bloomin' nut,
'E'd be waitin' fifty paces right flank rear.
With 'is mussick on 'is back,
'E would skip with our attack,
An' watch us till the bugles made "Retire,"
An' for all 'is dirty 'ide
'E was white, clear white, inside
When 'e went to tend the wounded under fire!
It was "Din! Din! Din!"
With bullets kickin' up dust-spots on the green.
When the cartridges ran out,
You could hear the front-files shout,
"Hi! ammunition-mules an' Gunga Din!"

I sha'n't forgit the night
When I dropped be'ind the fight
With a bullet where my belt-plate should 'a' been.
I was chokin' mad with thirst,
An' the man that spied me first
Was our good old grinnin', gruntin' Gunga Din.
'E lifted up my 'ead,
An' he plugged me where I bled,
An' 'e guv me 'arf-a-pint 'o water-green,
It was crawlin' and it stunk,
But of all the drinks I've drunk,
I'm gratefullest to one from Gunga Din.
It was "Din! Din! Din!"
'Ere's a beggar with a bullet through 'is spleen;
'E's chawin' up the ground,
An' 'e's kickin' all around:
For Gawd's sake git the water, Gunga Din!

'E carried me away
To where a dooli lay,
An' a bullet come an' drilled the beggar clean.

'E put me safe inside,
An' just before 'e died:
"I 'ope you liked your drink," sez Gunga Din.
So I'll meet 'im later on
At the place where 'e is gone—
Where it's always double drill and no canteen;
'E'll be squattin' on the coals,
Given' drink to poor damned souls,
An' I'll get a swig in hell from Gunga Din!
Yes, Din! Din! Din!
You Lazarushian-leather Gunga Din!
Though I've belted you and flayed you,
By the living God that made you,
You're a better man than I am, Gunga Din!

"Gunga Din"
by Rudyard Kipling

4. Against the prisoner at the bar, as an individual, I cannot have the slightest prejudice; I would not do him the smallest injury or injustice. But I do not affect to be indifferent to the discovery and the punishment of this deep guilt. I cheerfully share in the opprobrium, how much soever it may be, which is cast on those who feel and manifest an anxious concern, that all who had a part in planning, or a hand in executing, this deed of midnight assassination, may be brought to answer for their enormous crime at the bar of public justice.

Gentlemen, this is a most extraordinary case. In some respects it has hardly a precedent anywhere—certainly none in our New England history. This bloody drama exhibited no suddenly excited, ungovernable rage. The actors in it were not surprised by any lion-like temptation springing upon their virtue, overcoming it before resistance could begin. Nor did they do the deed to glut savage vengeance, or satiate long-settled and deadly hate. It was a cool, calculating, money-making murder. It was all "hire and salary, not revenge." It was the weighing of money against life; the counting out of so many pieces of silver against so many ounces of blood.

"Crime Its Own Detector"
by Daniel Webster

5. Is this a dagger which I see before me,
The handle toward my hand? Come, let me clutch thee.

I have thee not, and yet I see thee still.
Art thou not, fatal vision, sensible
To feeling as to sight? or art thou but
A dagger of the mind, a false creation,
Proceeding from the heat-oppressed brain?
I see thee yet, in form as palpable
As this which now I draw.
Thou marshall'st me the way that I was going;
And such an instrument I was to use.
Mine eyes are made the fools o' the other senses,
Or else worth all the rest; I see thee still,
And on thy blade and dudgeon gouts of blood,
Which was not so before. There's no such thing:
It is the bloody business which informs
Thus to mine eyes. Now o'er the one half-world
Nature seems dead, and wicked dreams abuse
The curtain'd sleep; witchcraft celebrates
Pale Hecate's offerings? and wither'd murder,
Alarum'd by his sentinel, the wolf,
Whose howl's his watch, thus with his stealthy pace,
With Tarquin's ravishing strides, towards his design
Moves like a ghost. Thou sure and firm-set earth,
Hear not my steps, which way they walk, for fear
Thy very stones prate of my whereabout,
And take the present horror from the time,
Which now suits with it. Whiles I threat, he lives:
Words to the heat of deeds too cold breath gives.
I go, and it is done; the bell invites me.
Hear it not, Duncan: for it is the knell
That summons thee to heaven or to hell.

from *Macbeth*
by William Shakespeare

INDEXES

Selections by Authors

(Titles or first lines used for identification)

ANONYMOUS

Esau Wood sawed wood 265

THE BIBLE

Job XXVIII 46

Corinthians XIII 111

Psalm XXIV 263

Psalm CXXI 264

Isaiah LX 282

Psalm XXIII 319

St. Luke XV 336

Job I 344

BURKE, EDMUND

"The Impeachment of Warren Hastings" 302

BYRON, GEORGE GORDON (SIXTH LORD)

"Childe Harold's Pilgrimage" 111

CARROLL, LEWIS

"A Strange Wild Song" 305

CLEMENS, SAMUEL

"The Babies" 337

DICKENS, CHARLES

Out upon merry Christmas! (A Christmas Carol) 301

In came a fiddler with a music-book (A Christmas Carol) . 306

Dora had a discreet friend (David Copperfield) 332

I confess standing here in this responsible situation 335

EMERSON, RALPH WALDO

"The Rhodora" 112

FERBER, EDNA AND KAUFMAN, GEORGE S.
I don't expect him to be like other people (Stage Door) .. 310
Terry! Wake up! We're in the movies! (Stage Door) 311

GILBERT, W. S.
My object all sublime 184
I siezed him by his little pig-tail 184
In other professions in which men engage 185
I am the very model of a modern Major-General 185
Then a glance may be timid or free 185
If any well-bred youth I knew 185
As I go out the door 186
A magnet hung in a hard-ware shop 186

GRATTAN, HENRY
"Grattan's Reply to Mr. Cory" 302

HENRY, PATRICK
"The War Inevitable" 110

INGERSOLL, ROBERT
Liberty is not a social question 281
Shakespeare exceeded all the sons of men 312
The loved and loving brother 319

IRVING, WASHINGTON
"Knickerbocker's History of New York" 333

KIPLING, RUDYARD
"Gunga Din" 345

LINCOLN, ABRAHAM
Gettysburg Address 109
Farewell to Springfield 334

MACY, JOHN
"About Women" 44

PALMER, GEORGE HERBERT
"The Glory of the Imperfect" (The Ideal Teacher) 43

PIRANDELLO, LUIGI
But don't you see that the whole trouble lies here
(Six Characters in Search of an Author) 280

POPE, ALEXANDER
"Essay on Criticism" 45

ROSTAND, EDMOND
You might have said, dear me, there are a thousand things
(Cyrano de Bergerac) 314

RUSKIN, JOHN
I tell you earnestly and authoritatively 262
SCHOPENHAUER, ARTHUR
A library may be very large (The Art of Literature) 281
SCOTT, SIR WALTER
Breathes there a man with soul so dead 312
SHAKESPEARE, WILLIAM
Speak the speech, I pray you (Hamlet) 45
To be, or not to be: (Hamlet) 114
Now I am alone (Hamlet) 316
Romans, countrymen, and lovers! (Julius Caesar) 108
Friends, Romans, Countrymen (Julius Caesar) 108
Villians, you did not so (Julius Caesar) 301
Well, honour is the subject (Julius Caesar) 343
How sweet the moonlight sleeps (Merchant of Venice) 113
The quality of mercy is not strained (Merchant of Venice) 264
If to do were as easy as to know (Merchant of Venice) .. 281
The curse never fell upon our nation (Merchant of Venice) 300
If I can catch him once upon the hip (Merchant of Venice) 300
You come to me, and you say (Merchant of Venice) 309
God's bread! it makes me mad (Romeo and Juliet) 304
O, then I see Queen Mab (Romeo and Juliet) 307
He jests as scars (Romeo and Juliet) 317
To-morrow, and to-morrow, and to-morrow (Macbeth) .. 263
Avaunt! and quit my sight! (Macbeth) 300
Is this a dagger which I see before me (Macbeth) 347
I'll tell thee: Life and death! I am ashamed (King Lear) .. 301
Most potent, grave, and reverend signiors (Othello) 308
It is the cause, it is the cause, my soul (Othello) 318
All the world's a stage (As You Like It) 334
SHERIDAN, RICHARD B.
Observe me, Sir Anthony (The Rivals) 310
STEVENSON, ROBERT LOUIS
"My Shadow" 305
SUDERMANN, HERMANN
You blame me for living out my life (Magda) 315
THAYER, ERNEST L.
"Casey at the Bat" 313
VAN DYKE, HENRY
Christ chose an image (Salt) 280

WEAD, FRANK
Eddie, since the day you were hired here (Ceiling Zero) . . 315
WEBSTER, DANIEL
"Crime Its Own Detector" 347
WORDSWORTH, WILLIAM
"The Daffodils" 113

Topic Index

Air
Through which sound waves travel, ... 47
Amplitude
A characteristic of sound waves, ... 52
Articulation
Training objectives, ... 36
(See also Pronunciation and Enunciation)
Aspirate
A vocal quality fault, ... 100
Auditory
Observation and judgment, ... 90, 156
Memory and guidance, ... 158
Babbling
Stage in learning to talk, ... 22
Breathiness (See Aspirate)
Breathing Mechanism
Lungs, ... 67
Diaphragm, ... 67
Rib Cage, ... 68
Muscles controlling breathing, ... 69
Air passage, ... 71
Soft palate, ... 71
Larynx, ... 71
Breath Support
Motivating power, ... 74
Improvement of, ... 94

Communication
Types and relative dominance, 15
Contrasted with expression, 16
Levels of difficulty illustrated, 19
Skills normally acquired, 27
Training objectives, 36

Consonants
As a type of speech sound, 119, 122
Classified, 122-125

Continuant
A type of consonant, 124

Critical Judgment of Voice
Factors determining judgment, 91
Criteria of a good voice, 93

Demonstration
As a teaching device, 161

Diacritical Markings
As used by dictionaries, 117
Used with phonetic transcription, 127

Diaphragmatic Breathing
Described, 69
Relative value, 94

Diphthong
Defined, 119
Symbols representing diphthongs, 121

Duration
A variable attribute of sound, 61
Means of controlling vocal durations, 82

Ear Training
Effects of, 153
Improving auditory observation and judgment, 156

Eating and Drinking Mechanism
The lips, 73
The mouth, 73
The jaws and teeth, 73
The tongue, 73
The throat, or pharynx, 73
Muscles used in swallowing, 73

Emphasis
Types defined and illustrated, 249
Force emphasis, 286-287
Pitch emphasis, 289
Quality emphasis, 296
Time emphasis, 323

Enunciation
Defined, 172
Of vowels, 173
Of consonants, 174
Modes of enunciation, 174
Reasons for poor enunciation, 175-176
Types of poor enunciation, 178
Methods of improvement, 181

Expression
Contrasted with communication, 16
Developing skill in, 37-38

Force Variations and Emphasis
Motivation of, 285
Types of, 286

Frequency
As a characteristic of sound waves, 54

Fricatives
A type of consonant, 123

Glide
A type of consonant, 125

Glottis
Illustrated, 67
Defined, 72
Use causing a breathy quality, 100
Use for voiced and voiceless sounds, 122

Harshness of Vocal Quality
As a fault, 101

Hearing
Variations in, 152
Factors involved in understanding speech, 153
Interdependence with speech, 155
Improvement of, 156-157

Impersonation
Dependence on memory images, ... 159
Intensity
A characteristic of a sound wave, ... 52
Loudness
As an attribute of sound, ... 52
Means of controlling vocal loudness, ... 81-82
Lungs (See Speech Mechanism)
Mimicry
Use of, ... 159
Value as ear training, ... 161
Nasal Consonants
Symbols and description, ... 123
Nasality
As a vocal fault, ... 98
Natural Voice
Described, ... 88
Means of changing, ... 90
Noise
Defined, ... 50
Optimum Pitch
Defined, ... 290
Overtones
Defined, ... 57
Pectoral Quality
As a vocal fault, ... 102
Personality (See also Speech Personality)
As it limits development of speech skill, ... 29
Phoneme
Defined, ... 118
Phonetic Alphabet
Advantage of, ... 118
Symbols of, ... 119-121
Use of, ... 144
Phonetic Unit
An element of speech, ... 171
Phonetic Writing
Use of, ... 157

Phrase
An element of speech, ... 171
Physical Communication
Relative dominance, ... 15
How learned, ... 21
Pitch
A variable attribute of sound, ... 54
Means of control, ... 55
Control of vocal pitch, ... 82
Pitch Emphasis
Defined, ... 249
Types and strength of, ... 289
Motivation of, ... 292
Pitch Key
Defined, ... 290
Pitch Range
Defined, ... 290
Means of extending, ... 291
Pitch Variations in Speech
Kinds of, ... 288
Kinds of inflexions, ... 288
Development of, ... 291
Plosives or Stops
Type of consonant defined, ... 122
Projection of Speech
As a training objective, ... 37
Explained, ... 180
Methods of improvement, ... 181
Pronunciation
As a training objective, ... 37
Defined, ... 171
Factors involved in, ... 215
Pronunciation standards, ... 215
Dictionary as reporter not an authority 218
U.S. standards of, ... 219
Relative beauty of standards, ... 222
Improvement of, ... 225
Quality
A variable attribute of sound, ... 56

Factors determining natural vocal quality, ... 88
Motivation and control of vocal quality changes, ... 294
Quality emphasis, ... 296
Developing flexibility of vocal quality, ... 297

Resonance
Types of, ... 58
As a means of controlling vocal quality, ... 78

Rhythm of Speech
Defined, ... 325
Determining pleasantness of speech, ... 326
Communicative function of, ... 326

Self-Consciousness
Limiting development of speech skill, ... 36

Sense of Timing
And time emphasis, ... 325
And speech rhythm, ... 327

Simplified Spelling
As means of representing pronunciations, ... 117

Social Inhibitions
Limiting the development of speech skills, ... 31

Sound
As distinguished from sound waves, ... 49

Sound Waves
Defined, ... 49
Types of sounds, ... 50
Effect upon the ear, ... 51

Speech Content
Variations in, ... 19

Speech Intonation Patterns
Evaluation of, ... 157
Nature of, ... 246
Factors determining variations, ... 247
Variations and meaning, ... 248-251
Inevitability of, ... 254

Speech Mechanism
Primary functions of its parts, ... 66
Motivating power, ... 74
Vibrator, ... 76
Resonators, ... 78

Articulators, ... 80
Factors determining vocal efficiency, ... 88

Speech Personality
Determining Intonation pattern, ... 29
Defined, ... 266
Effective speech personality, ... 268
Not based on pretense, ... 275
Ineffective speech personality, ... 276
Acting and speech personality, ... 277

Speech Situation
Defined, ... 268
Determining factors, ... 268

Speech Skills
Development in schools, ... 26
Factors limiting normal development, ... 27

Spontaneity
Determining factors, ... 328-329

Stage Fright
Factors determining degree of, ... 33
Means of controlling, ... 34-35

Stops (See Plosives)

Subordination
Defined, ... 249

Syllable
An element of speech, ... 171

Talk, Learning To
Stages of development, ... 22-24

Tempo of Speaking
Defined, ... 324
Changing one's natural tempo, ... 329

Time Emphasis
Defined, ... 323
Two types of, ... 323

Time Variety
Motivation of, ... 321
Improvement of, ... 327

Tonal Communication
Relative dominance, ... 15
Normal development of, ... 21

Tone
Defined, ... 50
Variable Attributes of Sound
Listed, ... 52
Explained, ... 52-57
Verbal Communication
Relative dominance, ... 15
How acquired, ... 22-24
Vocal Cords (Folds or Lips)
As part of the vibrator, ... 76
Improving the adjustment of, ... 95
Vocal Faults
Weak, thin quality, ... 96
Nasality, ... 98
Breathiness, ... 100
Harshness, ... 101
Muffled, pectoral quality, ... 102
Vocal Instrument (See Speech Mechanism)
Vocal Flexibilities (See Force, Pitch, Quality)
Vowels
Described, ... 119-125
Phonetic symbols for, ... 120-121